John Sittema has pro
Himself a shepherd c
Sittema opens his hear
Chief Shepherd. It will help to equip, encourage, and edify pastors, elders, and laypeople both young and old. Every man in seminary would be wise to read this book before he takes one step into the pulpit and then read it again every year of his life. It is a passionate call to the entire church, from any denominational tradition.

Burk Parsons
Editor of Tabletalk Magazine
Associate Minister of Saint Andrew's

At a time when the church is abuzz about being "missional," *With a Shepherd's Heart* is a timely reminder about the urgency of simultaneously being "pastoral." Dr. Sittema persuasively argues that elders are primarily called to be shepherds of the flock, not administrators. Here is a realistic perspective on contemporary eldership that is biblically informed and culturally relevant. Rich with practical helps for hands-on ministry, this book is a comprehensive roadmap for leaders written by a gifted shepherd who has watched the sheep for many years.

Dr. S. Donald Fortson III
Assoc. Prof. of Church History and Practical Theology
Reformed Theological Seminary

John Sittema agonizes over the gap between what the Bible says about elders and the realities of the eldership in today's church. He does not despair, however, because he enjoys gospel clarity (understanding both the depth of our need and the greatness of God's grace) and applies it to elders in a way that is challenging yet encouraging. This is the kind of gospel-centered training that elders need to be gospel-centered shepherds.

Alan D. Strange
Moderator of the 75th General Assembly (OPC)
Associate Professor of Church History
Mid-America Reformed Seminary

I have used this excellent book to help train the elders of our church. And now, I am blessed to serve alongside elders who refuse to see themselves as a board of directors who run an organization, but rather as a team of shepherds who love and serve the flock of Christ together. We could not be more thankful for elders who have the hearts of shepherds, for elders who love the flock of Christ with the love of Christ. I highly commend this invaluable resource to every elder, and especially to pastors who need to train new elders!

Owen Lee
Pastor, New Life PCA
Burbank, CA

John Sittema persuasively and practically cultivates the biblical notion of the elder as a pastor and shepherd. It is a vital message if the church is to prosper. Having had the privilege to work with John and use his book to train elders at our church, I gladly commend it to you.

Bernie Lawrence
Pastor of Shepherding and Discipleship
Christ Covenant Church
Matthews, NC

This book has completely changed my heart and perspective on what it means to be an elder. John Sittema has done an amazing job of leading you to really immerse in the Scriptures to understand what God has to say about pastoral care and shepherding. At the end of every chapter, the practical application and the case studies are invaluable. Being an elder is accepting a call to the front lines of service. This should be part of every church leadership curriculum.

Larry Kaye
Businessman and Ruling Elder
Jacksonville, FL

WITH A SHEPHERD'S HEART

Reclaiming the Pastoral Office of Elder

John R. Sittema

Published by Reformed Fellowship, Inc.
Grandville, MI

Reformed Fellowship Inc.
www.reformedfellowship.net

Unless otherwise noted, all Scripture quotations are from the Holy Bible, New International Version. © 1973, 1978, 1984, 1996, 2009, International Bible Study. Used by permission of Zondervan Bible Publishers.

© 1996, 2005, 2010 John R. Sittema
Printed in the United States of America
All rights reserved

ISBN 978-0-9653981-0-7

Preface

My wife and I were strolling hand in hand along the beach in The Gambia, West Africa. We had spent a week with a group of forty missionary families gathered for an annual sabbatical retreat. It was our last day, and we would soon pack to leave.

It happened to be the prophet Mohammed's birthday, and a group of six or eight young shepherd boys had brought their sheep in from the plains for a salt water bath in honor of the prophet. The oldest, a boy of about fourteen, was wrestling with the larger rams and ewes in knee-deep water, while the younger ones, between eight and ten, shuttled the beasts from the sand to the water.

We watched in fascination for perhaps twenty minutes. Emerging from the gentle surf, the sheep reminded me of our little terrier after his bath. Suddenly very frisky, each vigorously shook off the water and cavorted at full speed for a while before settling down for a drink at a nearby watering station.

We began to wonder how fifty or so sheep could be sorted, for it soon became apparent that the shepherds represented not one flock, but at least three. There were no tags, brands or collars, nothing to distinguish the animals of one flock from those of another. Things seemed a bit disorganized, the shepherds apparently more interested in adolescent trash-talk than anything else. I expected a bit of pubescent conflict to erupt any minute.

I was wrong. One shepherd simply began to walk east, another headed north along the beach, and a third strolled south. Each was talking or singing in a low voice. Within seconds, every shaggy head lifted, cocked an ear to listen, and then began to move. Within one minute, the flocks were completely separated. Each simply followed the shepherd's voice.

In the increasingly urban world of the twenty-first century, a book that defines elders by looking back to a shepherd metaphor from ancient Bible times seems strangely out of place. Surely, we can come up with something more relevant, something that fits the "leadership style" of the current world. Yet, if the church is, in fact, counter-cultural, made up of "citizens of heaven, colonizing the earth," it is not the leadership style of the world the church ought to adopt, but that of heaven's King. His name is Jesus, and he is the Good Shepherd.

Such "leadership" is not, by definition, old-fashioned. It suggests instead that elder-shepherds are to be highly relational. Each is to know the lives of God's people in his charge: the health of marriages and families, their struggles at work, their spiritual burdens, doubts and fears. God's people are to know the elders, too, so well in fact that they will come to trust a "recognized voice" because it sounds so much like Jesus'. In this isolated and lonely generation, relational shepherding is not just a good idea, but is absolutely essential and desperately needed.

I'm grateful that over the years the interest in this volume continues, and pleased that its usefulness has led to this third printing. Not surprisingly, the book has also generated critique. Some think I ask too much of elders, most of whom are volunteers, already too busy in their demanding careers. "Besides, that's preachers' work," suggested a dear friend and mentor. "You can't expect untrained volunteers to do what seminary-trained pastors should!"

I vigorously disagree, even more now than when I first wrote the book. It is not our right to shelve the biblical definition of elder because we've become too busy, or because most churches (in the West) have ministers who went to seminary. The fact is that elders are to do the work of pastoral care. Current practices must align with the biblical portrait, not the other way around. It's time we train elders to be what the Bible assigns them to be: relational shepherds who sound the Good Shepherd's voice.

This book stands in grateful testimony to the wonderful elder-shepherds who have enriched my own life and ministry. I pray that it will also serve as encouragement to those elders who are not yet the shepherds they are called to be.

Jacksonville, Florida

August, 2009

Table Of Contents

Part One: The Shepherd's Heart ~ Regaining Pastoral Purpose
1. Out of the Board Room 1
2. Check Your Aim 10
3. Giving Yourself an EKG 22

Part Two: The Shepherd's Eye ~ Sharpening Pastoral Vision
Section One: Knowing the Enemy
4. The Wolf's Teeth ~ Secularism 49
5. The Wolf's Teeth ~ Materialism 55
6. The Wolf's Teeth ~ Relativism 61
7. The Wolf's Teeth ~ Pragmatism 66
8. The Wolf's Teeth ~ Feminism 70

Section Two: A Strategic Blueprint for Pastoring Families
9. Foundational Principles of Family Care 79
10. Coming Apart at the Seams ~ Families in Crisis 91
11. Focus on the Marriage ~ Not the Wedding 98
12. Tend to the Lambs 107
13. Polishing Your Lens ~ Homework on Family Ministry 115

Section Three: A Strategic Blueprint for Pastoring Seniors
14. Retirement: Vacation or Vocation? 127
15. Pastoral Care in the Nursing Home 135
16. Polishing Your Lens ~ Homework on Ministry to Seniors 139

Part Three: The Shepherd's Hand ~ Developing Pastoral Skills
Section One: The Elder and Teaching
17. "Apt to Teach" 151
18. Teaching the Lambs of the Flock 157
19. A Catechism on Sex ~ Helping Parents Establish Biblical Values 161
20. "Old Dogs, New Tricks" ~ Training Adults in Christ 166

Section Two: The Elder and Member Visiting
21. Visiting to Encourage 175
22. Visiting to Rebuke 181
23. Visiting to Admonish 186
24. Visiting to Guard 192
25. Plotting A Pastoral Strategy 198

Section Three: Biblical Discipline ~ The Ministry of Accountability
26. Church Membership ~ Committed to Follow a Recognized Voice 209
27. Discipline: Face to Face with the Word! 217
28. The Elder's Meeting ~ a Structure for Mutual Accountability 232

Appendices: Tools For Group Study 243

Part One
THE SHEPHERD'S HEART
Regaining Pastoral Purpose

OUT OF THE BOARD ROOM

I lived in Texas for many years. When I crossed the Red River some years ago when moving from the Midwest with my family, I had to learn many new things and learn them quickly. I had to learn a new language that folks here actually call "Texas friendly": what I had known as "baptists" were actually "babdists"; where I had "done business" before, I would now be "doin' bidness"; and where previously I had referred to a group standing before me as "you," I would have to learn to say "y'all" instead. (Actually, "y'all" is an all-purpose pronoun serving as both singular and plural, though local linguistic "purists" insist that the plural of "y'all" is "y'alls.") I had to master the difference between "tote," "fetch," and "carry"; I had to learn that soft drink is not "pop" but that all varieties are called "cokes" ("What kind of coke do you want? Orange?"). I had to learn the strange Texas lilt that raises the end of each sentence a note or so, so that to my Midwestern ears, very indicative sounded more like an interrogative. I learned to say "fixin'" a lot (as in "I'm fixin' to fetch a six-pack of cokes").

I also learned an important lesson in Texas-style home maintenance; to "water my foundation." Since most of you don't know what that means, a brief lesson is in order. (Y'all listen up, I'm fixin' to make a point here.) The soil in Texas, especially in the Dallas region, is of such a kind that it expands and contracts rapidly—almost violently—with the increase or decrease of moisture. This soil volatility is so pronounced that there are few if any basements; homes are constructed on specially prepared slabs. Now I'd seen cracked and parched earth before in Midwestern droughts, but I'd never seen half inch cracks fracture a lawn only days after a 5 inch rain! Unless the soil around one's foundation is kept moist, the expansion and contraction cracks the slab, and wall damage results. Repairs can be very costly, so wise homeowners all water their foundations faithfully.

The church of the Lord has a foundation too. God's Word says in Eph. 2:19-20, "you are...members of God's household, built on the foundation of the apostles and prophets, with Christ Jesus himself as the chief cornerstone." This book is written to train and equip elders because to them is assigned the important task of caring for the foundation. They must keep the church firmly fixed on the Word—as the inspired apostles and prophets transmitted it—and see to it that no cracks weaken the walls and damage the holy temple in which God dwells on earth. Their task is an urgent one, not only to preserve what God has already given us, but also because the church is always under construction: "...in him you too are being built together to become a dwelling in which God lives by his Spirit" (Eph. 2:22). The church is our Lord's; she is precious in His eyes. He paid a high price for her redemption—His own blood.

This study aims to be Biblical. We will analyze what the Bible says about the tasks assigned to elders, and how the men who hold this office must do them. It will also be practical. We will target the "bottom line," providing insights and skills to enable elders to fulfill their calling before the Lord and among the membership of the church. It is designed to challenge the reader to study on his own at home with the Bible open on lap or table, and with heart open to the Spirit of Christ. It will also challenge the reader to gather for discussion with others to share insights and for mutual encouragement.

ELDERS ARE PASTORS

You may wonder why so much emphasis is placed on the word "shepherd" throughout this study. More than just a convenient handle, it defines what the office of elder really is, a shepherding—that is, pastoring—duty. The work of elders properly understood is nothing other than the pastoral care of the flock of God. That Biblical imagery is one that is repeated from Genesis through the New Testament. It describes both God's description of His care and the needs of His people; it is dominant in both Jesus' description of Himself and His work and in His assignment to the Apostles of His Church.

"Wait a minute," you may say. "Pastoral care is the minister's job, isn't it? After all, he is the one *called* "Pastor." He has the training and the experience, and he receives a salary for his work. Elders are busy laymen who have full-time jobs and many other responsibilities. Their term of office is only for a few years (in most churches). They simply can't do the job like "the pastor" can. We shouldn't expect them to try!"

There is no doubt that a preacher ought to be busy pastoring the flock, tending to their feeding and their care as a representative of the Good Shepherd. But is it just he (or, in the case of multiple-staff ministries, "they")—the paid "professional"—who is to do the work of pastoring the flock?

The Bible won't allow it! Scripturally, the elders are the pastors of the church just as much as any paid, seminary-trained preacher. The elders themselves must understand that, the people of God must understand that, and the church must shape its life and ministry accordingly. In fact, it is a central thesis of this volume that the raging spiritual infection within the fevered body of Christ that has left so many churches weak, flaccid and ineffective, can be traced directly to the loss of the Biblical understanding and practice of the office of elder. As we shall see, the Bible assigns to the elders in each local church the awesome duty to protect and secure the health of the flock. It also speaks some of its most frightful judgments to the shepherds who fail in this assignment. If the local church fails to insist upon obedience to this Scriptural teaching simply because its elders aren't paid "professionals," that church will wither under the Evil One's assault.

Why have churches in our time lost the pastoral office of elder in exchange for the paid religious professional? The problem runs deep. Cultural analysts of our age have observed the radical transformation of our society from a rural agrarian base to an information base, from a "hands on" style of work involvement to a "managerial" style of involvement, from face to face and person to person communication to that of phone, fax, modem, voice-mail and e-mail.[1] And the changes are coming faster than ever. Two hundred years ago, 95% of the US work force was involved in farming, compared to less than 4 percent today.[2] But the greatest impulse for such radical change has been in the last 50 years, and the majority of *that* change has been in the last 15, tied directly to the

---

[1] Many authors have written on the subject; perhaps the most popular is John Naisbitt, *Megatrends: Ten New Directions Transforming Our Lives* (New York: Warner Books, 1982).

[2] *Net Results*, September 1994, cited in REACH, Vol. 20, No. 6, Church Development Resources of the Christian Reformed Church, Grand Rapids, MI.

development and explosive growth of the personal computer. Make no mistake; these changes are not only changes about how we make our money and communicate with one another. These changes affect how we view ourselves as people, how we understand our purpose on earth, our way of living before the face of God and our fellow man. These changes also affect the way we view the church, and within the church the way we interact with each other and care for one another in Christian love.

We've become profoundly individualistic as a society, and that individualism has penetrated the church to her very marrow. American religion has become private, and sadly, irrelevant as a shaping influence for public life. It is fascinating—and grievous—that during the decade of the 80s, the pollsters report that "religion is up" but "morality is down." (You can read all you can handle on the subject by picking up a book by Chuck Colson,[3] for example, or one of the research reports by George Barna,[4] or the thorough and excellent study of American religious beliefs and practices entitled *Habits of the Heart*, written by Sociologist Robert Bellah.)[5]

The changing nature of American religion as a whole is reflected as well in the changing role of the life of the church for both society and the individual. Instead of looking to the church for spiritual vigor, to shape fundamental societal values, and to nurture core moral beliefs and practices, modern Americans view the church with fear, distrust and suspicion.[6] After all, most of her "leaders" have revealed their own corruption, and the Supreme Court has reminded us of the "wall of separation" that exists strong and tall, seemingly to keep the church in her place. Instead of viewing the church as God's "family," the heart of one's religious and social life, central to one's identity, and thus a large part of one's schedule, today's Americans view the church much the way a suburban housewife (should I say house-husband?) views cereals. There are

---

[3] For example *Faith On The Line*, Victor Books, 1994, p. 11-54. Also see *Kingdoms in Conflict* and *The Body*, both by Colson.

[4] *The Barna Report: An Annual Survey of Life-Styles, Values and Religious Views.* (Ventura, CA.: Regal Books), and Barna and William Paul McKay, *Vital Signs: Emerging Social Trends and the Future of American Christianity.* (Westchester, IL: Crossway Books), 1984.

[5] Robert Bellah, *Habits of the Heart: Individualism and Commitment in American Life* (Berkeley: University of California Press, 1985).

[6] Colson, *Faith on the Line*, pp. 58-59.

hundreds of options, all tailored to different tastes and preferences. So too with churches. Several researchers report that the generations coming of age in the 80s and 90s are generations that don't make commitments, but rather seek value. Gone is "brand loyalty" to GM or Ford, Zenith or RCA, and with good reason; a family is as likely to have an American automobile manufactured in Mexico as one made in the USA, and not one single VCR manufacturer makes cassette decks in the US any longer. Gone as well is "brand loyalty" to church and denomination. An individual or a family may well choose to worship at one church on Sundays, attend Bible Study in another church, an inspirational "power lunch devotional" at still another. For such folks, the concept of "church membership" that has served for nearly two millenia to give visible testimony to spiritual commitment and communal "belongingness" has gone the way of the dinosaur.

With such profound societal and cultural transformation going on all around us, it ought not to surprise us that many within the church have begun to think more as the world does than as Scripture would have us think. Not without reason does Paul implore us not to "conform any longer to the pattern of this world, but be transformed by the renewing of your mind. Then you will be able to test and approve what God's will is..." (Rom. 12:2). And much to the point of this volume, such penetration of worldly ideas into the church's way of thinking is especially evident in the way modern churches have begun to think about the role of elders in the life of the church. Simply put, elders are viewed today in an administrative role, as the corporate officers of the business known as "church such and such." In fact, many churches have even adopted names that reflect their new "insights"; they call their elders "board members" or "trustees." And, of course, along with the shift in emphasis and the change of name comes a corresponding change of qualifying prerequisites for the job. Gone the way of the Do-Do bird are the *spiritual* qualifications for the office of elder that are explicitly set forth in I Timothy 3 and in Titus 1. They have been replaced instead with the technical "skill set" necessary to be an efficient corporate officer.

Acts 20:17ff: Elders, Bishops or Pastors?

Recall, if you will, my thesis. Elders are pastors, not administrators. They are to care for the flock of the Good Shepherd, not merely to "manage the affairs" of a corporate entity. Let's look at Scripture, specifically at Acts 20:17-38. In this passage, we read Paul's well-known farewell to the Ephesian elders whom he had summoned so as to give them his final instructions (v. 13ff). In this important passage, Paul uses several words to describe the men to whom he speaks:

- in v. 17 he refers to them as "**elders**" (using the Greek word "presbuteros," from which comes the English words "presbyter" and "presbyterian")
- in v. 28 he calls them "**overseers**" (from the Greek word "episkopos;" the root word for "episcopalian," in English "bishop")
- also in v. 28 he charges them to be "**shepherds**" (the Greek word is "poimein," the word for "shepherd" or "sheepherder").

What are we dealing with in these verses? Must we speak of elders, bishops *or* pastors, or must we speak of elders, bishops *and* pastors? Several interesting observations could be made here. For example, we could observe that entire denominations and ecclesiastical systems have arisen depending only on which word one chooses to emphasize while reading this chapter. (A stress on "episcopos" has led to the episcopalian system of church government, with authoritative and hierarchical bishops ruling the church instead of elders. Likewise, an emphasis on "presbuteros" has led to the presbyterian [lit. "rule by elder"] form of church government. And a neglect of both of these words in favor of an emphasis on the word for "pastor" could well lead to the benign dictatorship of the local preacher who alone is considered to be pastoral.)

Beyond these observations, what is more important to note is the relation of each of these Biblical words to the others. Read the passage carefully. The *office* (commission, authoritative assignment) is that of elder (v. 17). The passage simply but significantly calls these men "the elders of the church"; a few chapters earlier, in Acts 14:23, we were told that "Paul and Barnabus appointed elders for them in each church." (Also see Titus 1:5.) The point is clear; the apostles and members of the early church viewed these men as "elders." The *work* or *duty* of that office and of those elders holding it is described in v. 28 as the "oversight" of self and of flock ("episcopos," from "epi," meaning "on" or "over," plus "scopos," referring to "vision" or "sight" [like "microscope" means "small vision"]). Finally, the *spirit, the character,* or, if you will, *the heart* with which the elders are to do the work of oversight is that of "shepherd" (an English equivalent is "pastor").

What may we conclude? *The Elders who oversee the flock are the pastors of the church!* The Lord's church is a flock that faces savage wolves who would tear the sheep and devour the lambs with the bloody fangs of false doctrine and worldly life-style (vv. 29-30). Caring for that flock requires diligent oversight and alert watchfulness. Yet the oversight and watchfulness assigned to the elders of the church is a waste of time if it does not arise from a genuine and hearty *caring* for the flock. Pastoral care—shepherding—is never content with mere management of livestock resources. It demands genuine concern and love (look at Paul's own example in v. 31. For further insights, read the delightful little volume by Phillip Keller, *A Shepherd Looks at Psalm 23*).[7] Pastoral care demands the involvement of the elder's total being in careful attention to the well-being of each individual of the flock. It requires heart—a shepherd's heart, one quite different from the reluctant spirit and diffidence of the hired hand. (Read John 10:11-13 to refresh your memory of the profound and important difference between the two.)

In contrast, what we see in today's churches are *administrators*. The senior pastor functions like a CEO who "markets the vision"; the deacons (usually by committee) fulfill the corporate role of the CFO (Chief Financial Officer); and in such a modern corporate or business model for the church, the elders become the Board of Directors. To them falls the administrative responsibility of setting direction for the life of the corporation. They commission or develop a "marketing plan" for church growth, and hold the CEO accountable for the implementation and success of that growth plan. They oversee and direct professionally-run fund raising programs for building or operation budgets. They delegate any and all pastoral duties to the professionals trained to handle such contingencies.

All genuine followers of Jesus will agree that the church must preach and teach the Word of God so as to evangelize the nations, incorporate them through baptism into the body of believers by way of repentance, conversion and faith, and disciple them thoroughly unto disciplined Christian living. That's the mandate of the Great Commission in Matthew 28. When trying to fulfill the Great Commission in our rapidly changing age, the church meets

---

[7] Grand Rapids: Zondervan Publishing Co., 1970.

new ideas, embracing some of them. Not all are bad, either. The corporate business model, for all the criticism I level against it, often arises out of a desire for an efficient use of the church's resources and a visionary and purposeful approach to reaching Biblically-assigned goals. But efficient or not, goal-oriented or not, it has come at a high price; the transferal of her "pastors" to the new department of "administration." And the flock suffers for it.

I Peter 5:1-4:
Organizational Passion or a Willing Heart?

The pastoral character of the eldership is a theme not only found in Acts 20. It is perhaps put even more forcefully in I Peter 5:1-4. "Be shepherds of God's flock that is under your care, serving as overseers—not because you must, but because you are willing, as God wants you to be." Here the radical difference between administering and pastoring is most clearly seen. Administration is a *managerial* function, applying resources to reach carefully articulated goals. It is preeminently organizational and intellectual. Pastoring however is a *nurturing* function, involving care, demanding both strength and tenderness, arising out of a passionate love for the well-being of the flock.[8] While good shepherding will involve the shepherd's calloused feet (today bald tires?), his skill with both rod and staff (both the ability to discern, and the communication skills necessary to challenge, rebuke and call people to repentance), and courage as he faces the predators of the flock (willingness to make the tough calls that generate "cotton mouth" fear?), good shepherding is preeminently a work of the heart, and depends greatly upon the intimate bond between the flock and the shepherd as they hear and follow His voice. "My sheep listen to my voice; I know them, and they follow me" (John 10:27). Pastoring focuses the flock on the *voice of Jesus*—the Bible as it shapes understanding and faith, and directs the flock to *follow*—to live in faith as the people of God.

In subsequent chapters, we'll examine each of these dimensions of

---

8 When I entered the ministry twenty-some years ago, the most sage advice I received was from an old elder who counseled me: "Make sure you love the people of God. You might become a great preacher, you may become an astute theologian, you may have the skills to be an effective administrator or church program manager, but if you don't love God's people, they'll know it, and your ministry will suffer." Sounds like he took it right out of I Cor. 13, doesn't it?

pastoring more carefully. Before I close this chapter, I leave the reader with the following questions. I challenge you to wrestle with them personally; let them stimulate you to self-examination and church-examination in your local congregational setting.

If you are currently an elder, what occupies most of the time you spend in your official duties: administration (meetings, committees, organizational details) or pastoring (meeting with God's people, praying with and for them, admonishing them, instructing them, etc.)? Discuss with others how those time demands might be adapted so as to reflect a more Biblical view of office.

If you are not an elder in your local church, think about the visible work of the elders who hold office. Are they involved in pastoral care, or is their visibility only that of "meeting attender" or "committee member"?

On paper, make a list, based on Acts 20:28-31 and I Peter 5:1-4, of specific duties that arise from an understanding of the eldership as a pastoral office. Discuss this list with others, comparing your findings with your perceptions of the practice of elders in your congregation.

Ask yourself whether you genuinely love the people of God in your local church? (Yes, warts and all, lovable and unlovable alike! Be honest, and admit it if you view them more as porcupines or skunks than as precious lambs.) If you can't state that you do, allow me to challenge you today to pray that God will forgive your sin, and that God will grant you the grace to enable such love!

2

CHECK YOUR AIM

Whenever I've had opportunity to train new elders, I tried to show them what Scripture says about the pastoral character of the work they are called to do. When I do, I usually meet wide eyes, dry mouths, and panic-stricken expressions. It's one thing to be elected to a board that meets the 1st and 3rd Monday of the month for a couple of hours to talk about "church problems, programs and issues." It's quite another thing to be expected to provide Biblical pastoral care to a group of individual believers who aren't much different than yourself, altogether frail sinners who are only in Christ by grace. Who is up to such a task?

The only way an elder can keep his bearings in the face of such great responsibility is to keep his mind on his assigned *purpose*. He must be clear in his own mind about God's purpose for having elders in the first place. After all, God moved the Apostle Paul and Barnabus to "appoint elders in every city" (Acts 14:23; Titus 1:5). It is clear that He wants to care for His people in this way.

Yet in most churches when an elder is ordained to office he faces an array of duties that are at best confusing and at worst completely unrelated to God's pastoral purposes both for him and for the flock. He spends much time in meetings, hears reports from the preachers and other program staff members, is placed on several committees, or may even be asked to serve in some public relations or fund-raising position. Seldom these days is he asked or assigned to pastor people, to become involved personally and deeply in their life struggles and joys.

The reason for this, I'm afraid, is that we often confuse ministry *style* with pastoral *purpose*. In fact, this confusion has been so prevalent that in many churches the various styles represent ecclesiastical "political parties" that in turn represent "voting blocs" within the congregation. Consider the following (admittedly caricatures, but certainly accurate to my years of experience):

The "Dots and Crosses" Man: Inevitably, all who serve in Christ's church will run across an elder who is consumed with details. He is the one that is often assigned to be clerk of records, because he's very fussy about taking minutes of meetings and "dotting the 'i's' and crossing the 't's'" of membership records. When the eldership deals with a difficult pastoral case, he'll be the one who wonders aloud what formal step of discipline you are up to in the sequence prescribed in Matthew 18 or by the denomination's book of church order. He'll be the elder who will view his purpose as that of explaining the church's "policy" regarding public sins to someone caught up in one. His intentions are honorable. He's not "cold"; he just wants to make sure things are done properly—"decently and in good order." To him, membership in the church is a technical, organizational thing; there are rules to follow, just as in the Rotary Club. Pastoral care for the flock is to be understood as careful "regulation" of the organization.

The Law and Order Man: Another character-type of elder in many churches today is the hard-nosed disciplinarian, more evident some years back, but still around (although less vocal these days). His approach is simple and straightforward; the elders are charged with preserving the faith and keeping the faithful in line. Since the devil tries to undermine both doctrine and life-style, the only defense against his treachery is a frontal attack. This type of elder willingly goes on the tough calls, the visits made to rebuke members who are weak in doctrine and/or living in sin, the awkward and confrontational situations. His approach in every such situation would be simple and straightforward; "you sinned, you must confess your sin and find forgiveness." Period. He's not unloving, but he is blunt and tough. To him, membership in Christ is like belonging to an army: Christ's church is at war with the Evil One, fighting against all his treacherous schemes. The elders are there to keep the soldiers of the Lord well-disciplined. Without discipline any army will fail.

The Sympathizer: Another character-type often seen in the eldership is the sympathizer. His name comes from his remarkable ability to identify emotionally with the church member with whom he is dealing. If he visits someone suffering from depression, he is very sensitive to all the depressing details of the individual's life, and can understand completely why he or she is suffering. If he meets an adulterer, the sympathizer will be most sensitive to the troubles at home that drove the man or woman into the arms of another for support. If he must deal with a young couple pregnant prior to marriage, his focus will minimize confrontation over the sin of premarital sex, and will be directed instead to the feelings the young couple will experience as they face becoming the subject of gossip as well as the parents of a baby they probably aren't ready to raise. This elder doesn't believe for a minute he is soft on sin, but focuses his gaze on the hurts and the misery sin has caused. He considers the practice of assessing blame and responsibility to be counterproductive; he believes sensitivity and understanding will build relationships with Christ much more effectively. To the sympathizer, membership in the church is much like a horizontal human relationship with all its emotional ups and downs. To keep the relationship alive is not a technical thing, nor a legal matter. It requires sensitivity, understanding, patience and love.

DIVINE PURPOSES FOR ELDER CARE

Perhaps you've seen these character-types at work in the life of the church. Admittedly, individual elders in the local church are more likely to be amalgams of several types, but I'm sure you recognize the stereotypes. Sadly, Biblical elders aren't supposed to be representatives of voting blocs within the church, the one more tough, the other more loving, the former ecclesiastical republicans, the latter ecclesiastical democrats. They are to represent God's interests, God's assigned purposes for the care of God's precious people, the flock under His ultimate care.

Let's examine just what God's purposes are. I suggest six, each clearly set forth in Scripture.

DEFENSE

The first is the defense of the flock. Notice the priority given the work of defense in Paul's instructions in Acts 20:28-31:

> Keep watch over yourselves and all the flock of which the Holy Spirit has made you overseers. Be shepherds of the church of God, which he bought with his own blood. I know

that after I leave, savage wolves will come in among you and will not spare the flock. Even from your own number men will arise and distort the truth in order to draw away disciples after them. So be on your guard! Remember that for three years I never stopped warning each of you night and day with tears.

Set against this background of expected attacks upon the flock both from the outside ("savage wolves") and from within ("from your own number..."), the work of shepherding the flock can only be appropriately understood as defense. And the practices both prescribed and described in the next verse serve to underscore this work: "Be on guard" and "warning."

The shepherds in Israel in Biblical times knew that defense of the flocks was of paramount purpose. They knew what the Psalmist meant when he referred to God's "rod and staff" being a comfort. Listen to this extended description of just what that meant.

Every shepherd boy, from the time he first starts to tend his father's flock, takes special pride in the selection of a rod and staff exactly suited to his own size and strength. He goes into the bush and selects a young sapling which is dug from the ground. This is carved and whittled down with great care and patience. The enlarged base of the sapling where its trunk joins the roots is shaped into a smooth, rounded head of hard wood. The sapling itself is shaped to exactly fit the owner's hand. After he completes it, the shepherd boy spends hours practicing with this club, learning how to throw it with amazing speed and accuracy. It becomes his main weapon of defense for both himself and his sheep.[1]

If the rod of the shepherd boy was a tool for defense, then the "rod" given to the NT elder for the defense of the flock of God is none other than the Word of God. That's the point of Paul's apostolic "warnings" referred to in v. 31—the words of the apostles becoming the NT Scriptures for the church of today. This squares as well with the message of Eph. 6:10f. Faced with the painful truth that "our struggle is not against flesh and blood, but against the rulers, against the authorities, against the powers of this dark world and against the spiritual forces of evil in the heavenly realms," the apostle Paul challenges the church to "put on the full armor of

---

[1] Phillip Keller, *A Shepherd Looks at Psalm 23*, p.93.

God." Central to that armor is the Bible: It provides both the "belt" and the "breastplate" of truth and righteousness that prepare the man of God for the conflict; it is the "gospel of peace" that readies him for battle; it provides the protective material for the "shield of faith"; it is the "sword of the spirit, which is the Word of God" (Eph. 6:14-17).

In a later chapter, we'll explore the ways in which elders must read and apply the Word in the lives of the sheep and lambs. For now it is enough to say that elders who are in tune with God's assigned purposes for their work and for His flock will be men who diligently use the defensive tools God has provided, central among them is the Word of God.

RECONCILIATION

If defense is primary among the duties assigned by God to the shepherd, reconciliation is close behind. Who can forget Jesus' gripping parable of the lost sheep?

> What do you think? If a man owns a hundred sheep, and one of them wanders away, will he not leave the ninety-nine on the hills and go to look for the one that wandered off? And if he finds it, I tell you the truth, he is happier about that one sheep than about the ninety-nine that did not wander off. In the same way your Father in heaven is not willing that any of these little ones should be lost (Matt. 18:12-14).

So many elders are content to manage church programs, chair church committees and all enjoy local church stability. But an elder who will not diligently pursue the church's lost sheep is failing miserably to live up to the pattern of the Good Shepherd. Ask yourself whether you (if an elder) or the elders of your congregation are faithful in chasing down the wandering "blacksheep"? That's really the measure of whether you fulfill divine purpose. Remember the closely related passage of Luke 15, in which Jesus teaches 3 related parables, all of which place the focus on seeking and finding the lost (object), and *celebrating when it is found*. That's the "punch line" of the Parable of the Lost Son (often called the "Prodigal Son"); the elder brother refuses to celebrate! Can that parable be told of you? Of your church family? God forbid!

Returning to the Matthew 18 passage, it is instructive to notice the shape of reconciliation. It is not seen as tolerance, overlooking differences or ignoring sins. It is not "peace at any price." Rather, in the section immediately following the parable of the lost sheep, Jesus launches into urgent instruction about rebuking a brother who sins. This effort unto reconciliation, seeking both to "win" a brother back to the church and to the church's "Father in heaven," is crucial to the work of reconciliation which the elders are called to do in the name of the Lord. [2]

The mandate of reconciliation appears several other times in the NT, none more important than II Cor. 5. In this passage the apostle is referring to his own divine appointment when he exults:

> All this is from God, who reconciled us to himself through Christ, and gave us the ministry of reconciliation....And he has committed to us the message of reconciliation. We are Christ's ambassadors, as though God were making his appeal through us.

Some may argue that it is *only* to the work of the apostles of the early church that this passage applies, but that is an unnecessary restriction. It is clear from the passage that the mandate is the ministry of the Word of God. That, in our age, is entrusted to the church as a whole (I Tim. 3:15) and especially to her pastors and teachers (II Tim. 2:2, 4:2).[3]

The point must be clearly understood. The "workers with the Word" in the church of the Lord must be gripped firmly by the pastoral purpose of the Lord to "seek and to save" the lost, to bring about reconciliation. The world and all its inhabitants are at enmity with God because of sin; only by the reconciling work of Christ the "logos," proclaimed in the preaching of the Word ("logos") of

---

[2] Although commentators differ in interpreting just who is meant by "the church" in v. 17, since Jesus' words in this passage predate the church after Pentecost and thus predate the institution of elders and deacons, it is fair to assume that by "the church" is meant more than the aggregate gathering of believers. Key to the passage is the role of legal witnesses—the "two or three" mentioned in v. 16—on the basis of whose testimony God promises to act from His heavenly judgment seat. At the very least the passage suggests formal and official representatives operative within the church, which in the later NT pastoral teachings embrace the eldership (See e.g. I Tim. 3:5).

[3] The NIV rendering *"message* of reconciliation" is a translation of the Greek word "logos" or "word." The theological importance of that word is well understood to refer both to the Word-made-flesh in John 1 and to the Word-inscripturated that the NT church preaches and teaches. The ministers of the Word, originally the apostles but later to include the pastors and teachers of the church, are none other than "workers with the Word" (II Tim. 2:15). It is to them that the "ministry of reconciliation" is entrusted in our age.

the NT church, can and will they be reconciled, that is, receive rebirth, new hope, new life and a new covenant in His blood.[4] The elders must keep in mind this purpose. They are not merely to "solve problems," if in solving that problem they do not seek to bring the person into intimate fellowship with the Living God. In fact, the contrary is often true. Frequently an individual's problems (like marital problems or other family difficulties, depression, financial stress, or any one of a number of other such immediate crises) are circumstances that drive the person to their knees, and ultimately to the Lord. Such is the powerful teaching of both Psalm 32 and I Cor. 10:11f.

Restoration

Close on the heels of reconciliation is the divine purpose to restore repentant and forgiven sinners to fruitful service within the Lord's church and world. Several passages make the point poignantly. Consider first of all John 21, where the thrice-denying Peter is not only forgiven by the Lord Jesus, but is *restored* to a position of trust and great pastoral responsibility in the wonderful and touching story that unfolds on the shores of Galilee and is recorded in vv. 15-17. He who denied thrice is now asked *twice* "do you love me unconditionally."[5] To each query, Peter answers in the affirmative, but with a twist; each time he declares his love, but uses a different word, the Greek word "phileo," a less-intensive form of love that word books often render as "affection."[6] Only after this exchange does Jesus change His question, asking the *third time* only "do you have affection for me." Yet, even though thoroughly-humbled Peter can only pledge a lesser form of loving commitment (gone is the brash assurance that "even if all fall away on account of you, I never will!" Matt. 26:33), nonetheless he is restored with the thrice-repeated commission "feed my lambs," "take care of my sheep," "feed my sheep."

---

4 Notice the inseparable connection between the Word preached on the one hand and spiritual rebirth and faith on the other, reflected in Romans 10:14-17 and I Peter 1:23-25.

5 The Greek word used by Jesus in the first two questions is the word "agape," meaning self-denying, self-sacrificing, unconditional love.

6 s.v. "phileo" in Bauer, Arndt and Gingrich, *A Greek-English Lexicon of the New Testament and Other Early Christian Literature.* (Chicago: The University of Chicago Press, 1957).

Look next at Acts 9, the marvelous account of Saul's conversion on the road to Damascus. Don't stop in your reading however with what God did *to* him and *in* him. Read on to note carefully what God was to do *through* him. Listen:

> But the Lord said to Ananias, 'Go! This man is my chosen instrument to carry my name before the Gentiles and their kings and before the people of Israel' (vv. 15-16).

Not only did God save Saul; not only did God forgive the sin of his stubborn-hearted and cruel persecution of the church; God *restored* Saul to a ministry of great responsibility. I often wonder how quickly we'd do the same? I know of godly and mature men and women who sinned, some grievously, in their lives. All of them dealt with their sin Biblically, that is, through genuine repentance and humility before God and others. Yet what characterizes the way their local churches have dealt with them is determined more by their past sin than by their status as forgiven and restored in Christ. Some of these dear people are never allowed any position of trust and responsibility, as if we who bear the legacy of the Reformation still believed and practiced the assignment of penance for sin! This ought not to be. God's purpose and goal is restoration to service!

The third passage to which I direct your attention is Philemon, Paul's little letter to his friend in Colossae. Sent along with Tychicus and the letter we know as *Colossians* (Col. 4:7-9), Paul returns runaway slave Onesimus to Philemon with a declaration and with a charge. The declaration is that, since Onesimus has now become converted to Christ, he is now "useful both to you and to me" (v. 11).[7] The charge is to restore, rather than to punish this new brother: "Perhaps the reason he was separated from you for a little while was that you might have him back for good—no longer as a slave, but better than a slave, as a dear brother...welcome him as you would welcome me" (vv. 15-17).

I trust the point is clear. Elders must follow this NT pattern set by the Lord in both His earthly ministry and through His apostolic instruction. Those whom the Lord forgives, the Lord restores to fruitful service and ministry in His church. So must elders endeavor to do. Challenge people with their sin? Of course. Rebuke and call

---

7 The name Onesimus means "useful"; before he was in Christ, he was more of a problem than a help to his master Philemon.

them to repentance? Absolutely! But never to stop there, the elders must seek to restore these now-transformed people into ministers of God! Such is God's purpose.

Equipping for Ministry

If those who are reconciled to God are restored, then those who are restored are to be "equipped for ministry." That is the teaching of Eph. 4:11-12, and is the next in the list of divine purposes God establishes for the work of the NT pastoral elder. The passage says: "And he himself (Christ) gave some to be apostles, some prophets, some evangelists, and some pastors and teachers, for the equipping of the saints for the work of ministry, for the edifying of the body of Christ..." (Eph. 4:11-12 NKJV).

I would make several observations about this important passage. First, this text is often used to argue against the unbiblical practice of separating clergy from laity, thus establishing firmly the principle of the "priesthood of all believers." The real weight of the passage is to be found in recognizing that, while all of God's people are to exercise and utilize the "grace" given to each (v. 7), it is assigned to the special office-bearers known as "apostles... prophets...evangelists...pastors and teachers" to "*prepare* (equip) God's people for works of service." Often overlooked in the verse is that "pastors" in these verses is the same word used to describe "elders" in Acts 20 and I Peter 5.

This is to say that elders are given by God to train His people for their own work in the Kingdom of God. The work of elders enables and equips the works of the saints. It is a shameful indictment of most churches that the "80-20" rule is an accurate description of their deployment of the gifts of the Spirit: 80 % of the work is done by 20% of the people. The purpose of God in and through the eldership is precisely the opposite: the few assigned the duty of preparing and training the many for the ministry of all!

Edification

One of the most powerful images of the Old Testament—the central place and function of the Temple in the lives of the people of God—carries over and is developed in the New, and serves as the fifth purpose to which we give our attention. In Christ, the temple changes from a place to a people (I Cor. 3:16). Yet, in several passages in the NT, the development, strengthening and cultivation of the church is referred to as the work of "edification." In Ephesians 4:12b, on the heels of the expression of God's desire that His people be equipped for ministry, we read of yet another purpose: "...so that the body of Christ may be built up...." Connected to the previous, it is nonetheless a distinct point. Here the Greek word connotes construction, the building of an edifice. When seen in connection with other Scriptures like I Peter 2:5 and II Tim. 2:15,[8] it becomes clear that the pastoral work assigned to the elders of the church aims to build God's people into a towering edifice of faith, a temple within which God delights to make His dwelling, a people/place of holiness and worship 24 hours a day, 7 days a week. And once again, the construction method to be employed is that of the pastoral ministry of the Word. People are built by the Word.

Interestingly, and seldom acknowledged, are the corollaries of upbuilding. In Eph. 4:13, three are expressly identified. They are *unity, knowledge* and *maturity.*

In the *first* place, when the elders of the church are pastorally faithful in building up the church through the truth of the Word of God, pastorally faithful in equipping the membership for its ministry-service to Christ, the church and her members will and must exhibit dynamic *unity.* This unity will not be superficial, but will run deep into the bedrock of both commitment to Truth and shoulder-to-shoulder striving for Christ. This must serve as a pastoral goal for the local church, and one that is often overlooked by elders. So often, in the pursuit of the "truth" (sometimes only a term used for the self-justification of proving that one was "right") the local elders would allow for the breaking up of the body of believers. Those whose pastoral strategy seeks God's purpose will seek instead a faithfulness to the Truth that is evidenced by unity, not by division.

In the *second* place, the church will reach the *knowledge* of the Son of God. This is a profound notion, far beyond the mere knowledge of the text of Scripture (although certainly including it!). This knowledge reflects the intimacy between the believer and the Lord, about

---

[8] I Peter 2:5 explicitly describes the members of the Lord's church as the "living stones" of the temple, who are also the priests of that temple, and whose lives are the spiritual sacrifices offered to the Lord. II Tim. 2:15, on the other hand, is more implicit, employing the imagery of the brickmason to describe the men who work with the Word.

which the writer to the Ephesians wrote a couple of chapters earlier when he used compound words to describe vividly the believer's unity with Christ: "made-us-alive-with-Christ," "raised-us-up-with-Christ," "seated-us-with-him." The pastoral strategy for the local elders that best reflects the divine purpose for the church is a strategy that sees the people of God becoming truly and passionately pious, in the most intimate sense of that term.

And in the *third* place, the church that is properly equipped and built up will be a church that exhibits *maturity*, defined here (v. 13) as "attaining to the whole measure of the fullness of Christ." The concept of mature manhood is best understood when contrasted with the "infant" behavior of the next verse. The mature will stand firm in Biblical doctrine and will not be blown about by distortions and new teachings; the mature will speak the truth lovingly and will not bite and devour each other verbally; the mature will participate in mutual encouragement and upbuilding and not in tearing down and the pursuit of individual aggrandizement.

HOLY LIVING

Finally, one cannot conclude any discussion of God's purposes for His church and her members without mentioning the primacy given to the goal of "holiness." Remember the words of Heb. 12:14, which reminds us that "without holiness no one will see the Lord." And as a careful study of the Old Testament roots of the concept will reveal, holiness embraces twin emphases: first, *separation* from sin and moral corruption, and second, *consecration* to the Lord's devoted service. Elders who are pursuing God's purposes will always aim to develop genuinely holy living among God's people. That means confronting sin and calling for repentance of course. But it means more. It means teaching the high yet rewarding demands of service to a High and Exalted King. It means insisting that the profession of faith that people make with their mouths must be matched by the expression of faith revealed in their day-to-day existence. It means following up instruction with specific application that works out the details of the radical distinction between the citizens of the Kingdom of God and the citizens of this world.

* * * *

I began by observing that many confuse eldership style with pastoral purpose. I caricatured common styles of elder work as "Dots and Crosses," "Law and Order," and the "Sympathizer," and noted that when the focus of attention is laid instead on the divinely-ordained pastoral *purpose* of the elder's task, questions of style fade into secondary or even tertiary priority. In Biblical metaphor, the elder is not a microscope; his vision must never to be limited to narrow confines of a very specific and immediate problem, isolated on the glass slide placed beneath the lens of his examination. The elder is not a hammer: his purpose is not limited to striking hard and clean on the nailhead of a specific sinner and his sin. Nor is the elder only an ear: his task is not just to listen sympathetically to the emotional cries of a believer in difficult circumstances. The elder is a shepherd, nothing more, nothing less. As shepherd, his work and his purpose must be guided by nothing other than the purposes of the Good Shepherd for the care and tending of His sheep. When those purposes are kept in mind, the elder will be a faithful shepherd; when those purposes are lost, the elder will be unfaithful, and open to the withering judgment of God pronounced over all who fail the flock.

3

GIVING YOURSELF AN EKG

In the previous chapters, I argued for a pastoral definition and understanding of the office of elder, pointing to Acts 20, I Peter 5, and Eph. 4:11-12 for a clear and Biblical understanding of the role and purpose of the elder in the care of the flock. At the same time, it is important to note that the *first* assignment given by the Apostle Paul to the elders of the local church is *not* that of pastoral care of the flock, but oversight of one's self! Acts 20:28 begins: *"Keep watch over yourselves...."*

This is no accident. The Apostle Paul, who in Romans 7:7ff would painfully but incisively describe the powerful role of sin in the life of every believer, allows the local elder no room for self-deception. He knows full well sin's ability to cloud one's self-assessment. He knows well the Psalmist's prayer, "Search me, O God, and know my heart; test me and know my anxious thoughts. See if there is any offensive way in me, and lead me in the way everlasting" (Ps. 139:23-24). He knows that unless God grants us insight into our sins, we will delude ourselves with the pretense of self-righteousness. That is true of elders as it is of any other sinner before the face of God.

It is especially urgent for elders to see themselves correctly, to view themselves as God sees them, and that for several reasons. *First*, if the elder does not see himself with spiritual accuracy, he risks spiritual arrogance, and the flock suffers. Arrogance in the shepherd leads to a despising of the sheep and lambs, an attitude of superiority that allows no room for genuine loving care, no place for patience, no desire for forgiveness or restoration. *Second*, if the elder does not test himself rigorously, he falls under some of the most frightful curses of God to appear on the pages of Scripture. When God tests the false shepherds in the time of the prophet Ezekiel, He finds that they "did not search for my flock but cared for themselves rather than for my flock." God then declares, "I am against the shepherds and will hold them accountable for my flock" (Ezek. 34:9-10). That is a frightening word, one that every shepherding elder in our generation will do well to take to heart.

How does an elder see himself correctly? There are many Scriptural diagnostic tools. One could, for example, use Colossians 3 to assess whether he has his mind "on things above," as opposed to being mired on earthly things. He could use I Timothy 3 or Titus 1 as the standard by which to judge his own spiritual maturity. If he does not find himself sufficiently mature to meet God's criteria for the eldership, he has reason to fall on his knees in repentance and confession and to plead for God's mercy and grace. He could assess his own spiritual gifts and his use of them according to the standard of Romans 12:3: "Do not think of yourself more highly than you ought, but rather think of yourself with sober judgment, in accordance with the measure of faith God has given you."

Each of these passages and countless others provide spiritual tools with which to test one's own heart. All of them are worthy of careful and humble study and application.

Yet, some passages of Scripture speak directly and specifically to and about the heart of the pastor, the heart of the shepherd. They drive us inexorably to the Good Shepherd Jesus Christ. They also provide the standard for both shaping and ultimately judging the heart of those who shepherd His flock in His name. In the next pages, then, you must do your own work, you must give yourself a spiritual EKG. It will not do for me merely to explain what the many passages say; you must hold your own heart and life under the light of God's words so as to subject yourself to the thorough and unyielding scrutiny of God's own eye. Testing yourself in the light of these passages will reveal clearly to you whether you have a *shepherd's heart*.

So, take out your Bible, sharpen your pencil, and get to work. But before you do, pray that God will keep your heart humble, your mind teachable, your spirit malleable under the workmanship of the Potter Whose clay you are.

24 / With A Shepherd's Heart

Materials for Individual Study

Individual Study #1:

Lessons From The Old Testament

1. Throughout Scripture, God uses metaphors to reveal His heart for His people, His way of dealing with them. Think of the well-known imagery of Father or of Judge. From early in the history of God's people, the picture of God as Shepherd has been crucial to the understanding of His heart and to the pattern of His care.

Read Genesis 48:15 and 49:24 in context. From these passages, describe what it means that God is Israel's shepherd.

He Has always been w Jacob (and Joseph) as the Good, Sovereign guide before whom we walk, A cornerstone that cannot be moved, and, thus, always able to be trusted.

2. After Moses brought God's salvation from Egypt (a powerful picture of the coming "exodus" from sin through Jesus Christ for all who believe), God appointed Joshua to provide leadership and care for His people. Again, Scripture uses the image of shepherd.

Read Numbers 27:15-23. What is the reason given for Joshua's appointment? What does Jesus' use of the same phrase in Mark 6:34 tell you about God's heart-concern for His church in every age? *Asked for someone who will go before the people, who shall "lead them out and bring them in", that the people will not be "sheep w/o a shepherd". They need a shepherd's voice.*

3. The Bible calls David the "man after God's own heart." It is no coincidence that David grew up as a shepherd boy, nor that his background equipped him to be a shepherd-king whose responsibility to the nation was that of a shepherd looking after his flock. In fact, the shepherd image came to define what a godly king in Israel was to be!

Read all of the passages in context and answer the following questions:

Giving Yourself an EKG / 25

- II Samuel 5:2 — How is the kingship defined?

  "shepherd of my people"

- II Samuel 7:7-8 — What is kingly leadership called? How is the servant-leadership described in these verses different from the totalitarian authority of the typical ruler of that day?

  he had commanded the judges to "shepherd my people" my servant, David, to be prince ("leader") over my people..

- II Samuel 12:1-6 — How does Nathan the prophet describe Bathsheba, with whom David sinned? How does the picture used in these verses describe the nature of David's sin?

  little "lamb" — Treated people as things. Had "no pity" on those less fortunate

- I Kings 22:17 — What does Micaiah prophesy will be the result of King Ahab's death?

  The people will be "scattered" as sheep w/ no shepherd

- Psalm 23 — David, the shepherd-king, penned these words. How do they reveal God's heart? How should they shape a leader's heart and ways? Always sees that goodness and mercy is following His flock. He is good. He is sovereign, always with us, always guiding, protecting, even overflowing our cup and anointing our head in the midst of enemies

- Psalm 28:9 — To whom does David cry for help? Why?

  God — "Be their shepherd". The people need to be carried, need strength, need refuge

- Psalm 78:71-72; Psalm 80:1 — How do these verses describe both the Lord and the Lord's chosen leaders? What lesson is there in these words for the church in our age?

To be a shepherd - "with upright heart" and guiding people "with his skillful hand"
- Leaders ought to be chosen for their known integrity and evident skills

4. From what you've just read, you know that the "heart of the Shepherd" was the standard God would use to test the faithfulness of the leaders of His people. Faithful leaders were faithful shepherds. Unfaithful shepherds fell under the stern indictment of the prophets, whose words would test prophet, priest and king alike to see if they had the heart of God. Listen to prophet Isaiah thunder forth against all who threaten God's own flock:

> See, the Sovereign Lord comes with power, and his arm rules for him. See, his reward is with him, and his recompense accompanies him. He tends his flock like a shepherd: He gathers the lambs in his arms and carries them close to his heart; he gently leads those that have young (Isaiah 40:10-11).

Read the following passages and answer each of the questions:

- Isaiah 56:10-12 — Who is described, and what is their sin?

His "watchmen" (the leaders). Laziness, idleness, without knowledge/understanding, turned to their own gain.

- Jeremiah 23:1-4 — Who is addressed, what is their sin, and what will God do about it?

"Shepherds" (leaders). Scattered and drove away the people. Did not attend to them. He will gather and bring them back. Set shepherds over them who will care for them. So they will not fear or be dismayed or be lost.

- Jeremiah 25:34-38 — What does this reveal about God's reaction to unfaithful leaders?

"Fierce anger". A holy wrath in response to these shepherds.

- Ezekiel 34 — Read the entire chapter carefully.

    1) verses 1-4 — What was the sin of the leaders?

    Feeding themselves instead of the sheep — not strengthening, not healing, not bringing back those strayed. ruling ē harshness & force

    2) verses 7-8 — What was its spiritual cause?

    3) verses 5-6, 11-13 — Because of the leaders' sin, what happened to the flock? Were scattered over all the face of the earth

    4) verses 17-21 — How did the flock follow their wicked example?

- Ezekiel 34:23; 37:24 — Who is promised in each of these prophecies? David

- Micah 5:4 — From the context, are you able to determine when this prophecy will be fulfilled?

Individual Study #2:
LESSONS FROM THE LIFE AND TEACHING OF THE GOOD SHEPHERD

Introduction: The life and teachings of Jesus of Nazareth are replete with shepherd imagery. The Gospels reveal that the heart and will of God, the Shepherd of Israel, come to complete expression in the ministry of His Son Jesus. In one of the most vivid descriptions of who He is and what He has come to do, Jesus calls Himself "The Good Shepherd" — both claiming an identity with His Father, and revealing the sharp contrast to the false leaders of God's people in that day.

[margin note: Moses ask God for a successor, a shepherd]

Consider carefully (in context) the following passages, and answer each question:

1. Matthew 9:36 (compare Mark 6:34) — How does this passage reveal that Jesus possessed a heart like that of His Father (see Numbers 27:17)? In Mark's account, Jesus' compassion led Him to do something specific. What? Why?

Had compassion on the crowds & recognized that they need guidance, help, protection. Healed them. They were sick, some with demons that he cast out

2. John 10 — Read this entire chapter before proceeding.

[margin note: What was sheep, K.J.V. destroy]

- Describe concretely the differences Jesus identifies between Himself and false shepherds (verses 1-10).

Thiefs, robbers. He calls & they know his voice. Will flee from stranger but will follow Jesus. He identifies himself as the only one by which sheep can enter, that they can be saved & have "find pasture" or have life abundantly

- What do the following verses reveal about Jesus' motives?

  - verse 10 - *to give abundant life is to love others rather than want from others*

  - verse 11 — *This love occurs through "laying down life"*

- verse 16
  motivated towards unity of flock under one shepherd
  - bringing others in

- verse 18 of laying down life
  - Motives are of his own will, accord & given authority by the Father.

- verses 27-30
  - Motives are to give eternal life, to never lose them — which is not possible as He is one with the Father.
  - He knows them — sounds deeply personal

3. Matthew 26:31 — How does this passage (and its parallel in Mark 14:27) describe Jesus' view of His upcoming death?

- the shepherd (himself) will be struck

4. Luke 15:1-7 — What does this parable (and its 2 companion parables in chapter 15) tell you about the heart of God's shepherd?

This compassion goes out of its way leaving things untended to go find a lost one w/ diligence

- Waits & eagerness, compassion watching for the lost one to come home
- Rejoices & joy at the return

Individual Study #3:

LESSONS FROM THE APOSTOLIC CHURCH

Introduction: In the Old Testament, the Shepherd of Israel (Psalm 23:1, Psalm 80:1, etc.) appointed prophets, priests and kings who were to care for, defend and preserve the flock of Israel.

In the New Covenant, Jesus — the Good Shepherd — commissions men to represent Him and to care for His flock (the church, the new Israel-Galatians 3:29) after His ascension to heaven.

A frightening thought, I'll admit. How can sinful men, with all of the hidden motives of their heart, hope to avoid the indictment and condemnation God had heaped upon the false shepherds of the Old Covenant? No wonder that those most familiar with the work of the eldership are most burdened by the thought of being ordained to that office.

1. Study John 21:15-17 in context (especially read John 13:31-38 and John 18:15-18, 25-27).

- How does the reinstatement of Peter (boastful but thrice-denying; humble then thrice-commissioned) give hope to your heart? *I have done what Peter did, and was still Peter used to build & shepherd the church. Even one who walked on water & knew him intimately failed & denied.*

- The commission given to Peter (21:15-17) focuses his attention away from his own failure and on to something else. What is that new focus? *The sheep. Feed them, Tend them.*

- What is the connection between Jesus' questions about Peter's heart-love and His commission to care for the flock?

Your love for Jesus will show itself through action - feeding, tending the people

Giving Yourself an EKG / 31

2. After the Lord's Ascension, recorded in Acts 1, the church grew quickly as "the Word of the Lord grew." Wherever the Apostles preached, God prepared hearts to receive His Word (Acts 16:14). But the Apostles and their companions could not stay for long where they preached. They had to travel, to preach throughout the world. The book of Acts is a blur of apostolic travel, preaching, teaching, equipping...and moving on again!

That's why it is of such great importance that we read of the appointment of elders "in each church of the region" (Acts 14:23; compare Titus 1:5). The elders were necessary because the Apostles' unique work was coming to an end. Soon they would be gone, replaced by others appointed to carry on after them.

- Why are elders to be appointed "in each local church" (Acts 14:23)? *Shepherd flock through tribulations.*

- How does Titus 1:5 and the verses following shed light on the reason for and function of locally functioning elders? *"Order". Steward. Instruct. Hold firm. Rebuke those who contradict*

3. In Acts 20:28-35 we read *the most significant passage regarding the eldership* in all of Scripture. Nowhere else is the task and responsibility of the elder of the local church so clearly defined. In few passages are the spiritual foes so clearly identified and so graphically described as in this one.

Please note in the first place, that the Apostle is speaking to the elders of the church in the city of Ephesus (verse 17). It is these elders to whom he gives the charge, "Be shepherds..." (verse 28). No mistaking the identity or the assignment! Take care of the Good Shepherd's flock! It is elder's work.

Note second, that several names are used (verse 28) for these men. As noted in the opening chapter, these men are called "elders" (presbuteroi) in verse 17; they are called both "overseers" (often translated "bishops" — episkopous) and "shepherds" (poimein) in verse 28. Sadly, the church has often, through the ages and in many places, missed the point; elders are the bishops and (pastoral) shepherds of the flock; these are not different offices reflecting the difference between protestant and catholic or episcopal churches. Bishops are not some hierarchical authority figure in a church bureaucracy; nor are "pastors" ("shepherds," literally) an office distinct from the eldership. "In every town" elders are to oversee the lives of the flocks representatives of the heart of the Good Shepherd.

Note finally, that the essential work of an elder is to watch over the flock in order to defend it (verses 28-31). The Apostle Paul holds up his own work among the church at Ephesus as an example for them to follow (verses 31-35), and teaches them specifically what it is they are to watch for (verses 29-30), both from within and outside the body of believers.

Your turn. **Carefully study the passage (read verses 17-38) and answer the following:**

1. What 4 specific commands appear in verses 28-31?

   Pay careful attention to yourselves
   "   "   "   to all the flock
   Care for the church of God
   Be alert
   Remembering Paul's gracious admonishments

2. Why is each command both relevant and urgent?

3. From the following verses, deduce specific practices or methods employed by Paul which can serve as an example for godly elders today:

   - 20:20

   - 20:27

- 20:31

- 20:32

- 20:35

- 20:36

Individual Study #4:

THE HEART OF A SHEPHERD

If Acts 20:28f provides the principle set of *instructions* for the duties of the eldership, then I Peter 5:1-4 is the preeminent appeal to the *heart-motives* of those entrusted with this office. In it, the Apostle Peter, commissioned by Jesus to "feed my lambs" in John 21, now passes along to the elders in the churches the same charge: "Be shepherds of God's flock" (I Peter 5:2). And just as Jesus had linked Peter's commissioning to Peter's profession of love ("Do you love me, Peter?"), so Peter in turn, addresses the heart-motives of those called to care for God's precious people.

Read I Peter 5:1-4 (also note the context of 3:8-chapter 4), and answer the following:

1. Why does Peter list his "qualification" in verse 1? How do those words add weight to the charge to follow?

2. What do these 4 verses tell us about the relationship between elders and Christ Himself in regard to the care of the church?

3. What were the church's circumstances (see the context) in that day? How would they affect shepherding work? What lessons are contained in this truth for the church today?

4. What must be the motivation of a Christ-like elder? Why is motive so important?

Giving Yourself an EKG / 35

5. What motivations (attitudes) are inappropriate for a Christ-like elder? Why?

6. Why is the example of the elder's own life-style so crucial to his shepherding work (verse 3)?

7. What is the promise in verse 4, and why is it so important?

Individual Study #5:

AIM AT GOD'S TARGET!

Please read and study Ephesians 4:11-16 (include a careful reading of the prior context).

As you study these words, note first of all the list of offices that appears in verse 11: "...apostles, prophets, evangelists, pastors and teachers." It is important to understand that not all of these are given by Christ to the church in every age. Apostles and prophets, for example, functioned in the first generation of the church after Pentecost, but died and were not replaced. They dominate the pages of the New Testament writings and the life of the early church but were not necessary for the ongoing life of that church. For subsequent generations of the church, the office(s) of pastor and teacher are especially relevant. Hence, the "Pastoral Epistles" of I - II Timothy and Titus were written to the church specifically to equip such men.

It is also important to note historically, that the term "pastor" has often been used to refer to ordained "clergymen" (as distinct from laymen). This is unfortunate, unwarranted and unbiblical. The term "pastors" in Greek is "poimenas" and as we've seen, means "shepherds." The term used here is the same one used in Acts 20:28 to prescribe the work of elders.

Some have understood the phrase "pastors and teachers" in Eph. 4:11 to refer to separate offices. Calvin saw the latter as referring to "Doctors of Theology," or professors. Others view pastors and teachers to refer to two kinds of elder: "ruling" (or pastoral) elders and "teaching" elders (meaning preachers). (See also I Timothy 5:17). The important thing to remember is that God wants His church to be well cared for, and provides representatives of His own loving protection as His gracious gift. Some of these were necessary in the process of laying the foundation just after Pentecost; others during the hectic and rapid spread of the church; and others in the preaching, teaching and shepherding care of the flock every since. In every age, the one constant is that they who serve the flock in God's Name are to be shepherds, following after the heart of the Good Shepherd Himself.

Read the previous chapter, carefully studying the various passages referred to in the discussion of the pastoral purposes for elder work and answer the following questions:

Giving Yourself an EKG / 37

1. From Ephesians 4:12-16, identify the *purpose* for which God granted the church the gifts of the offices listed in verse 11.

2. How, according to the next verses in this text, does one evaluate whether the divinely established pastoral purposes are being achieved?

3. Based on your study of this and the other passages discussed in chapter 2, evaluate the following specific activities. Assess which of these activities are in harmony with the purposes discussed in the chapter. Of those that are, try to identify *which purpose* each activity seeks to pursue.

   - visits to the homes of each church member or family

   - one-on-one discipleship visits

   - leading Bible Studies in your home with immature believers who wish to grow

   - rebuking a member who has a long-standing habit of using coarse language

- excommunicating a woman member who is living with her boyfriend and refuses to see you despite repeated attempts

- referring a potentially difficult marital problem of members of the local church to an area psychologist (alternatively, counseling the couple yourself)

- challenging a member's involvement in a psychotherapy self-help group

- challenging a 40ish single woman's membership in a computer dating service

- defending the proposed ordination to the office of deacon of a godly man who, prior to conversion and years earlier, had been alcohol-dependant (alternatively, who had been previously married and divorced)

- assigning/appointing members to work in various local church ministries

- mediating disputes between church members

- mediating disputes between a church member and an unbeliever

Giving Yourself an EKG / 39

MATERIALS FOR GROUP DISCUSSION

The material presented in this section is offered with a view to use in meetings of elders, or in sessions offered as preparatory for nominees to office or potential office holders. It is designed to stimulate analysis of Scripture, promote discussion among godly men, and enable the existing elders to gain a glimpse into the hearts of the trainees. Hopefully what they see there will be *shepherd's hearts!*

Group Seminar 1:

DEVELOPING A HEART FOR THE CHURCH

1. What is the Church, according to Scripture? That is a big question today, one for which many have no clear answer. It may help to wrestle with the Biblical word-pictures or metaphors that God uses to teach us. **What is the metaphor used in each of the following? How does that metaphor instruct us concerning God's view of the church and how you should view it?** (The first one is done for you as an example.)

- Luke 8:21 (The church is a *family*. God's family is defined, not by blood, but by hearing and doing God's Word. Christ thinks of us as his brothers and sisters.)

- John 10:11f

- I Timothy 3:15

- I Corinthians 12:12f

- Ephesians 2:19; Philippians 3:20

- I Peter 2:9-10

2. Do people in your area or congregation employ *worldly* concepts or patterns when they think of church leadership? (For example, do your people view leaders in the church as *trustees* of a Board? As *businessmen* in charge of the corporation? As *democratic representatives* of various interest groups?) How would you suggest the church combat such thinking?

What does Matthew 20:20-28 say about leaders in the church?

3. Read and Discuss one of the Case Studies from the Appendix to this volume. (Suggested: Case Study 1 and 2.)

Group Seminar 2:

UNDERSTANDING GOD'S REQUIREMENTS FOR ELDER

Read once again the following passages, reprinted here for your convenience:

> *Be shepherds of God's flock that is under your care, serving as overseers — not because you must, but because you are willing, as God wants you to be; not greedy for money, but eager to serve; not lording it over those entrusted to you, but being examples to the flock. And when the Chief Shepherd appears, you will receive the crown of glory that will never fade away (I Peter 5:2-4).*

> *Now the overseer must be above reproach, the husband of but one wife, temperate, self-controlled, respectable, hospitable, able to teach, not given to drunkenness, not violent but gentle, not quarrelsome, not a lover of money. He must manage his own family well and see that his children obey him with proper respect. (If anyone does not know how to manage his own family, how can he take care of God's church?) He must not be a recent convert, or he may become conceited and fall under the same judgment as the devil. He must also have a good reputation with outsiders, so that he will not fall into disgrace and into the devil's trap (I Timothy 3:2-7).*

> *An elder must be blameless, the husband of but one wife, a man whose children believe and are not open to the charge of being wild and disobedient. Since an overseer is entrusted with God's work, he must be blameless — not overbearing, not quick-tempered, not given to drunkenness, not violent, not pursuing dishonest gain. Rather he must be hospitable, one who loves what is good, who is self-controlled, upright, holy and disciplined. He must hold firmly to the trustworthy message as it has been taught, so that he can encourage others by sound doctrine and refute those who oppose it.*

> *For there are many rebellious people, mere talkers and deceivers, especially those of the circumcision group. They must be silenced, because they are ruining whole households by teaching things they ought not to teach — and that for the sake of dishonest gain (Titus 1:6-11).*

1. Compile a list on a blackboard of the basic qualifications stipulated as requirements for the office of elder in these passages.

2. In what way are these qualifications *pastoral* in character? (Discuss how each qualification you have listed on the blackboard enables an elder to do the work of a shepherd, or conversely, how would the absence of each hinder shepherding work?)

3. Does *popularity* function as an (unwritten) qualification in any of these passages? How about in your church? Are there any steps that you should take to change the way your church selects elders so that the process is based on uniquely Biblical requirements? Be specific.

4. Read and discuss one or more Case Studies that appear in the Appendix to this volume.

(Suggested: Case Studies # 3-5.)

Part Two
THE SHEPHERD'S EYE
Sharpening Pastoral Vision

THE SHEPHERD'S EYE

Section One:
KNOWING THE ENEMY

THE WOLF'S TEETH—*SECULARISM*

Any shepherd in the hill country of Judea must be aware of what wild animals he's up against as he tries to care for the flock under his care. Will he deal with lions? Bears? This knowledge affects how and where he leads the flock to graze, how he "enfolds" them at night, whether or not he will get any sleep himself. He also needs to know if disease has weakened the flock from within. Do they need special nourishment, special care and attention, isolation from each other?

The same issues demand the attention of spiritual shepherds. What enemies does the flock face today? How is Satan working his devious schemes in our generation? We know from Scripture that he operates "like a roaring lion, seeking whom he may devour" (I Pe. 5:8), and that he masquerades as "an angel of light" (II Cor. 11:14). What are the external attacks he launches against the people of God in our time? With what humanistic germs does he corrupt from within? Most of us agree that though Satan is the same enemy against which the church does battle in every age, his tools and strategies in this decade are decidedly different than they were in the 50s.

While seeking to understand Satan and his ways, and also to operate with the same imagery I've used throughout this volume, I want to take a close look at "the wolves' teeth." This graphic picture comes from Paul's descriptive statement that "savage wolves will come in among you and will not spare the flock" (Acts 20:29). It is imperative for elders to know just what those fangs look like, just how they work. Knowing the Enemy's strength is the first step in avoiding trouble, both for one's self and for the flock.

With what fangs do the wolves tear the flock of Christ? I would observe 5: secularism, materialism, relativism, pragmatism, and feminism. (Although others arrange the material in different categories and use different terms, my analysis does not conflict with theirs.[1])

THE WORSHIP OF THE HERE AND NOW

R.C. Sproul's book *Lifeviews*[2] contains an instructive discussion of secularism. Most folks think of "secular" as the opposite of religious, accepting the US Supreme Court's distinctive approach to the wall of separation between church and state and extending that separation to apply to religion and the rest of life. But the word "secular" implies more. It traces back to two Latin words for "world"; *saeculum* and *mundus*. The former, origin of the English "secular," referred to the "when" of life, the here-ness and now-ness of this life as opposed to the eternal; the latter, origin of our "mundane," referred to the "where" of life, this place earth as opposed to heaven or hell. The distinction between the two aspects is immensely important. Clearly, God has put us in a place called earth. It is His creation. And just as clearly, when He created it He built time into it. Genesis 1 speaks of "evening and morning," the first day, the second day, etc. There is *timed-ness* to God's creation; and according to God's own assessment, it is good!

But when that *timed-ness* of creation, when the here and now of our creatureliness, gobbles up any sense of our eternity and occupies all of man's heart and mind and attention, you have *secularism*. Secularism denies the eternal; it will not allow for the thought that anything in the here and now has eternal consequences. Secularism happily allows people to go to church, to "be religious," but believes with all its heart that the important things in life, the valued things, the godly things, are in the here and now. Only if religion has value for the here and now is it of any real significance.

---

1 It is not unique to this volume to attempt to categorize demonic influences on our culture and their influence on and penetration into the Christian church. R.C. Sproul, in his book *Lifeviews* (Old Tappan, N.J.:Fleming H. Revell Co., 1986) identifies Secularism, Pessimistic Existentialism, Sentimental Humanism, Pragmatism, Positivism, Pluralism, Relativism, and Hedonism in his list of spiritual and ideological foes. Charles Colson writes of the "prevailing worldview" of our time, and identifies the components in that world-view: it is secular, antihistorical, naturalistic, utopian, and pragmatic, and arises out of the relativism that holds modern man in its death grip (*The Body*, pp. 172-182). Herbert Schlossberg, historian and cultural critic, uses the paradigm of idolatry with which to evaluate our age, and finds the following idols alive and functioning: idols of history, of humanity, of mammon, of nature, of power and of religion (*Idols for Destruction: Christian Faith and Its Confrontation with American Society* [Thomas Nelson Publishers, 1983]).

2 Sproul, pp. 29-42.

A culture in the grip of secularism has certain visible features. First, it exhibits a passion for instant gratification, satisfaction in the here and now. It won't wait for food, so it develops fast food restaurants, guaranteed 15 minute lunches, and microwave ovens. It won't wait for wealth, so it glories in "get rich quick" schemes, frequent job changes for monetary reasons, and lottery tickets instead of developing the discipline of saving hard earned dollars. It won't spend the time to develop disciplined learning habits, choosing instead to spend money on video- and audio-cassette tapes that promise children higher grades in school, and on SAT tests with just a few hours' attention.[3] Secular people may note the dangers of deficit spending and of personal and federal debt, but they keep on borrowing, using credit cards and worrying little about the payback.

Second, a secular culture is dualistic. By that I mean that it observes a rigid dichotomy between the *realms* of the sacred and the secular, between the natural and the supernatural, between the here-and-now and the eternal. We all make such *distinctions* easily; but a secular culture erects an impenetrable wall between them. Different gods rule in each; different laws operate in each; different ethics function in each. A man who wouldn't hesitate to use strong-arm tactics in the secular world of work wouldn't think of using such in a church committee. The Lord Christ is not allowed to be Lord of all of life; if He is given any position at all, it is only in the "sacred" part. Listen to Harry Blamires' description:

> No Christian thinks it possible to live without secular activities. No Christian wants to abolish building houses or eating meals. But secularism, by definition, excludes Christian faith and practice. No Christian is trying to prohibit ploughing fields or selling potatoes on the grounds that these are secular activities, but secularists are committed to reject every activity that is religious. Christianity wants to *claim* the secular sphere; secularism wants to *abolish* the religious sphere."[4]

---

[3] Popular as I write these words are such programs as, "*Where There's a Will There's an A*" and "*Math-a-magics*" for children, plus several "memory improvement" programs available on video for adults. These in themselves could well be very helpful; my concern is the insistance on "instant learning" that demands the development of such programs in the first place.

[4] Harry Blamires, *Recovering the Christian Mind: Meeting the Challenge of Secularism* (Downer's Grove: Intervarsity Press, 1988). See also Bradshaw Frey et.al., *All of Life Redeemed* (Jordan Station, ON: Paideia Press, 1983) Mark Noll, *The Scandal of the Evangelical Mind* (Grand Rapids: Wm. B. Eerdman's Pub. Co., 1994).

If Blamires' observation that secularists from their "side" seek to abolish the religious sphere (keep Christ out of daily life), it is noteworthy that certain theological camps of the Christian church end up at the same place, albeit for different reasons.

> Dispensationalists traditionally viewed their task in the present epoch as rescuing unbelievers from sin and keeping themselves unspotted from the world. The supernaturalism of dispensationalism has always been intense. The unmediated agency of God is thought to lie behind all wholesome activities on earth; the mediated agency of Satan is perceived behind all natural and human evil.[5]

Churches also can be profoundly affected by the spirit of secularism. On the one hand, many go into long term debt to finance elaborate building programs while giving little more than passing thought to questions of responsible Biblical stewardship, spending much more energy defending the immediate impact of the new facility on their "relevant" and growing ministries. On the other, the *content* of such ministries bears the mark of compromise with secularism. Living in a world preoccupied with the here and now, members of many contemporary churches are obsessed with "relevance," evaluating sermons and other forms of discipleship and training almost exclusively according to that standard of judgment. Never mind the careful process of discipleship; of apprenticeship to a mature believer, learning slowly by observation what it means to be a disciple, growing patiently in grace and knowledge as one learns the Word and all its implications. "Meet my needs now! If you don't, I'll go somewhere else!"

PASTORING IN A SECULAR AGE

So what's the point? How does knowledge of the spirit of secularism better equip the pastoral elders of the church to defend the sheep from the satanic wolf's fang? How does such knowledge help you guard yourself against attack? Gal. 6 provides a most powerful reminder and application:

> Do not be deceived: God cannot be mocked. A man reaps what he sows. The one who sows to please his sinful nature, from that nature will reap destruction; the one who sows to please the Spirit, from the Spirit will reap eternal life" (vv. 7-8).

Both for yourself and for God's people entrusted to your care, you

---

5 Mark Noll, *The Scandal of the Evangelical Mind*, p. 119.

must sound the alarm that rings in the presence of deceit! You must alert God's people to the destructiveness of worshiping the here and now and neglecting the eternal. You must teach clearly the Lordship of Jesus Christ over every thought, action, and sphere of life (Eph. 1:15f.; Col. 1:15f.). You must pound home the lesson that behavior now has consequences later, that seeds sown now will produce a harvest eternally!

Specifically, I offer the following suggestions for your pastoral consideration:

1. Take note of the presence of the spirit of "instant gratification" on the part of God's people under your care. Listen to them speak; try to discern their purchasing habits; observe the way their children operate. Point out to them, young and old, the spiritual dangers of such a spirit. Many will not even realize that it has gripped their life or home. They cannot fight without knowing the enemy!

2. Make sure that you, perhaps through the local deacons, provide careful and thorough instruction concerning the Biblical principle of stewardship. Nowhere has the bug of secularism bitten the sheep more painfully than in their attitude and practices toward finances. Disciplined and generous giving, careful saving, avoiding personal debt; all are practices that are rare these days, and must be cultivated. Overdependence on credit cards, buying homes that require mortgage payments that financially enslave God's people, testing one's "success" by how many (and what kind of) cars are in the driveway; all are practices that must be exposed as sinful and spiritually dangerous. Instead, elders (and deacons) must sound the trumpet that calls God's Kingdom citizens to the virtues of contentment, generosity in giving, and patience in saving and investment.[6] Additionally, take a long

---

6 Several contemporary Christian authors have provided excellent material for stewardship training in the local congregation; among them are Ron Blue, whose books are available in most Christian bookstores, and Larry Burkett, whose ministry produces a variety of training materials suitable for church classes or individual work, including *Debt-Free Living, Your Finances in Changing Times, The Complete Financial Guide for Young Couples, The Complete Financial Guide for Singles, Dollars and Sense* and *Surviving the Money Jungle,* (a wonderful training manual in Biblical stewardship for Junior and Senior High School aged children). The first 3 are available from Burkett's Christian Financial Concepts Materials Department, PO Box 100, Gainesville, GA, 30503 (800-722-1976). The last is available from Focus on the Family in Colorado Springs, CO (1-800-A-Family).

and careful look at your local church's debt load. Perhaps it is appropriate to borrow some money (short term) for construction of a needed sanctuary or educational facility, so long as it is truly needed. At the same time, churches that wish to avoid being torn by the fang of secularism will studiously develop policies about long-term debt, about mortgaging the ministry future to pay for the present wants. Such practices take our eyes off the eternal, teach us that we don't need to pray or sacrificially give as II Cor. 8-9 teach us to do, and cultivate a thoroughly secular spirit among the believing community.

3. Listen carefully to people when they talk, and listen to them when they pray. Their words will give you a window into their hearts. Ask yourself the question; do they (do *you*!?) divide life into sacred and secular, nature and grace? Do they limit the realm over which Christ rules to church, piety and ethics, or do they believe He is Lord of all? Do they give indication of viewing life dualistically?

Knowing the answers to these questions will give you a good indication of your pastoral obligations as you care for people attacked by the enemy and infected by the germ of secularism.

THE WOLF'S TEETH—*MATERIALISM*

"Whoever Dies With The Most Toys Wins." (bumper sticker, c. 1993)

"Greed is good; greed works." (Gordon Gecko in the movie "Wall Street," c. 1985)

"A Man's Life Does Not Consist in the Abundance of His Possessions" (Jesus, Lk. 12:15).

Today the West and especially North America, is squeezed tightly in the grip of materialism. As secularism focuses its gaze on the here and now, materialism puts its heart on the *stuff* of the here and now, the quest for the attainment of things that satiate the 5 senses, the accumulation of mammon. Materialism is not merely an idea; materialism is an idol, a master that demands worship. And like all idols, it does not give life; only the Living God does that. It devours life, consuming and destroying the life of all who give it a place in their heart. It is not merely a misplaced emphasis, an overindulgence by people blessed with many possessions, an imbalance in lives otherwise balanced. It takes hold of the heart, and is absolutely inconsistent with Biblical faith. Remember our Lord's words:

> ...where your treasure is, there your heart will be also...No one can serve two masters. Either he will hate the one and love the other, or he will be devoted to the one and despise the other. You cannot serve both God and Money (literally "mammon," wealth or possessions, "stuff" to be owned) (Matt. 6:21,24).

How are we to understand the rise of materialism in our culture? And more importantly, how can we understand its penetration into the church of the Lord? I think the answer is rather easy—and uncomfortably so. We are wealthy people! Compared with most of the population of the earth, those of us in the West are undeniably rich. That's true whether or not we feel rich, whether or not we think we are wealthy compared to our neighbors.

The reality of our wealth was recently brought home to me most poignantly. A young couple in our congregation were able to adopt twin Romanian boys soon after the opening up of Eastern Europe. When they went to Romania to bring home their sons, they were greatly aided by a gentleman in that country whom they called "Mr. Black" (his name was difficult to pronounce in English). When he later had opportunity to visit them in this country, he looked with wide-eyed amazement at our homes and at their contents. His comment? "You have so many things you don't need. Look at all the pictures on your walls, the things on your tables, the chairs you don't sit in, the clothes you don't wear!" For Mr. Black, wealth was defined by utility: if one has more than he really, actually needs, he is wealthy!

Given that definition, who among us isn't wealthy?

Sadly, in times of prosperity the church has never done well. Throughout history, the church has always been more faithful to her Lord under persecution and hardship than she has been in times of wealth and ease. She has always been drawn closer to Him when she had to pray in utter dependence than when her eye and heart was drawn away from Him by the pleasures and joys of this life. Jesus knew that. That's why He warned that we must not "store up for yourselves treasures on earth" (literally, "stack up" like cordwood, piled up for storage but not for immediate use).[1] That's why He spoke so boldly about the inability to serve both God and the stuff of life. That's why He spoke the unnerving words of Matt. 19:23-24: "I tell you the truth, it is hard for a rich man to enter the kingdom of heaven. Again I tell you, it is easier for a camel to go through the eye of a needle than for a rich man to enter the kingdom of God." Few words in the Bible should bother us in the wealthy West more than these!

What are the symptoms of a materialistic society? Consider a few:

- the health of our society and the well-being of our people are measured by purely economic standards: Consumer Price Index, consumer confidence (measured especially by the level of consumer spending), inflation, interest rates, etc.

---

[1] John MacArthur, Jr., *Overcoming Materialism* (Panorama City, CA.: Word of Grace Communications, 1983), p. 28.

- *success* to most minds is measured by the accumulation and possession of things
- *ethics* are shaped by economic goals, not by absolute standards: if "things" mark success, their accumulation is good, and whatever it takes to gather them is good; anything that hinders the goal of "more" should be jettisoned, including a "bad" marriage or even children that get in the way of "success"; it is expected, understood and sometimes even justified, that people living in poverty will be caught up in violence, robbery and theft
- the media feed a pervasive *dissatisfaction* with one's lot in life, fueled by "infomercials" promising easy ways to become rich through real estate, thin through diet fads or gimmicks, or smart through video courses
- the word "greed" no longer connotes a sinful spirit; it's been replaced by "*profit motivated*," considered a positive trait, not a sinful one
- in many cities, police report youth being beaten, even killed, for their new "Air Jordan" sneakers
- consistently, "Life-styles of the Rich and Famous" and similar shows lure large TV audiences
- and, lest you think I unfairly suggest that materialism is a peculiarly American evil, you should know that it is a non-discriminating corrupter. We in the West export this sinful spirit internationally; although there are only a few programs broadcast on television in Eastern Europe, the one that has the largest audience is reruns of "Dallas," the American soap opera series. So dominant is the program in that land that many Christian churches have had to change the time of mid-week meetings to accommodate broadcast schedules, or face empty pews.

Clearly, many more characteristics could be listed. I could tell you of the young man I met in a 7-11 while buying gas, who boasted of having enough credit on his VISA card that he bought a $18,000 sports car on it—and he was proud of that! Or of the many folks I've met who are constantly on the look out to "upgrade" their house to the newer and larger variety in a more upscale neighborhood. (This despite the fact that they have no children, are seldom in their home [both work, and long hours too], and already have 4 bedrooms, 3 bathrooms, and such a large yard they have to hire out the lawnwork.) Or, I could speak of contemporary home architecture; "family rooms" that do not enhance family life, but are arranged around electronic entertainment centers, organized to display the latest "stuff" accumulated by the family, but that require a placement of seating so as to make it impossible for the family to talk or communicate with anything except the video or audio system.[2]

OVERCOMING MATERIALISM

How do you battle such a powerful spiritual foe? How do you as elders strengthen the flock so that they can win victory over such "principalities, powers, world rulers of this present darkness?" Allow me to suggest several very practical tools, each of which arises from Scripture.

1. First, use the wonderful prayer in Proverbs 30:7-9 to teach God's people under your care that *materialism is profoundly dangerous, especially because it denies the spiritual dangers inherent in wealth.* Listen to the words of the wise: "Give me neither poverty nor riches, but give me only my daily bread. Otherwise, I may have too much and disown you and say, `Who is the Lord?'" If only all of us would know that and believe it! If only we learned our perspective on wealth and poverty from God instead of from TV. And, speaking of TV, use the opportunities God gives you (visiting families in their homes, deacons visiting with those struggling with budgets and personal debt , etc.) to make a point about this intrusive medium. If you can't get the people to throw it in the trash (and realistically you can't), you can teach them how to watch it! Call attention to the deception of Hollywood; challenge them to observe how writers and producers portray life so that it appears that wealth is always desirable; observe that the commercials are perhaps the most deadly item on the screen, especially to the tender minds and hearts of the youth, because they sow seeds of discontent and greed, and intentionally and viciously aim at younger "consumers."

---

[2] Bob De Moss provides insightful analysis of this phenomenon in a Focus on the Family video entitled *Learn to Discern*. I highly recommend showing it to teens and parents in local churches; it addresses the influence of various media on Christian families today, including insights into the impact of materialism. Available from Focus on the Family: call 800-A-Family.

2. Second, point to the insightful observations of the preacher in Ecclesiastes 2:1-11 to teach God's people *the emptiness of wealth unless it is used in the service of the Lord.* Listen: "I built houses for myself and planted vineyards. I made gardens and parks and planted all kinds of fruit trees in them...I bought male and female slaves...I also owned more herds and flocks than anyone in Jerusalem...I amassed silver and gold...I denied myself nothing my eyes desired; I refused my heart no pleasure...Yet when I surveyed all that my hands had done and what I had toiled to achieve, everything was meaningless, a chasing after the wind; nothing was gained under the sun." Indeed! What frustration to achieve, to have, to amass, to accumulate...and to come to realize it doesn't really matter. It's like trying to catch the breeze. Futile! Vanity! The only lasting meaning in things, in possessions, is in their use in the service of the Lord and His people.

3. Remember yourself, and remind your people of the words of Paul to Timothy about priorities: "Command those who are rich in this world not to be arrogant nor to put their hope in wealth, which is so uncertain, but to put their hope in God, who richly provides us with everything for our enjoyment. Command them to do good, to be rich in good deeds, and to be generous and willing to share. In this way they will lay up treasure for themselves as a firm foundation for the coming age, so that they may take hold of the life that is truly life" (I Tim. 6:17-19). Learn from such a passage that materialism is not a spiritual force that afflicts only the rich. None of us is immune, for it is not a sin of *having*, but one of *wanting*. It grips one in the heart, not in the wallet.

4. *Teach your people diligently the principles and practices of Biblical stewardship.* "The earth is the Lord's and everything in it" (Ps. 24:1) is not only a nice memory verse, but it is a much more important and urgent life-principle. God's people must learn to live as if all they have—all they have enjoyed and all they will have, all they give and all they keep for their own use—belongs to the Lord, and we must give account to Him for its use. Such a life-principle is hard to cling to in a materialistic age, particularly so in such a wealthy culture. But maintain it you must, and more than that, you must teach it to all of God's people. The good news is that you don't have to invent the wheel in this matter. There are many resources available, not

to mention the most important and immediate one you have—the deacons who labor alongside of you. It is their high calling to develop and administer Biblical stewardship. If they do it well, you will be well-served in the battle against the spiritual foe of materialism.[3]

5. Finally, *don't just talk about the dangers of materialism; actively oppose it.* Don't just cluck your tongue at this younger generation and its passion for expensive electronic gadgets; teach them Biblical priorities. Don't shake your heads at people who "just don't know the value of a dollar"; instruct them about the dangers of debt. Don't lament the sin of greed; call attention to its destructive effects in the lives of all who are controlled by it. Fight back with all the weapons at your disposal. Remember, such is your duty: "Keep watch over yourselves and all the flock of which the Holy Spirit has made you overseers...be on your guard!" (Acts 20:28, 31).

---

[3] I refer you again to the excellent material I mentioned above (e.g., in fn. 6 of chapter 4); in addition, see *Overcoming Materialism* by John MacArthur, Jr., and note the existence of The Barnabus Foundation, an organization created to serve as independent stewardship advisor to Christian churches and individuals. This organization can be consulted for help with estate planning, presentations to churches, etc. They also produce good training material for stewardship education entitled *Firstfruits*. (To order, call 708-532-3444. Fax 708-532-1217)

The Wolf's Teeth—Relativism

Woe to those who call evil good and good evil, who put darkness for light and light for darkness, who put bitter for sweet and sweet for bitter (Isaiah 5:20).

...God...gave them over to a depraved mind...they are senseless, faithless, heartless, ruthless...Although they know God's righteous decree that those who do such things deserve death, they not only continue to do these very things but also approve of those who practice them (Romans 1:28-32).

Not only does the devil tear at the flock of God with the dripping fangs of secularism and materialism, but he also attacks their inner strength with the erosion of commitment that occurs because of *relativism*. In a secular and materialistic society, when a culture's heart has been given over to the here and now and in particular to the "stuff" of the here and now, what is it that drives its ethics? Every culture possesses and exhibits its basic values in the way it lives its life. Those values are shaped by its heart convictions. To say it a bit differently, secular materialists *are* religious and they *do* have ethics, but their religion and their ethics are shaped by their secularism and their materialism. Cannibals eat the flesh of their enemies, but not of their fellow tribesmen. That is taboo. Al Capone killed many people, but never failed to stop at the Catholic church each morning for confession and Mass. And so it goes. Everyone has a set of values, a way of determining right and wrong. But in a world in which the eternal has been excluded from having a decisive role and in which the here and now has been elevated to divine status, such values are determined exclusively by the individual himself and for himself. No longer may we appeal to an eternal and sovereign God who has revealed Himself in His Word, and Whose Word is absolute truth and functional law (Ps. 19:7ff)! No, in a culture that denies the eternal and worships the here and now, any eternal and absolute truth is rejected in favor of a here and now judgment. It's "ethics on the fly!"[1]

Perhaps you recall the heated discussions surrounding Supreme Court appointments in recent years. Robert Bork and those following his approach to constitutional law have been excoriated and pilloried because they believe that the Constitution of the United States, *as the framers wrote it*, is normative for us today; it does not evolve in meaning with each passing generation. The legalist's attack on such an approach to the constitution parallels the theologian's attack on a high view of the Scriptures as God's authoritative and eternal truth. To think that the Bible, penned over two millenia ago, could be the absolute standard of right and wrong is viewed as nonsense, plain and simple. Such a belief is met, in the mind of today's relativist, with disbelief and indignation.

A reading of Chuck Colson's recent work *The Body* hears Colson reserve some of his most acerbic judgments for modern TV talk show hosts like Phil Donahue, Geraldo Rivera, Oprah and their clones, and columnists like Ellen Goodman. Why? Because they perpetuate relativistic ethics.[2] Recently, I caught a few minutes of Sally Jessie Raphael's show. She was interviewing a mother and her 13 year old daughter, discussing with them the teen's insistence on having sex with her boyfriend in her room without the intrusion or interference of the mother. Sally Jessie's only comment: "I surely hope you are using protection!" Not a word about wrongdoing, let alone the Biblical word "sin"; not a word about the destructive effects of such selfish and hedonistic behavior upon family, the marriage relationship or the physical body; not a word about the corrosive effect of such sin upon a society choking on its own permissiveness. In fact, as Colson observes, the only thing that our relativistic society holds as an absolute is that there are no abso-

---

1 Professor Allan Bloom dropped an a-bomb on our cultural establishment in his definitive work, *The Closing of the American Mind* (New York: Simon and Schuster, 1987). Consider these perceptive words from his opening chapter: "There is one thing a professor can be absolutely certain of: almost every student entering the university believes, or says he believes, that truth is relative...They are unified...in their relativism and in their allegiance to equality. And the two are related in a moral intention....The study of history and of culture teaches that all the world was mad in the past; men always thought they were right, and that led to wars, persecutions, slavery, xenophobia, racism and chauvinism. The point is not to correct the mistakes and really be right; rather it is not to think you are right at all" (pp. 25-26).

2 Charles Colson, with Ellen Santilli Vaugn, *The Body* (Dallas: Word Publishing, 1992). The portions relevant to this discussion are contained on pp. 157-200.

lutes, and that those of us who believe that such absolutes exist are absolutely wrong!

What does the above have to do with the work of elders who must shepherd God's precious flock? A great deal, since the people of God in North America live in a relativistic age, in a time when TV, radio and the print media scream the values of relativism at the top of their lungs. And because some of it inexorably sinks in. Consider:

- Many people in the church have lost all respect for church discipline. "After all, who are you to judge me or what I do? My life is my own; leave me alone." Along with the individual's rejection of Biblical standards applied by God's appointed shepherds to their lives, comes the ease with which the discontented lone sheep can find refuge in another fold. For you see a corollary of relativism is *pluralism*. Don't like the church where you receive God's care? Move to another one. They are moral equivalents. Virtually any church will take any person with a pulse into full and free membership without so much as a raised eyebrow.

- Many church members have lost the conviction that the Bible is true. Replacing that conviction is the relativistic notion that the Bible *contains* truth, but that since Christians have never been able to agree completely on what the Bible says, none of us really know what truth is, anyway. Besides, "other religions contain a measure of truth, too." That's been the point of the World Council of Churches for many years, seeking to accord respect to any and all religions[3]

- Don't forget the corollary; if the Bible is no longer confessed to be absolute truth, then there is nothing the Christian church may declare to be absolute error, either. Pastoral elders are no longer expected to denounce as sin errors of doctrine; they must likewise tread lightly when applying ecclesiastical sanctions to people living in moral sin lest they find themselves embroiled in a defamation lawsuit. "Who do you think you are, telling me that abortion is wrong?" cries the relativistic church member. "The Christian faith is about love, not about judgment!" cries the homosexual pastor of the Metropolitan Community Church downtown. "Leave me alone; quit has-

---

[3] This despite recent revelations on network news broadcasts that the Soviet KGB spy agency had infiltrated the WCC at the highest levels with planted and controlled intelligence agents. Incredibly, relativistic ecumenists are able to ignore this contradiction to their foundational premise.

sling me!" demands the child of a long-standing church member who has been living with his girlfriend without the benefit of marriage. If there's no truth, there's no such thing as heresy either!

What can pastoral elders do in such a time as this? It is incumbent upon the elders of the local church not to flinch in this head-on collision with relativism. They must not waver from the truth; they must not throw up their hands in hopelessness. Christ demands that His church be holy (I Peter 2) and entrusts the elders with the duty to see to it that holiness is pursued.

A few suggestions may help.

1. Make clear, both from the pulpit in your local church and in personal pastoral meetings with the members of the flock under your care, that your church holds firmly to the Bible as the infallible and inerrant Word of God.[4] Teach clearly what these terms mean. Declare loudly and often, both in principal and in practice, that you consider the Bible to be the absolute and infallible standard for both doctrine and life.

2. Whenever the Bible and what it teaches is contradicted, either by doctrinal affirmation, expression of doubt, or blantantly sinful practices, call it what the Bible calls it; *sin!* Be careful about language; sin is sin, not just a "mistake." Heresy is untruth, not just a difference of opinion.

3. Teach the Bible! This radical notion stems from my growing experience and conviction that so many people in the church drift into unbiblical belief and practice because they don't know what the Bible says in the first place. (How did the prophet say it? "My people are destroyed for lack of knowledge" Hosea 4:6.)

4. Rebuke sinners with the Bible. Pastoral care of sinful people demands a clear reference to the Scriptural teaching that was disobeyed; elders ought not to rebuke or admonish or call to repentance without pointing out what God expects in His own words.

---

[4] I deliberately use both terms "infallible" and "inerrant," since one of the interesting breaches in the high view of Scripture in recent decades has come as a result of the work of so-called evangelicals who argue in favor of Biblical infallibility, but consider inerrancy to be a modern rationalistic term, inconsistent with the Bible's view of itself. I reject the distinction as a dangerous semantic game.

5. Lead by example, not just talk. Make clear in your own life that you are a person of the Word. Immerse yourself in it daily, reading eagerly to see the glory and majesty of our covenant keeping God, and with careful attention to learn the specifics of His will for you in your life. Read the Old Testament to grasp the sweep of the covenant promises and warnings; read the New Testament to awaken the thrill of sufficiency in Christ. The more you are yourself a man of the Word, the more those whom you seek to pastor will learn from your example.

The Wolf's Teeth—Pragmatism

George was a deacon in the church. He had been married for some years to Connie; everyone had thought their marriage was solid. Solid, that is, until he abruptly moved out. The strain of the separation added to the now-obvious marital tension was telling on their faces, even as the tear streaks left seemingly permanent marks on the cheeks of their children. When their elder finally figured out what was going on (often elders are among the last to know!) he went to talk to Connie, then to George.

Connie sobbed with emotion. Trying to make some sense out of what she was experiencing, she finally blurted out, "I guess I wasn't making him happy enough. That's all I can figure!"

George was much more rational. In fact, he possessed a chillingly cool and analytical demeanor when he acknowledged, "It's all over with Connie. I've been seeing Fran for over a year now. I feel better with her than I ever did with Connie; Fran makes me happy. My marriage didn't work very well, but my relationship with Fran does. I've filed for divorce and plan to marry Fran as soon as the divorce goes through. The decision is final, and it is best for both of us."

Wendy was shattered. Pregnant? Her folks would kill her! Dave was no "father material," and she knew it. He was a jerk! Pleasant company for a night, but certainly not the man she planned to marry. She really didn't like him, but had to admit she enjoyed sex with him. But this!?

Well, she thought, she'd just have to have an abortion. After all, the Planned Pregnancy counselor had spoken so sensitively about "unwanted" and "unplanned" babies and their difficult lives. And boy, was her life going to be difficult! Besides, it was more compassionate for her to terminate the pregnancy now. Surely this baby was "unplanned" and "unwanted" if any child ever was. The preacher's sermon last week about "pro-life" values and commitment really made her squirm, but if he was in her shoes, he'd change his tune. Having a baby now, at this stage in my life, just won't work out!

Pragmatism: "A philosophical system or movement stressing practical consequences and values as standards by which concepts are to be analyzed and their validity determined" (Webster's Encyclopedic Unabridged Dictionary). Charles Colson calls it *utilitarian individualism*, the system whereby individuals make moral judgments by rationally calculating what will multiply their pleasures and diminish any pain.[1]

Understand that? It translates into common language like this. Pragmatism means first you determine whether an act seems practical, whether its consequences bring you pleasure or pain, and by that process you determine what is right or wrong. Have an unplanned child in your womb? First determine whether the consequences of that pregnancy "work out" practically. If not, it is not wrong to abort the child. Locked into a marriage relationship you don't like? Remember, "you have a right to be happy!" (A so-called "christian" marriage counselor, deeply infected with pragmatism, once said that to a couple from a church I was serving. Needless to say, that ended any referral plans I had for him!) If staying in a marriage brings you pain rather than pleasure, if it does not bring the desired consequences, divorce is not wrong. In fact, it may be the best choice among the available options.

THE WORLD'S WAY

Before you lament such logic as unbiblical, remember that this is the world's way! This is the way the soap operas and the sitcoms on TV resolve their character's problems. This is the way of Hollywood, the way of your neighbors, the way of the folks at work.

And the world's way is penetrating the church. The examples I used above aren't fictitious inventions. They are real life situations I've dealt with. They reveal the way of the world, but they are lived out within the life-styles of the people of the Kingdom. The fang of the wolf has bitten deeply into the flesh of the sheep of the

---

1 *The Body*, op. cit.

Good Shepherd. The church in North America, for all her talk about values, for all her cry for a return to old-fashioned morality, has been more influenced than influential. George Gallup's terse phrase, used to describe life in America today, is eerily accurate; "religion up, morality down." Despite record numbers claiming to be Christian, a diminishing percentage believe their religion to have a direct bearing on the way they make moral decisions.[2]

Pragmatism Is Not Practical

Part of the difficulty of dealing with pragmatism is that it has a close cousin who is so nice; everyone likes her. Her name is "practical." How can anyone oppose "practical"? After all, if we want to be good stewards of God's resources, we'd better be practical, not frivolous, with our spending. And so it goes.

But being *practical* isn't the same as operating from a commitment to *pragmatism*. They are not really close relatives. Pragmatism changes moral values, it doesn't seek to apply in an efficient manner existing values that have been shaped by Biblical truth. Two examples will suffice to highlight the difference. Dr. C. Everett Koop, eminent Surgeon General of the United States for many years, was *practical*. He knew AIDS was predominantly a disease related to homosexual behavior; he also knew that the US had to do something about it before it swept through the entire populace. He did *not* believe nor declare that homosexuality is morally-acceptable alternative behavior; he *did* believe something must be done to protect the population. So he strongly encouraged a promiscuous adult populace to make responsible use of condoms. In contrast is Dr. Jocelyn Elders, President Clinton's 1994 nominee to be Koop's replacement. She's a *pragmatist*. She is on record as having said that unwanted and unplanned pregnancies are a blight on women. Result? Not easier *adoption* rules, of course. She declared, with fire in her eyes and passion in her voice, that the unpleasant consequence of an unwanted child demanded preventative measures; condom distribution to children in school-based clinics. It also demanded remedial measures; the unquestioned right for any woman to have access to abortion, and government funding to provide such remediation to those who couldn't afford it on their own. The "unpleasant consequence" demands a fundamental change in morality and a throw-away view of human life!

---

2 Bellah, *Habits of the Heart*, op. cit.

What's An Elder To Do?

Your people live in such a world. You'd better know it and be ready for it. If you haven't noticed pragmatism at work yet, you may live in an isolation bubble. If not, perhaps you haven't been sufficiently aware of what to look for. Pragmatism is all around and it is in your church.

What to do?

1. For one thing, keep your eyes and ears peeled. Recognize the penetration of the evil one in the "situational ethics" of pragmatism when you see it. Ask "why" a lot, as you visit among the flock; listen closely to the reasons people give for their behavior choices. Try to determine if they really function with Biblical principles, or "fly by the seat of their pants."

2. But do more. Begin now to raise the issue in every visit to a family home, in every discussion group. Make clear to God's people in your charge that this rewrite of morality is a grievous wrong. God's Word is eternal. Its standards do not change. His glory is what we must seek; our immediate pleasure and comfort are not the standards of right and wrong. His Law determines right and wrong, and life lived by His standards brings joy, comfort and contentment. To make moral choices merely by analyzing the potential for pleasure or pain is to play into the devil's hand.

3. Work especially with the young people in your church. Use examples like I used above, but tailor specific ones to the issues facing your youth. Discuss such "case studies" in youth group meetings. Point out the radically different ways to make moral choices that exist in their world. Make clear to them what God says, and call them to faithfulness.

The Wolf's Teeth—Feminism

So God created man in his own image; in the image of God he created him; male and female he created them (Gen. 1:27).

Haven't you read...that at the beginning the Creator made them male and female...For this reason a man will leave his father and mother and be united to his wife, and the two will become one flesh (Matt. 19:4-5)?

You may be surprised to find in these pages that I identify feminism as one of the fangs of the wolves that Satan unleashes upon the flock of God. After all, isn't feminism merely a minor ripple in the ebb and flow of history, a pendulum swing that seeks to balance out the extremism of "machismo," that male super-domination that treats women like chattel? Isn't feminism really no more than a synonym for justice?

In fact, feminism in these pages does *not* refer to matters of justice and equity; it does *not* describe attempts to apply Biblical righteousness to situations in which there has been unrighteous discrimination against people because they are female. Those issues are not feminist issues; they are simple yet profound issues of Biblical obedience!

Feminism is different. It is a belief system; it embraces values and ethics; it seeks to shape behavior far beyond the mere quest for justice and righteous. And it is evil. I include this "tooth" of feminism in my analysis of the enemy's fangs precisely because it gives us a profoundly important example of how the Evil One adapts his attack from generation to generation. His strategy evolves; it is not sufficient to be prepared to face the temptations and heresies of yesterday. In every new age the people of God must recommit themselves to stand square on the foundation of the Word of God which is the Shepherd's voice, and live out of its absolute Truth. In every new age, the shepherds of the flock must keep eyes peeled to discern how the wolves will attack the flock that hearkens to the Shepherd's voice. In our age, an age of secularism, materialism, relativism and pragmatism, one of the strategies of demonic attack is that of feminism.

GENDER FEMINISM: WAR ON BIBLICAL CHRISTIANITY

Real feminism, as the most ardent feminists would define it, is a much more radical concept than you may be aware of. Often, known as *Gender Feminism*, it seeks nothing less than a rewriting of the Divine blueprint for human interaction. Dissatisfied with maleness and femaleness, chafing under traditional understandings of male and female relationships within marriage and family, Gender Feminism seeks to "deconstruct" those roles and relationships, replacing them instead with a frightening and humanistic set of alternatives that redefine marriage, family, sexual right and wrong, and even theology. Consider the following lengthy recitation of gender feminist goals and beliefs:[1]

- Marriage is seen as the root of all evil for women...Everything related to traditional male and female relationships is despised. Men are seen as oppressors and exploiters whom women should regard as lifelong enemies.[2]

- The family is also blamed for most of the violence suffered by women and girls. Nowhere is it acknowledged that men and women should be partners in the procreation, care and nurturing of children.[3]

---

[1] A recent letter from Dr. James Dobson to supporters of Focus on the Family—actually, an 8 page "white paper"—describes in great detail the upcoming United Nations Fourth World Conference on Women, to be held in Beijing, China. The US delegation is made up of a virtual "who's who" of leading and radical gender feminists. Dobson exposes the feminist agenda of the conference, quoting extensively from a document released by the US Department of State entitled "Background on the UN conferences on Women Leading to the Fourth United Nations World Conference on Women: Action for Equality, Development, and Peace." Much of what appears in these pages is informed by this letter and this document.

[2] Dobson, op. cit., p. 3.

[3] Dale O'Leary, Gender: "The Deconstruction of Women: Analysis of the Gender Perspective in Preparation for the Fourth World Conference on Women in Beijing, China," p. 21, cited in Dobson, p. 3.

- Gender Feminism proposes "a new way of looking at human sexuality. The notion that babies come into the world as male or female based on the size and shape of their genitalia is anathema. Sexual identification, they say, is something *society imposes on children and then expects them to play out in their behavior ever after.* One feminist writer expressed it like this; 'Although many people think that men and women are the natural expression of a genetic blueprint, gender is a product of human thought and culture, a social construction that creates the "true nature" of all individuals.'"[4]

- The political agenda of gender feminists even seeks the elimination of "such terms as *wife, husband, son, daughter, sister, brother, manhood, womanhood, masculine* and *feminine*. These references to sexual identity are being replaced with gender-neutral terms, such as *parent, spouse, child* and *sibling*."[5]

- Once this redefinition of terms and identity has been accomplished, social life will radically change. "All household responsibilities will be divided 50/50 by governmental decree. Every business will be governed by strict 50/50 quotas. The military will also be apportioned equally between men and women, including ground combat assignments and any future selection of draftees. There will be absolutely no differences tolerated between the sexes."[6]

- Gender Feminism demands a high priority be given by governments and cultures to "reproductive rights," a byword for safe-sex ideology, including condom distribution and especially abortion rights for all women.

- Gender Feminism walks hand in hand with the homosexual and lesbian lobby. Listen to their own words: "We, the undersigned, call upon the Member States to recognize the right to determine one's sexual identity; the right to control one's own body, particularly in establishing intimate relationships; and the right to choose if, when, and with whom to bear or raise children as fundamental components of all human rights of all women regardless of sexual orientation."[7] The

---

4 Ibid., p. 6. (*emphasis added*).

5 Ibid.

6 Ibid., p. 23.

7 From the Declaration of the Gay and Lesbian Human Rights Commission to the UN Conference, cited by O'Leary, p. 6, and quoted in Dobson, p. 4.

The Wolf's Teeth—Feminism / 73

"deconstruction of gender" is so in tune with the homosexual/lesbian agenda that "homosexuality is considered the moral equivalent of heterosexuality. For women however, the preferred love relationship is lesbian in nature. In that way male oppressiveness can be negated. Artificial insemination is the ideal method of producing a pregnancy, and a lesbian partner should have the same parenting rights accorded historically to biological fathers."[8]

- Gender Feminism is extremely hostile to traditional "fundamentalism" in religion. They seek to mow down any religion in their path that they consider "fundamentalist," including "Catholics, Evangelicals, Orthodox Christians, Orthodox Jews, Muslims, and any other persons whose religious views contradict feminist dogma. Nothing, they say, has done more to oppress women or limit their aspirations than these patriarchal religious beliefs and teachings."[9]

- More to the point, even within Reformed and Presbyterian confessional circles - traditionally bastions of Biblical conservativism - Gender Feminism has made inroads. Cynthia Campbell, herself a leading Presbyterian feminist, describes feminist theology as that which seeks to give religious expression to the female "experience"[10] (That experience? Oppression by men.) Not only does theological feminism find that "The Reformation maintained the subordination of women...," but that "For some Christians with a feminist perspective, the Bible presents significant problems. Alongside the story of God's liberation of Israel from slavery is a story about human sin in which the woman is often interpreted as the culprit. Alongside the good news of Jesus Christ are passages that command women to keep silent in church, that forbid women to teach or bear office and that charge a wife to submit to her husband 'as to the Lord'."[11] How do gender feminists deal with a Bible that presents problems? They redefine the way in which they will read it. Listen: "This conviction about women's experience...leads many

---

8 O'Leary, p. 7, cited in Dobson, p. 4.

9 O'Leary, p. 25, cited in Dobson, p. 4.

10 Cynthia Campbell, *Theologies Written From Feminist Perspective: An Introductory Study* (Study Paper commended to the churches of the 199th General Assembly of the PCUSA, [1987]), p. 17-18.

11 Ibid., p. 21-22.

feminists to formulate a principle of interpretation applicable both to Scripture and to Christian doctrine; where Scripture and tradition do not speak to women's experience, or speak in such a way as to demean women, they are not authoritative."[12]

- Gender Feminists suggest a rewrite of major Christian doctrines:

    1. a transformation of the *doctrine of man* which they see as having been male dominated and requiring inclusive language to help redress the sins of the past

    2. a rethinking of the *doctrine of God* which has been thoroughly corrupted by male imagery to the exclusion of female, again requiring, among other things, new language (God as "father" must always be supplemented by the word "mother"; Rosemary Ruether suggests using the new term "God/ess.")[13]

    3. a redefinition of the *doctrine of sin* that is breathtaking: "Women's sin is precisely the failure to turn toward the self. The sin of women is submitting to the view that she is powerless or helpless"[14]

    4. and, of course, a radical change in the understanding of the *doctrine of redemption and Christology*; redemption is liberation (strong parallels to "liberation theology" should be noted), and is understood as "empowerment or becoming able to take responsibility for one's own life."[15] The work of Christ undergoes the greatest reworking. Rosemary Ruether puts the question succinctly: "Can a male savior save women? Does not the worship of a male figure reinforce the stereotype that women cannot be whole persons without the intervention of or relationship to a man?"[16]

---

12 Ibid., p.24.

13 Rosemary Ruether, *Sexism and God-Talk: Toward a Feminist Theology* (Boston: Beacon Press, 1983), cited in Campbell, p. 29. See also *An Inclusive-Language Lectionary*, Division of Education and Ministry, National Council of Churches.

14 Judith Plaskow, *Sex, Sin and Grace: Women's Experience and the Theologies of Reinhold Niebuhr and Paul Tillich* (Lanham, MD: University Press of America, 1980), p. 151, cited in Campbell, p. 31.

15 Campbell, p. 33.

16 Ruether, op. cit. (chapter 5 of her book is entitled "Christology: Can a Male Saviour Save Women?"), cited in Campbell, p. 33.

If you read this catalog of feminist convictions and goals, you will be convinced, as I am, that feminism is a serious threat to the people of God. Not only does it undermine the doctrinal and confessional underpinnings of the faith ("Even from your own number men will arise and distort the truth..." Acts 20:30), but it directly challenges the way in which the people of God live out that faith in marriage, in family, in sexual purity and in interpersonal relationships in home, church, work and society in general. It is indeed a genuine threat and a very real danger to the flock.

WHAT TO DO?

What should you do as elders of the flock? Allow me to be specific.

1. *Teach Biblical principles about gender relationships.* Don't expend all your energies reacting negatively to feminist agitators in your local church or community or even in your denomination; rather, as elders you must teach positively and clearly, and insist that your preacher do so from the pulpit as well, the fundamental Biblical truths regarding male and female role relationships in marriage, home, church and society.[17] Of course, from the distortions evident in the way feminists rework crucial Biblical doctrines, it becomes clear that accurate and foundational knowledge of Biblical doctrine is essential to combat this and every attack of Satan. The prophet was right: "My people are destroyed for lack of knowledge." So, teach your people a full and balanced diet of Biblical Truth!

For further study in the entire issue of feminist theology, I refer the interested reader to a few titles in addition to those cited; this list is by no means exhaustive:

> Rosemary Radford Ruether, *Women-Church: Theology and Practice of Feminist Liturgical Communities* (San Francisco: Harper & Row, Publishers, 1985).
>
> Letty M. Russell, Editor. *Feminist Interpretation of the Bible* (Philadelphia: The Westminster Press, 1985) (Chapters written by a who's who of feminist theologians).
>
> Christin Lore Weber, *WomanChrist: A New Vision of Feminist Spirituality* (San Francisco: Harper & Row, Publishers, 1987).

17 As an example of what I mean, I offer to you the schedule of a teaching series I preached on the subject; the series included successive sermons on *Foundations*, using Gen. 1:26-31 and Gen. 2:18-25; *The Godly Husband*, using Eph. 5:21,25-33 and I Peter 3:7; *The Godly Wife*, using Eph. 5:21,22-24 and Prov. 31:10f; *Men and Women in Worship and Witness*, using I Tim. 2:8-15 and I Cor. 11:2f, 14:33f; *Gender and Office in the Church*, using I Tim. 3:1-3. More could be added

2. *Don't overreact.* Not all of God's people who have been influenced by a feminist agenda embrace all of the planks of the platform of Gender Feminism. In fact, some are righteously caught up in a pursuit of Biblical justice; they have merely adopted dangerous words and concepts because they are the currency of today's debate. Be patient with these folks; teach them that "ideas have legs," that much of today's rhetoric arises from thoroughly unbiblical notions. Expose those invisible notions.

3. *Use women and their God-given gifts Biblically and appropriately in the life of the church.* One theologian once observed that "cults are the unpaid debts of the church," that cults arise where the church has failed to be thorough in her obedience. If that is true of cults, it is surely true of feminism. It has arisen in no small measure because appropriate ministry by women in the life of the church has been stymied, often by mere tradition and certainly in conflict with Scripture. For instance, I Cor. 14:33 clearly prohibits women from preaching (the literal meaning of the verse suggests a prohibition, not of speech itself, but of "being the speaker" i.e., the preacher. See also I Pet. 4:11). That does *not* mean that a woman may not be used wisely and appropriately to speak or to teach under the Biblical supervision of the eldership within a Sunday School class. Again, the I Tim. 2:12 prohibition against a woman "having authority over a man" does *not* require men to chair every single committee within a local church, nursery committee included! Rather, the text prohibits the usurping of authority, particularly within the context of authoritative teaching.

4. *Make sure the "careers" of wives and mothers are honored within your home and your church fellowship.* Nothing combats feminism in our society and within our churches more effectively than the careful articulation of the high view of these roles in Scripture. To be sure, you may not convert a rabid Gender Feminist by referring to Eph. 5:22, but you will surely encourage godly women (and instruct godly men!) when you hold high the role of a wife as a gift of God who is a life-partner in the work of the kingdom, and that of a mother as a precious instrument in God's hand for the nurture and shaping of the next generation of His own servants, complete with prophetic, priestly and royal duties.

---

to the series; our local pastoral elders followed this series up by leading a several-week long Sunday School seminar-class in which they developed the application of the teaching series to the details of our lives as believers in home, church and society.

THE SHEPHERD'S EYE

Section Two:
A STRATEGIC BLUEPRINT FOR PASTORING FAMILIES

FOUNDATIONAL PRINCIPLES OF FAMILY CARE

A generation ago, "Leave it to Beaver," "My Three Sons," and "Ozzie and Harriet" were weekly fare in most homes. Today the diet has changed. Today, people watch "Roseanne," "The Simpsons," and the extended soap opera trials that are tragically not soap operas: the Menendez trial (brothers Eric and Lyle Menendez tried twice for murdering their parents), the O.J. Simpson trial (the famed NFL running back tried and acquitted on the charge of brutally murdering his ex-wife and her male friend), and the Susan Smith murder trial (a young woman convicted in South Carolina for drowning her two young sons, still strapped in their car seats, apparently because of fear of losing her illicit lover who didn't want to be bothered with the burden of children). All of these focus attention on the sad state of American family life.

The change in entertainment diet from one generation to the next is both urgent and instructive for all who must serve as pastors in the church of Christ. The devil is waging an all-out frontal attack on the marriages and families of your people. You as elders must do something to defend the flock!

In this chapter, we turn our attention to practical strategies for the pastoral care of the family, believing it to be the foundational institution of society and to lie at the heart of the life of the church. Please remember the focus of this part of the book: I am challenging you to *sharpen your pastoral perspective*, that is, to help you get a better view of the condition of today's flock under the devil's ferocious attack, and consequently, to help you learn to think strategically as you plan and carry out your pastoral work to defend the Lord's sheep.

FAMILY MINISTRY PAST AND PRESENT

The difference in television portrayals of the American family described in the opening words of this chapter reflects the world we minister in, a world of radically different needs than that of a generation or two ago. Then, the church's ministry did not target the family or marriage as the focus of her work; it *presumed* Christian marriages and families as foundational to its life. Today, the church's ministry cannot assume healthy home life, cannot assume a commitment to marriage fidelity, cannot even assume the nurturing presence of a father within a home. Instead, we must establish new categories; single and single *again* (due to divorce); single parenting; marriage and *re*marriage.

These days the painful and dysfunctional relationships in which many of God's people live have demanded the development of a focused family ministry in evangelical churches. Unfortunately not all local churches do a good job of family care. In fact, if you would ask many pastors to suggest ways to minister to the marriages and families of their people, you would hear the same monotonous refrain over and over; "show the Dobson film series."[1] In such a climate of pastoral ineffectiveness, allow me to suggest several positive principles to guide your pastoral work long before crises afflict your people.

Principle One: Ministry to the Family Must Equip Families to Serve the Lord

Overall, what most characterizes current ministry to marriages and families is that it is almost exclusively *crisis-oriented*. Christ's church and her shepherds have not usually been ahead of the problems, preparing and equipping His people for what they will face in such an age, working preventatively. Rather, they have treated the cases in reaction to problems; a divorce here, a tyrannical and abusive father there, a runaway teen or a suicidal adolescent thrown in all too frequently. And failing to minister consistently in a normative, foundational and preventative manner to strengthen, equip and warn God's people about the spirits of the age, today's church has too frequently failed in her pastoral responsibilities.

---

1 I focus here on the work of pastors *in churches*. It is not my intent to slight the powerful and effective work of such extra-ecclesiastical ministries as Focus on the Family. Indeed, I lean heavily on their work, as is evident from the frequency with which I quote their publications and statements from their founder and leader, Dr. James Dobson. Fact is, Focus on the Family was founded precisely because of the devil's attack on the family and because churches weren't getting it done in pastoral care. Thank God for this organization; but let's not default to them in pastoral care.

In an earlier chapter, I explored with you the *purposes* of pastoral care. One of them was shaped by Eph. 4:11-12; pastors must care for the people of God so that the people of God can themselves serve and minister before the face of the Lord. Theologically, this has been called the "priesthood of all believers." If this is a valid Scriptural goal of pastoral care (and it is), the implication of that goal for the pastoral care of families is striking. The reasoning goes something like this: *the Christian family is the greenhouse within which is nurtured the tender plant of obedient service to Christ; therefore the church should keep the glass clean, the temperature warm, and the soil well watered and fertilized.* In short, the church must give parents the Biblical tools to nurture their kids; husbands and wives the tools to live together in Christ-honoring love; children the tools with which to grow to maturity and service. Listen to the Christian family described in Scriptural language: "Talk about them (God's commandments) when you sit at home and when you walk along the road, when you lie down and when you get up. Tie them as symbols on your hands and bind them on your foreheads. Write them on the doorframes of your houses and on your gates" (Deut. 6:7-9). Such a home will be a tremendous greenhouse for faith. It involves both parental mouth and modeling alike in nurturing the young plant; it extends to daily work ("hands"), thought processes and decision-making ("foreheads"), and consistency of faith from front-door to back, from living room to bedroom, from kitchen to garage ("doorframes and gates" visibility).

If you add the admonitions of Proverbs, you get an even more detailed portrait of an equipping ministry at work. Consider the assignments:

- *begin young* (4:3) (go ahead, look it up!)
- *communicate God's Word, not just parental notions* (4:2, 7, 11)
- *provide both positive and negative direction;* both "setting the course" of right living (v. 11) and warning and correcting the child about deviations from "the way" (4:14f.)
- *focus on the important, not just the urgent.* Concentrate on *the heart* at all times (4:23)
- *be specific.* Correct the mouth (4:24); curb the wandering eye (4:25); redirect wavering feet (4:26-7)

- recall the wonderful wisdom of Prov. 22:6, which most directly addresses "preventative parenting": "Train up a child in the way he should go, and when he is old he will not turn from it."

Principle Two: Ministry to the Family Must Recognize the Covenantal Nature of Marriage and Family

In previous pages, I reminded you how the evil one works to tear the flesh of the flock. I identified several key fangs in his mouth: secularism, materialism, relativism, pragmatism, and I called your attention to a modern example of these spirits active in Gender Feminism. While pastoring in such an age, I have been helped greatly by the work of Paul Vitz,[2] who clarifies the basic issue even more. Vitz argues that all such "isms" have one thing in common; they evidence the worship of self. One cannot call such a thing "selfishness," which refers to a character trait; Vitz sees it as a spiritual force, calls it *selfism,* and sees in it a danger much more malignant.

A central theme in Scripture is the description of faith and religion as the direction and commitment of the *heart*. We are called to "love the Lord your God with all your heart" (Deut. 6:5); we are told that the sinful, unregenerate "heart is deceitful above all things and beyond cure" (Jer. 19:9); we are promised "a new heart of flesh" to replace the hard "heart of stone" (Ezek. 35:26-27), and we are challenged "above all else" to "guard your hearts" (Prov. 4:23). (A concordance study of the term "heart" is most valuable.) If the *soft heart* of the individual before the face of God is central to vibrant and humble Biblical faith, then "selfism" as Vitz describes it is that faith-commitment which stands in direct antithesis to such faith. It is the selfist heart direction which was evident in Adam and Eve's disobedience; it is the selfist faith which is evident in the repeated lament over Israel's sin throughout the book of *Judges*: "There was no king in Israel. Every man did what was right in his own eyes."

And selfism is a malignancy that eats away at marriages and families. A pastor-friend of mine once commented: "There is no sin that soft hearts in a marriage cannot overcome by love, repentance and forgiveness. No sin, that is, except selfism." He's right; that is

---

2 Paul Vitz, *Psychology As Religion: The Cult of Self-Worship* (Grand Rapids: Eerdman's, 1977).

exactly Jesus' point in Matt. 19:8 when He declared that "Moses permitted you to divorce your wives because your hearts were hard. But it was not this way from the beginning."

In fact, each marriage, every family, does indeed have a "heart" all its own. It is either a home with the heart of Christ and His service, or it is a home within which beats the pulse of the world. Understand me clearly: I am not suggesting that Christian marriages and families have fewer problems than non-Christian ones. Rather, what reveals the heart of the Christian home is that it *solves* its problems in a Christ-centered manner. The motive of such a home is to honor Christ; its manner is to follow His instruction to rebuke, to repent and confess, and then to forgive a "brother" or "sister" who sins.

This principle implies, first of all, that your ministry to marriages and families must be *corporate* in its approach. You cannot combat the antithetical faith of selfism by approaching only individuals; you must recognize the corporate dimensions of sin in marriage and families. Indeed, Scripture makes clear that God Himself deals with communal groupings and not merely with individuals. Blessing was promised to Abraham *and his family* in Gen. 12 and 17; the curse of the covenant was applied to Achan *and his family* in Joshua 7. Remember also the New Testament passage in Acts 16:31f., where the declaration of salvation and the consequent application of the sacrament of baptism were given to the Philippian jailor *and his household*. Though we are not sure just who was included in his "household," it is clear that the promise and grace of God were extended beyond himself as an individual!

Specifically, to minister in a corporate manner requires that you meet with entire families in their homes; it implies that to minister to husbands and wives is to minister to them together, so that they hear the claims of the Word of God upon each within their marriage. To approach individuals merely as individuals denies the covenantal nature of the respective institutions, and may well foster selfism. Instead, the obedient (covenant) *institution* must be in focus, not just the happiness or advancement of the individual.

Paul Vitz makes the same point when he examines popular counseling methodologies. He demonstrates the methodological bankruptcy of selfist psychology and family therapy (evidenced in Maslow, Rogers, Fromm and Rollo May) *precisely because* it is client-centered instead of objectively normative. Then he says: "The social destructiveness of much of today's psychotherapy can be attributed to characteristics of the therapy process itself, although psychologists assume that social or personality characteristics are to blame when a client's marriage ends in divorce, for example. *The problem begins with psychotherapy's neurotic preoccupation with the individual patient."*[3]

Principle Three: Because Marriage and Family are Divinely-Established Institutions, Ministry Must Always Seek Divine Goals and Use Divine Tools

Ministry to families is always and finally the ministry of the Word. By that I mean that God, who in paradise established the institution of marriage, provides standards or norms for that institution and for the family in His Word. It is the task and duty of the church and her pastors to preach and teach those norms, and to call for obedient response in the people of God. Consider some specific implications of this principle.

Scripturally-defined Family Relationships

In the first place, the Word of the Lord is normative for *relationships* within the institutions of marriage and family. It is evident that the current spirits of the age have undermined the traditionally-held understanding of the *offices* of husband, wife and parent.[4] These days, young people get married in the passion of infatuation (or worse, in the bloom of a pregnancy), not Biblical love. For years, ministers assumed that these youth, raised in the bosom of the church and in Christian homes, understood what loving each other involved. We can no longer take that for granted. You must rather build marriages from the ground floor up. In premarital instruction sessions, pastoral elders must deal with Biblical fundamentals: Eph. 5:22-24 on what wife-love looks like, patterned after the love of the church-bride for her heavenly Husband; Eph. 5:25-

---

3 Ibid. p. 83. (emphasis added).

4 Although not a widely used term these days in American evangelicalism, "office" is a concept rich and well-known in continental Reformed churches, and is used to convey the stewardship of a sacred trust. We readily acknowledge it when we speak of the "office of the presidency" (it was even reported that, after his own brother's inauguration, Bobby Kennedy was so impressed with the office that he could not bring himself to call him "Jack," but only "Mr. President"). A fine treatment of this Biblical concept can be found in K. Sietsma, *The Idea of Office* (Jordan Station, Ontario, Canada: Paideia Press, 1985), trans. by Henry Vander Goot.

33 on what husband-love looks like, patterned after the sacrificial leadership-love of Christ for that bride.[5]

The same must be said about sexuality. Pastoral ministry of the Word of God regarding the normativity of intimate relations within marriage is an urgent responsibility of the church. That may come as a surprise to you, but I mean it seriously. Perhaps we don't need to *inform* the members of the church about sexual matters, but we surely need to *norm* them! Once again, we must hold forth the fundamentals; the prohibition of sex outside of marriage, and the joyful and delightful holiness of sex within the context of marriage.[6] A balance in this area will do much to alleviate Victorian prudishness toward sex, on the one hand, and growing commonness and vulgarity about it on the other.[7]

Finally, we must pay serious pastoral attention to Scriptural norms about the burgeoning practice of an unquestioning acceptance and use of birth control. While it certainly can be argued that such methods may well be used as part of a godly couple's stewardship of the physical health of the mother and the resources of the family, it is also clear that blind and unthinking use will contribute to the selfism of the day, since it permits sexual self-indulgence without fear of consequence. We must, in the face of such attitudes and practices, uncompromisingly hold forth the value of the bearing of children for the coming of the Kingdom, reminding the people of God that children are "a heritage of the Lord, the fruit of the womb a reward" (see Ps. 127-128).

SCRIPTURALLY-DIRECTED *FAMILY STEWARDSHIP*

The foundational principle that our ministry must be a ministry of the Word can and must be applied to matters of stewardship. Not only are relationships normed by Scripture; our use of the resources entrusted to families by God must follow divine patterns. And this involves more than warning God's people against the idolatry of

---

5 More will be said about this in a later chapter dedicated to the subject of pastoral preparations for marriage.

6 I join with those who do not read *Song of Songs* as an extended allegory, but as OT wisdom literature. As *Ecclesiastes* expresses covenant wisdom about the quest for wisdom and knowledge, so too *Song of Songs* speaks about the righteousness, delight, even excitement, of physical relations within the context of marriage.

7 Detailed suggestions on providing Scripturally-shaped sexual nurture of adolescents will follow in a separate chapter, *infra*.

greed or the sin of waste. It includes setting values on time usage (the KJV translation of Col. 4:5 expresses the idea beautifully; "redeeming the time"), challenging the sinful notion that education is to be evaluated strictly on economic terms, and reminding the people of God that "a man's life does not consist in the abundance of his possessions."

SCRIPTURALLY-SHAPED *FAMILY ENTERTAINMENT*

Further, ministering the Word of the Lord to the marriages and families within the church involves teaching what the Bible says about the *recreational* life of the home. The line-item in most family budgets called "entertainment" has, without question, grown significantly in recent years. Today, entire rooms within the house are built and arranged around "entertainment centers." Today, the thought of spending an entire evening, much less *every* evening, at home without TV or a movie is anathema to most families. Yet, seldom does the family think seriously about what they welcome into their homes, their hearts and their minds by way of the TV screen. Such influences are no less insidious for all their commonness.

Without reducing Scripture to a superficial "do/don't" type of application, the warning against worldly amusements in I John ("Do not love the world or the things in it") cannot be overlooked. In the church in which I grew up, the general assembly (Synod) of the denomination issued, way back in 1928, a formal position-statement on "Worldly Amusements." Many then, and subsequent, have been free to criticize the document as overly simplistic, especially since the technology by which we are amused has changed and evolved so thoroughly. A recent rereading has convinced me that the statement is both Biblically comprehensive and quite helpful. Permit me to quote extensively from it:

> I. Synod reminds our people of the doctrinal and ethical principles which should guide the Christian in his relation to the world in general and in the matter of amusements in particular, and urges all our professors, ministers, elders, and Bible-teachers to emphasize these principles in this age of prevailing worldliness.

> Some of the most important of these principles follow:

> 1. The *honor of God* requires:
>
>> a) that the Christian's amusements should at the very least not conflict with any commandment of God;

b) that we and our children should be keenly aware, also in our amusements, of our covenant relation to God as His peculiar people;

c) that the Christian shall deem it a matter of loyalty to God not to further the interests of an institution which is manifestly an instrument of Satan for attack on the Kingdom of God.

2. From the consideration of the *welfare of man* we conclude:

a) that there is a legitimate place in life for such amusements as are recreative for body and mind;

b) that no physical recreation or mental diversion should be tolerated which is in any way or in any degree subversive of our spiritual and moral well-being;

c) that even when our amusements are not spiritually or morally harmful, they should not be allowed to occupy more than a secondary, subordinate, place in life.

3. The principle of *spiritual separation from the world:*

a) does not imply that Christians should form separate communities or should shun all association with ungodly men (I Cor. 5:9ff.);

b) forbids friendship, in distinction from fellowship, with evil men (James 4:4);

c) requires that we shun all evil in the world;

d) demands a weaning away of the heart from the transient things of this present earthly sphere (Col. 3:1,2).

4. *Christian Liberty:*

a) consists in freedom from the power of sin; in freedom from the law: its curse, its demands as a condition for eternal life, its oppressive yoke; and in liberty of conscience with reference to human ordinances and things neither prescribed nor condemned, either directly or indirectly, in the Word of God;

> b) is limited in its exercise by the law of love (I Cor. 8:9,13), the law of self-preservation (Matt. 18:8,9), and the law of self-denial, which often requires the renunciation of things in themselves lawful (Matt. 16:24).
>
> II. While *several* practices are found in our circles which cannot pass the muster of these principles, and while *all* our amusements, not only theatre-attendance, dancing, and card-playing, should be judged in the light of these principles, yet Synod feels constrained...to call particular attention to this familiar trio. It greatly deplores the increasing prevalence among us of these forms of amusement (and) urgently warns our members against them....
>
> III. Synod urges all our leaders and all our people to pray and labor for the awakening and deepening of spiritual life in general, and to be keenly aware of the absolute indispensability of keeping our religious life vital and powerful, through daily prayer, the earnest searching of the Scriptures, and through engaging in practical Christian works, which are the best antidote against worldliness." [8]

As you can imagine, the mere identification of the "familiar trio" of card-playing, movie-going, and dancing by the Synod of 1928 resulted in an overemphasis on them by church members and media alike, and the unfortunate neglect of the broader Biblical scope of the principles and practices contained in the rest of the report. May God grant us, in this age of Hollywood's attack on everything that is holy, such an attitude toward recreation, such Biblical hearts and such Biblical revival!

SCRIPTURALLY-INSPIRED *FAMILY WORSHIP*

I would be remiss if I did not also speak a word about the normativity of the Word of the Lord for the faith and worship of the family. The heritage of the faith both in this nation and in Reformed and evangelical Christianity the world over has long em-

---

[8] *Acts of the Synod of 1928 of the Christian Reformed Church*, pp. 86-88. For a further and comprehensive analysis of this document and particularly the issue of Christian liberty, see the dissertation by Nelson Kloosterman, *Scandalum Infirmorum et Communio Sanctorum: The Relation between Christian Liberty and Neighbor Love in the Church* (Neerlandia, Alberta, Canada: Inheritance Publications, 1991).

phasized the importance of the "family altar." My parents and most others of their generation followed the precedent of their ancestors and gathered with their families around the Word regularly—mostly but not always in connection with mealtimes. Some, admittedly, reduced the exercise to superficiality; most didn't. A devotional submission and commitment to learn the text of Scripture were part of each day.

If reports I hear from pastoral elders are accurate, such is no longer the case. Life is lived at a frenzied pace these days; a chilling statistic reveals that more than half of all family meals are eaten "on the go," and over 20 per week at restaurants. It's tough, in this world, to pay careful attention to such a pattern of Scriptural devotions. Still, if you take seriously the comprehensive requirement set forth in Deut. 6, you will challenge Biblical parents under your pastoral care to structure life so that such comprehensive nurturing in the words of the text of Scripture can take place. Challenge them to deliberately schedule meals together, even if it means getting up an hour earlier for breakfast. You may have to stimulate alternatives, such as the use of Sunday afternoons for family study of Scripture, or a change in the bedtime routine to allow for reading and talking about Bible stories. You may even need to prepare study guides and discussion sheets to assist them. One thing is for sure; if God's Word is Truth, and a "lamp to my feet and a light upon my path," neglect of the Scripture is not a legitimate option for any Christian family.

Family worship, of course, also involves attendance at worship services with the family of God. Several implications flow from this observation. In the *first* place, preachers must take note of those family units gathered together for worship in the same place, and not just preach to elicit individual (read: private) response. Specific application of the Word of God must be addressed to the different groups within the assembly. Unless Scripture is allowed to speak directly to families, to marriages and to children in and about their respective relationships, we will find that the people of God will embrace the reigning individualism of our culture and miss much of God's instruction for obedient, fruitful and joyous Christian life.

In the *second* place, I must discourage the widespread practice of dismissing the children from the services so that they may attend "children's church." To be sure, keeping children in church places a demand upon both parent and preacher. The latter will have to structure worship and preach so as to keep kids involved and listening attentively, or parents will have a difficult task of keeping kids focused on worship. But it is not impossible.[9] I remember a story a friend told about his boyhood preacher. When preaching about the plague of frogs in *Exodus*, the preacher described briefly but graphically the comprehensive nature of the curse of God by describing Pharoah's wife and her probable reaction to finding a frog in her housecoat! The young 5 year old boy in the pew never forgot. Likewise, I'll not soon forget the time I was teaching 3rd graders a survey of Bible doctrine using a compendium of the *Heidelberg Catechism* as my textbook. The lesson was on justification by faith, admittedly a difficult subject for 9 year olds to grasp. One youngster raised his hand and asked if I was talking about the same thing I had preached about some weeks before in a sermon on Zechariah 3, where the high priest Joshua had his garments changed from filthy to pure by the action of the angel of the Lord. Tears welled up in my eyes as I had to admit my own faithless miscalculation; I had not assumed little ones listened to God's Word, and therefore I had not spent much time trying to speak to their ears and hearts so that they could hear! That young boy's question changed my ministry.

In every sphere of life the spirit of unbelief threatens to undermine and fragment the institutions which God created and which reflect His covenant relationship and love. Your pastoral ministry to marriages and families in this culture must be ministry of the very Word of the One who created those marriages and families. It is His Word alone which is the objective, eternal law for the life of these institutions and which provides the principles by which they are to live. You must not fail to make that Word live for the people of God who must confront this unholy spirit every day!

---

[9] See Richard Bacon, *Revealed to Babes: Children in the Worship of God* (Audubon, N.J.: Old Paths Publications, 1993). In this volume, the author stresses both the obligation of parents to incorporate their children in individual and family worship, and that of the church to incorporate the children in the public worship of God. His argument is quite convincing.

COMING APART AT THE SEAMS - PASTORING FAMILIES IN CRISIS

The story is familiar to any pastoral elder with some experience: The phone rings at 9:30 PM. Chris is on the other end, his voice heavy with emotion, straining not to break down. They'd had another "explosion" at their home. In the background you hear his wife sobbing, their teenaged daughter having cursed her once again, now threatening to leave home for the umpteenth time. Carol Ann had always been a problem, but lately she had been much more difficult. Her demand to be "left alone" was coupled with a style of cruelty, verbal abuse and emotional manipulation of both her parents. All of this was usually well disguised in public; most people thought she was sweet. But the family was coming apart at the seams. Chris had few "normal" conversations with his wife any more; every one was dominated by the crisis, punctuated by the weighty burden that hung around their necks like a stinking albatross. "A Christian family," thought Chris, "should be a source of happiness and joy. What's happened to mine? It seems to be a source of nothing but grief." He began to be afraid that his wife, who took the brunt of the verbal abuse from Carol Ann, was thinking of suicide.

You'd just hung up the phone, having arranged to meet with Chris's entire family in a half hour (looks like another insomnia night, anyway), when the phone rings again. This time it's Marge, a friend of yours and part of one of the most solid families in your church. Her emotional outburst is like the release of a pent-up stream. "I just can't take the silence anymore. Bill won't talk to me anymore ever since I accused him of being an alcoholic. He says he's not, and has been angry at me ever since. The kids cry themselves to sleep every night. This morning, Billy asked me if we were going to get divorced like Mike's Mom and Dad did. I don't know what to do!"

Families in crisis. If you haven't faced their pain in your pastoring work yet, you will, and more than likely, soon. Such are the times we live and labor in. And such a different experience than the visit you make to the "normal" Christian family, where Dad and Mom reflect Biblical love and faithfulness, where parents live out the faith, albeit imperfectly and the kids emulate their example and profess Christ. How does an elder deal with such crisis situations short of throwing up his hands hopelessly or becoming angry at the people who "can't control their own homes"?

In this chapter we turn to the basics of dealing with such crises. Where does one begin? What are the secondary steps? How can you be sure you won't make things worse? When should you refer? How, in short, does one plan a pastoral strategy when he is "up to his armpits in alligators and doesn't have time to drain the swamp?"

WHERE TO BEGIN

First of all, let me suggest a few underlying convictions which should undergird your thinking for most family crisis situations.

1. Understand fully that the well-being of families in your district or care group is your responsibility, like it or not. Far too many of these kinds of problems are neglected in Christ's church because the pastoral elders look immediately for a "professional" to whom they can refer the case, happy to be rid of the burden. Unfortunately, too many of the "pros" to whom such cases are referred are unbelieving, and even if they are believers, they lack the spiritual authority to insist upon a response, an authority God has invested in the eldership. So on the level of competence, you are God's man for the situation!

2. Stick to the basics; any crisis could overwhelm you with a multiplicity of details, problems, and personalities unless you keep your eye on the central issues, the non-negotiables.

    - First, remember the Biblically-assigned *role-relationships*. When a husband or father fails in his God-ordained duty to give firm spiritual leadership (sacrificially, "as Christ loves the church") thus setting the direction the entire family is to walk, problems are inevitable. When a wife or mother usurps the husband's role or undermines his direction, refusing to "submit" Biblically to him "as the church submits to Christ," crises are likewise unavoidable. When children are not raised with loving discipline that aims at the development of spiritual self-discipline, but instead are over-disciplined (so that they never learn self-control because Mom and Dad make all their decisions) or under-disciplined (so that they receive no guidance or correction), grief and pain are sure to follow. When children show no respect "as to the Lord," harmony in the home is impossible.

- Second, keep the Biblical *purpose of the family* in mind; a Christian home is to be a place where Biblical principles shape decision-making and problem-solving and where spiritual growth and obedience in each member is nurtured. You may recall from a previous chapter the image of the family as a greenhouse within which each member is nurtured for Christ's service. If each of the members of a family isn't "bearing fruit" of knowledge, obedience and service to Christ, something is amiss.

3. Remember the Biblical dynamic of *rebuke, repentance, confession, and forgiveness*.[1] If you are convinced that it is truly Christian believers you are dealing with, you may need to remind them simply that many explosive crises, deep and interpersonal as well as immediate and emotional, can be defused harmlessly when the members of the family, with broken and contrite hearts, confess their sinful wrongs to one another and humbly ask forgiveness. If you find hard and stubborn hearts, on any side of any issue, you can expect no healing, no appropriate response to your counsel. It is a wise man, says the writer of *Proverbs*, who delights in a rebuke. He, on the other hand, whose heart is stubborn and closed, hates rebuke and correction.

4. *Lead in seeking Biblical reconciliation*. Of course, the previous comments beg the question; just who is responsible to rebuke whom? How does a family institute such a communication style that involves and embraces Biblical rebuke without itself degenerating into judgmentalism, carping and nagging

---

[1] Jay E. Adams, *How To Help People Change* (Grand Rapids: Zondervan Publishing Co., 1986) (pp. 12-16) affirms the same principle but uses different words, suggesting the application of what he calls "the 4-step Biblical process" of teaching, conviction, correction and disciplined training in righteousness taught in II Tim. 3:14-17.

criticism? What must the practice of rebuke seek as its end goal? Recently, a dear friend summarized Biblical teaching on this subject by calling it "the GO principle." After studying carefully both Matt. 5:23-24 and Matt. 18:15, he observed that in each case, the believer is instructed to "go" and seek reconciliation, *irrespective of who is at fault!* In every case of brokenness, tension and sin that affects human relationships, you as a child of the Father are expected to "go" to seek reconciliation. Such behavior requirements are intentionally patterned after what the Father in heaven did for us. Rather than to wait for us to seek reconciliation with Him, He sent Christ "while we were yet sinners." Nowhere does such a desire and pattern for reconciliation apply more urgently than within the Christian family. And no one bears a greater responsibility for starting and carrying out the practice of such reconciliation in a Christian home than the "spiritual head" of the home, the husband and father. As my friend says, "if your wife or kids beat you to the punch in confessing sins or seeking reconciliation, you aren't giving Biblical leadership!"

5. *Be prepared for long-term pastoral commitment.* Those families who are faced with "immediate" crises usually have had pressures building for a long time. (Much as "overnight success stories" usually labored in anonymity for 20 years.) While repentance, confession and forgiveness bring remarkable healing and grace, they do not immediately transform patterns and habits that have been in existence for a long time. You must help people discern and break old sinful habits and patterns; just as importantly, you must guide them to establish new and Biblical ones.[2] Few of these things can be done exclusively through the minimal "annual visit" to members' homes customary in many churches, especially if such visits are perfunctory and superficial; such pastoral care requires weekly contact, sometimes even daily. Happily, some of these contacts can be informal, even telephone calls. But don't neglect to keep in touch. Pastoral elders are the men God has called to "watch over the flock of God" (Acts 20:28) to protect and defend them from doctrinal error and sinful life. You

---

[2] For an extended treatment of this and related themes related to Biblical counseling within the context of the church and the responsibility of pastors to care for the flock see Jay E. Adams: *Competent to Counsel* (Grand Rapids: Baker Book House, 1970).

can't watch with your eyes closed, and a periodic glance from a distance isn't sufficient to defend against the wolf!

6. Finally, look for new "ingredients" in the recipe. In some homes you may know well, as in the second example above, you might be genuinely surprised to see sudden major crises crop up. You may have taught the children in catechism class or Sunday school, and prayed and studied with the folks in Bible studies, believing them all to be solid and faithful believers whose relationships are loving and Biblical. Yet, suddenly and unexpectedly, the marriage is in trouble, or one of the children runs away, or the character of the home changes from one of love to one of anger. In such a situation, be alert to new factors that enter the equation. An adulterous affair, though not yet revealed publicly, will reveal itself in guilt and a growing distance from the marriage partner long before the details of the sinful affair may become known. Alcohol dependency, though well disguised, will affect everyone in the family profoundly through transformed personality, denial, anger, guilt and the like. Drugs will sharply transform a previously normal child into a Jekyll and Hyde personality. So will the impact and influence of friends whose influence is negative. Keep your eyes and ears open to such new factors that the family itself may be too close to see.

WHEN TO REFER

Obviously, some situations will require more assistance than you are able to give. In that case, consult with someone else spiritually discerning. Some seminary-trained pastor/teachers are competent; many are not. Some Christian MDs are excellent sources of advice. Some have had much experience themselves pastorally counseling those people who come to them for physical care, because they understand the intimate connection between physical and spiritual well-being[3] and can refer you to someone who can help. But be sure that you aren't merely trying to dump off a problem because you are unwilling to spend the time and commit the effort that it will take to care for the flock. It is after all your responsibil-

---

[3] You must be sensitive to this connection which is clearly taught in such passages as Ps. 32 and 51, and which is the basis for a proper understanding of James 5:14. In that regard, see Adams, *Competent to Counsel*, p. 105-107. Also see Karl Menninger, MD, *Whatever Became of Sin?* (New York: Hawthorn, Inc., 1973).

ity. You are the shepherd of the flock. Even if you don't do the hands-on work of counseling, you are responsible to God to oversee the process. Such is the duty of oversight. May God grant you wisdom and give you perseverance to do your duty.

If you must refer a member or a family to someone with greater knowledge or experience, please be careful. Especially in this day and age, so many counselors who hang a shingle and advertise as Christian counselors are sadly, people who may have personal faith in Christ, but who operate in their professional lives with thoroughly secular presuppositions and methodologies. Unfortunately, many so-called "Christian" counselors take such a non-integrated approach to their faith; they believe that faith deals with "salvation issues," yet never allow its principles to direct the intimate details of their non-ecclesiastical lives.[4] Jesus' words in Matt. 6:24, "No one can serve two masters" are widely understood to apply to the conflict between materialism and Kingdom values. These words apply as well to the matter of the Lordship of Christ to all dimensions of life. Either He is Lord, or He isn't. No man can serve two masters, one in church and the other in business or in the professional counselor's life.[5]

Instead, any counselor's faith must shape his understanding of how he approaches the people of God. Does he believe "disease" lies at the root of all problems, or is he willing to look sin in the face and call it what it is? Is he willing to confront, rebuke, call to repentance and confession, or will he only work in a non-directive manner? Is he willing to isolate the help he gives to God's people professionally from the care God demands that the elders provide within the context of the family of God, or is he willing to work *with* the elders, believing them to be ultimately responsible to God. In the case of marital counseling, does he believe what the Bible teaches about marriage, about the roles of husband and wife, about the nature of love, about the importance of their mutual loyalty to the marriage bond, or does he buy into worldly definitions of roles, relationships and easy divorce. I've been "burned," frankly, by referring couples to "Christian counselors," only to see those coun-

---

[4] Please refer to the earlier chapter on "Secularism" for an analysis of such a non-integrated approach to life.

[5] See the comprehensive analysis of the dichotomy between Biblical (pastoral) counseling and counseling methodologies with secular bases (Freudianism and its legacy; Carl Rogers and "client-centered" therapy; etc.) in Adams, *Competent to Counsel*, pp. 1-104.

selors reveal unwillingness to insist upon appropriate handling of evident personal sins and sinful patterns within the relationship, and to encourage divorce because they saw the couple as "incompatible."[6] Such counselors work against the grain of what God has called you to do as pastors.

As a wise elder once said, "Don't put the club into the devil's hand!" Don't refer God's precious lambs to others who are merely "hirelings," men or women whose approach is that of the wolf, whose motive is financial and whose methods butcher, rather than heal the flock.

---

[6] All pastoral elders will be well-served to read Jay E. Adams, *Marriage Divorce & Remarriage in the Bible* (Phillipsburg, NJ: Presbyterian and Reformed Publishing Co., 1980). Such a volume establishes fundamental counseling approaches that are thorough, Biblically-balanced and most practical. Another recommended volume by the same author is *Solving Marriage Problems: Biblical Solutions for Christian Counselors* (Phillipsburg, NJ: Presbyterian and Reformed Publishing Co., 1983).

Focus on the Marriage, Not the Wedding

Sheep mate; humans marry. At least that's the way it's supposed to be. Though the church is Christ's flock, we're not animals. God made us in His image, and that means we can and should reflect a dignity and an ethical bond in our interpersonal relations that is not shown in the rest of the animal kingdom. Nowhere is this to be more evident than in marriage.

I wish more couples would spend as much time preparing for their marriage as they do making ready for their wedding. Literally hundreds of hours are invested in the making/purchase of a wedding dress, bridesmaids' gowns, tuxedo fittings, and floral arrangements, not to mention the time and money consuming details of a wedding reception. But when a pastor or elder suggests a series of 4 to 6 hour-long meetings to focus on preparing for the marriage, couples often find it hard to fit into their schedule.

Is such "premarital counseling" necessary? Is it important? Is it even worthwhile? After all, in the "dinosaur days" (you know, back 40 or 50 years), most pastors conducted "premarital counseling" like this:

> Is this fellow (or gal) you are marrying 'in the Lord'?
>
> Do your parents approve of the marriage?
>
> When is the wedding? I'll be there 15 minutes early so we can talk about the details of the ceremony.

And that's about all there was to it. Unthinkable today, yet 40 or 50 years ago it was often sufficient. Despite notable exceptions, society, not to mention Christ's church, held marriage and fidelity in higher esteem than today, and viewed divorce with disfavor. But no more. Marriage is considered by many to be the formalization of living arrangements, but little more than that. Divorce is a viable option and often seen as the best option. The marriages children and teens see "up close and personal" in their homes often aren't all that great, even in the church.

Pastoral elders must, as a consequence, concern themselves deeply with stemming this tide that threatens to overwhelm the Christian family, and with domino effect, the nurture of the next generations to come within that family. So the process of premarital preparation begins with you as you plan to care for the flock under your care.

Allow me to identify some basic strategic steps the wise elder will take.[1]

PREPARATION BEGINS WITH ANALYSIS

The wise elder begins by observing carefully the marriages within the church and particularly within his assigned care district. He sees which ones reflect the Scriptural patterns; which marriages are blessed with a husband who is a patient and loving leader, guiding his family with a firm but faithful hand through the spiritual minefield of our age, showing his wife tenderness, affection, love; which wives are secure in their calling to be Biblically submissive, respecting their husbands for Christ's sake, not rebelling against God's pattern, but not putting their gifts and talents on the shelf, either. When an elder sees a marriage like that, he knows that the pattern will be impressed upon the children. So, when spending pastoral time with the children, he encourages them to marry "in the Lord" like Mom and Dad.

On the other hand, the observant elder will also notice those marriages where the parents are merely surviving together but not living in joyful Christian love. You know the kind; the husband is impatient, insensitive, uncaring about the wife's desires, needs, or concerns. He wants things his way, and even claims divine sup-

---

[1] In what follows, my suggestions have in view preparing a previously unmarried young couple for marriage. Several circumstances will require elders to adapt the material in these pages differently: first, many wait until they are older before they first marry; second, in an age when life expectancy has grown, many live long after the death of their first spouse and remarry at a much older age; third, elders increasingly face issues of remarriage following divorce. Such circumstances demand special attention, certainly including a clear understanding of Scriptural teaching on marriage and divorce. See Adams, *Marriage Divorce &Remarriage,* op. cit. Also, see John Murray, *Divorce* (Phillipsburg: Presbyterian and Reformed Pub. Co., 1961) and Ray Sutton, *Second Chance: Biblical Principles of Divorce and Remarriage* (Ft. Worth: Dominion Press, 1988).

port- "after all, God made me the head of the house."[2] Sometimes he may even become violent, even defending such tendencies by lame appeals to his duty to be the head of his home. Meanwhile, the wife lives emotionally in a box. She goes through the motions of life, never feeling support, and consequently, finds herself unable to show her man much respect. Sometimes she responds by becoming manipulative, deceitful, or downright nagging. Tempers are often on edge. Blowups occur easily; he responds in angry silence, while she longs to "talk things out from the heart." Though they both claim Christ as Savior and Lord, they do not know how to subject this most intimate relationship of their lives to His healing touch and sovereign control. They're "boxed in."

In such a home, children cannot learn godly marriage patterns from their parents, except by negative example. The discipling model breaks down; the sinful habits become ingrained in yet another generation. The children marry, and the parents hope and pray that they will escape from the box, knowing down deep, however, that they never will.

When an elder deals with such a home, his burden and duty does not only encompass the "spiritual" side of life, as if one's "relationship with Jesus" does not also include one's "relationship with Jesus' teachings in His Word." Too often, when seeing such a marital disaster unfold before the eyes, an elder will confine his focus to the "safe" concerns of personal piety; what about Scripture reading and prayer practices? Are the worship services a blessing to you? Do your children learn much in Sunday School?

Instead, the elder must carefully but firmly observe the Biblical obedience or disobedience reflected in the marriage. One fine pastoral elder I know observed that in his "care group" most of the men did not exhibit the kind of qualities Scripture asks of husbands and fathers in the church. Rather than avoiding the issue, he committed himself to take each man out for breakfast, patiently and carefully calling them to loving leadership that shows a pas-

---

2 An interesting observation about this well-known phrase is that God never tells husbands to be the head of the house, or even to be the head of the wife! When God uses the phrase "head of the wife" in Eph. 5:23 *he is addressing the wives, not the husbands.* The point? Wives must understand the authority God has established in their husbands in order properly to submit; husbands, however, only receive the command to "love their wives as Christ loved...." A husband's temptation to sin by domination instead of love doesn't need divine encouragement!

sion for Christ, tenderness and understanding for his own wife, patient and careful concern for and involvement in the daily nurture of the children. After making his way through all the men of his assigned pastoral group, he began to visit families as units. By then, the process of revival had begun; hearts were soft, open to instruction and correction. Several of those "lock box marriages" experienced real renewal by the power of the Spirit!

THE POWER OF PASTORAL MODELING

What does this all have to do with "premarital preparation"? Because you as a pastoral elder must begin such work long before the pastor-teacher invites a young couple in his office to talk about Eph. 5, birth control, wedding ceremonies and the like. You are the "front line" soldier of the Kingdom of God. You see the kids when they begin dating, and when they get "serious" with someone. You must be the one who holds before them the blessed joy and satisfaction of a marriage lived well under God's pattern and in God's presence. You must let the kids who grew up in a positive marital atmosphere know that Mom and Dad are good examples to follow. Conversely, you must help the angry, sad, confused or frightened kids who grew up in a marital "war zone" know that the Biblical pattern for marriage is a happy, fruitful one. They're really not locked in a box. In Christ, there is hope!

How do you do this? Clearly, it is inappropriate to dump on teenagers or young adults your opinion of their parents' rotten relationship. But some things are appropriate, and necessary. Some kids need an ear; make sure you provide it. Some don't know how to behave on a date because they've never observed their parents treat each other with respect. You may be the "coach" who provides the game plan. Such young people have probably never wrestled with the question of the role of dating in the Christian life. You can help them understand the difference between sniffing before rutting season (the world's idea of dating) and testing someone's heart to ascertain the presence and character of Biblical love (that of the people of God). You can even give them some ideas of things to do on a date, activities that are wholesome and genuinely fun, and that release the tension level of worldly temptations about sex.

Of course, such advice is not welcome from some stranger even if he identifies himself as an elder. You must build a relationship of trust first; but that's not impossible or even difficult, especially with kids whose own home life is such a disaster that they long for a loving and stable refuge. Invite them to your home from time to time for a soft drink, or a cup of coffee, or even to watch a football game. You've heard of the program "Big Brothers and Sisters?" It tries to match good role models with kids who have none. The sponsor spends an afternoon or an evening with a youngster, hoping to let him know that all men don't desert their families, that all women aren't drunks or drug addicts. Let's learn a lesson from such a program, and apply it with elders willing to invest themselves and their time in the cultivation and nurture of young people whose ability to relate Biblically to a member of the opposite sex will either be learned on the street (God forbid!) or in some positive manner. Let the church offer the positive! So build relationships. Get them into your homes. Let them observe your marriage at work. One teen told me once "I thought all parents fought all the time." He'd never seen a marriage up close where a couple showed love and genuine respect for each other. As an elder, you must be "apt to teach," says Paul to Timothy. That means teaching, by example, the Biblical pattern for marriage as much as it means classroom instruction!

Think it's unnatural and unrealistic? That a teen won't come over to an elder's home? You're wrong! I know many kids who love it! They think it's great to have an elder who cares so much for them that the home is open for real, honest conversation. They think it's neat to be able to talk with an adult other than their parents. When my grandmother was well into her 70s, teens from our church and from other churches in the neighborhood, would drop by for coffee and talk. They knew she cared, that she really listened, that they were welcome; she didn't mince words, either, if she thought they needed advice. Kids will interact if adults will listen.

You object? Your family is too young, you're too busy? Sorry, I won't let you off the hook easily; it is your *calling* to model the faith, also in marriage. Even if you do have a legitimate alibi, you are still responsible! Find a couple in the church that is willing to be a mentor. Maybe it is the couple that sponsors your youth group. (It's essential that youth sponsors have good marriages!) Maybe it is a "youth elder." Maybe just a godly couple with a hospitable spirit. Ask them to work to start a relationship with dating young people who have no role models; coffee after church, some non-threatening activity together, whatever. The point is, those dating teens who have no Biblical role models need some, and if you can't function in that capacity, you must find someone who will.[3]

FORMAL PREPARATION: WHO DOES THE WORK?

I have always believed that I, as a pastor-teacher, am responsible in a direct way for the premarital training of young couples I agree to marry. I say that for a couple of reasons. First, I should screen couples before I agree to marry them. Despite public opinion to the contrary, most Christians recognize that the preacher is not merely a "servant of the state" in regard to marriage, but has a prior obligation to the Gospel. He is a minister of Christ, not just a "marrying Sam." Most expect the preacher to ask about their faith, their commitments, their loyalty to Christ and to each other. (There are exceptions. Those who are not committed to Christ as Savior and Lord are seldom interested in the sort of spiritual inventory I ask them to take before I agree to perform a ceremony.) There is one other reason, however, why I believe the pastor-teacher is the most logical choice, and that has to do with the nature of the "preaching" he has to do in the sessions scheduled. Clearly, the "instruction" to be given is instruction which is based on specific texts, and the counselor must proclaim them to the pair in his office.

At the same time, there are many good reasons for the local pastoral elder to do such work. Sometimes he must function in place of a pastor-teacher who is unable to do the work, or cares for such a large church that the work must be spread out simply because there are too many upcoming weddings! Certainly the elder must function in the absence of the preacher.[4] In my experience, elders often can do a better job than many preachers because they avoid some

---

3 A couple of assignments for your next elder's meeting: First, come up with a list of those young people in your congregation you believe to be dating "seriously." Determine whether they have good models to follow. If not, commit yourselves to making contact, to building relationship. Don't wait for them to come to you. In the process of pastoral care, make sure you face them with this question; does your boy/girl friend spur you on to greater Christian faith and service, or is your relationship with him/her a drag on your faith? Second, come up with a list of high school kids who are living in homes where the parents' marriage is unhealthy. Speak to the parents about the dangerous pattern they are setting, and commit yourselves to work with the parents to bring Biblical healing to their own relationships.

4 Pastoral needs of the flock do continue even after a preacher leaves one church, either by retirement or by relocation to another field! The preacher's departure does not change the elder's job description.

of the nonsensical psychological jargon familiar to seminary-trained men and get down to the real life issues exposed by God's Word. This is especially true when the elder has built the basic pastoral relationship described above. Based on that pastoral bond, these elders ask the tough questions, offer the hard-nosed advice, and aim to help people deal with the real issues they are going to face in their marriages.

Formal Preparation: What Must Be Covered?

In what follows, I offer a simple thematic outline of the subjects that ought to be covered in preparation that will equip God's people for their marriage in this day and age. Some might think this is overkill; others, not nearly enough. I prepare the list out of a sense of deep conviction of what Scripture demands, out of a realistic assessment of what a pastor or elder can actually accomplish, and out of the firm belief that the Word must remain central in the process.

Schedule For Pre-Marriage Preparation

Session 1: Assessment [5] (approximately 60 minutes)

- Determine the Biblical eligibility of the couple to marry. (Assess their basic commitments to Christ and to each other, their assessment of the maturity of their relationship, their personality traits, whether reasons exist that would forbid the marriage Scripturally, etc.)
- Assess family patterns influential in their lives. Use questionnaire if necessary.
- Assign homework; a careful study of Eph. 5:21ff.

Session 2: Bible Foundations (approximately 90 minutes)

- Teach, from Genesis 2, the nature and purpose of marriage.

---

[5] Excellent evaluative tools are available for elders in a variety of books. One that I have found particularly helpful is Howard A. Eyrich, *Three To Get Ready: A Christian Premarital Counseling Manual* (Phillipsburg, NJ: Presbyterian and Reformed Publishing Co., 1978). The section on evaluating eligibility for marriage is found on pp. 29-65. What follows in my "recipe" has been developed over the years of my ministry, but borrows heavily from Eyrich and many others whose ideas have become my own. Helpful in Eyrich's book is an annotated bibliography of books, tapes and tests to help you prepare folks for marriage.

- Teach, from Matt. 5 and Matt. 19, the permanence of marriage.
- Teach, from Eph. 5:21ff., the Biblically-assigned roles of husband, wife
- Teach, from Eph. 5:21ff. (and other passages) the Biblical definition of love (in contrast to the view of our world).

Session 3: Communication [6] (60 minutes minimum)

- Study Biblical principles of communication (Eph. 4).
- Reiterate the Biblical model of, repent, confess, forgive.
- Discuss lessons learned from the communication styles in their parental homes.

Session 4: The Place of the Bible and the Church (60 minutes minimum)

- the family altar; establishing Bible Study and Prayer routines
- family worship and the family of God; commitment to the local church

Session 5: Sex, Reproduction, and Child-rearing[7] (60 minutes minimum)

- Sex Concerns (a sensitive, but urgent, subject; especially so in a world where AIDS is so prevalent).
    1. determine whether a sexually-active past must be dealt with Biblically
    2. discuss the beautiful principles established in Gen. 2:24, I Cor. 7:1ff., Song of Songs

---

6 See Eyrich, p. 66f. Also see H. Norman Wright, *Communication: Key To Your Marriage* (Ventura: Regal Books, 1974).

7 Eyrich, p. 87-93. Also see Tim and Beverly LaHaye, *The Act of Marriage* (Grand Rapids: Zondervan Publishing Co., 1976) and Dr. Ed Wheat, *Intended for Pleasure*. Dr. Wheat also has produced a series of audio tapes entitled *Sex Problems and Sex Techniques in Marriage* (Omaha: Family Concern, Inc., 1975). The tapes are more suited to existing marriages than for premarital work. Finally, take note of Wayne Mack, *Strengthening Your Marriage* (Phillipsburg: Presbyterian and Reformed Publishing Co., 1977), which has chapters relevant to many of these matters, including one on developing a common philosophy of child-rearing. Discussing this matter prior to marriage is not premature; a common commitment to Biblical values in such matters is crucial to establishing spiritual oneness in the marriage.

- Birth Control (important in an age which believes in sex as recreation without consequences); also discuss legitimate/illegitimate reasons for, proper/improper methods of birth control.
- Discuss Biblical view of children in home and Kingdom (Ps. 127-128).

Session 6: Financial Stewardship[8] (60 minutes minimum) (could be led by a deacon)

- Stewardship foundations, including discussion of current financial circumstances, long-term goals
- Establishing a family budget (assign homework)
- Biblical teaching on giving, saving, investing, borrowing, etc.

Session 7: Planning the Ceremony (60 minutes minimum)

- Discussion of any unresolved questions from previous sessions
- Planning for the wedding ceremony (can be done earlier if time demands; however, I suggest waiting until this session, as many ideas may well change because of material studied and discussed in earlier sessions. This implies, of course, doing premarital work some months before the wedding).

---

8 Eyrich, p. 73-80, includes a budget-planning worksheet. You could also consult any one of the many resources published by Larry Burkett and Ron Blue referred to above in the chapters on secularism and materialism.

12

TEND TO THE LAMBS

In the land of Uz there lived a man whose name was Job....His sons used to take turns holding feasts in their homes, and they would invite their three sisters to eat and drink with them. When a period of feasting had run its course, Job would send and have them purified. Early in the morning he would sacrifice a burnt offering for each of them, thinking, 'Perhaps my children have sinned and cursed God in their hearts.' This was Job's regular custom(Job 1:1, 4-5).

George and Tena have three kids. Their oldest, Bill, is 25; his sister, Melissa, is 19; and the "baby," George, Jr., is 12. All of the children show signs of total commitment to worldliness. They hang around with worldly friends, delight in worldly activities and amusements, attend church functions (including worship services) only under duress from the parents. None of the children evidence a desire to seek God's face in daily devotion to Scripture and prayer, none show any sign of genuine repentance from sin or conversion of life. George and Tena obviously are concerned about these things; but, when the elders come for an annual visit with them about their walk in the Lord, they verbally affirm that "the kids were all baptized. God won't let them go. They'll be fine. All we can do is wait on Him."

Pete and Gloria have only one child, Pete Jr., who is 4. They're both faithful members of your home congregation. Gloria agonizes over the fact that Junior hasn't become a Christian yet, since she's prayed since his birth that he'd accept the Lord before he went to school. She can't bear the thought he might not be saved; in fact, every time he lies or sneaks a cookie without permission, it feels like a stab wound in her heart. She's becoming convinced he's an unbeliever.

WHAT'S WRONG WITH THIS PICTURE?

Ever see cartoons in magazines with the caption "What's wrong with this picture?" Usually some strange, illogical situation is portrayed as most natural (like a sunbather with mittens and snowshoes on). Well, something is wrong in the portrait of Pete, Gloria, and Junior. And that something is their theology. While waiting for "something to happen" to their son spiritually, they fail to understand what has already happened to him. God placed him in their believing home and bestowed upon him tremendous promises and covenant blessings.

Something is wrong as well in the picture of George, Tena and their kids. Again, it's their theology, their inappropriate presumption that since their children were baptized, all is fine with their souls, despite appearances to the contrary.

But Job seemed to have a different approach to his children, didn't he? He did not, perhaps, presume they were unregenerate, beyond hope, lost for all eternity. But he also did not presume they were regenerate, insured by baptism and thus secure for all eternity. Instead, he wrestled before God for them. Though he lived long before Christ, he seemed to understand two very crucial truths upon which Christ's coming was based. *First*, the reality and power of sin in the human heart, and *second*, the persistent and irrevocable call of God to conversion of life.

As a parent, this passage has both challenged me and humbled me for years. For a pastor it stimulates much insight. Imagine praying for forgiveness of sin *just in case* your children, or the children of the church, had sinned? Imagine such fear of sin blended with such a passionate love for the spiritual vitality of the children the Lord has entrusted to you? Such was the "regular custom" of Job, who "was blameless and upright," who "feared God and shunned evil." But such does not describe the usual practices of most people I know in the churches of the Lord Jesus regarding their own children, and sadly it is not the custom of most elders.

Why is this the case? Why is it that so few parents, not to mention elders, are exemplary spiritual prayers and nurture-providers? Why is it that so many solid believers stand on the sidelines of their children's lives, wringing their hands in hope that their kids won't be hurt by the Opponent, thrown for a loss by the Tempter? Or, on the other hand, why is it that so many seem to be blind to the spiritual coldness of their children, confidently assuming all will be well? I believe it is because of a pair of theological distortions that have afflicted both Reformed and evangelical churches for many years. On the one hand, a loss of the doctrine of the covenant; on the other, presumptive regeneration.

THE COMFORT OF THE COVENANT: *STANDING ON THE PROMISES*

In an earlier chapter, I challenged you to recognize that God deals with His people covenantally. That is to say, He does not only deal with us individually, as if, in faith, we each "cut our own deal" with the Almighty. Rather, He deals with us as a corporate people both in Christ, and through subordinate covenant "heads" like fathers. As you may recall, I referred you then to the wonderful passages in Gen. 12 and 17 in which God bound Himself in covenant promises to Abraham *and his children* for generations to come. What a wonderful truth! At the same time, God maintains His covenant in all its dimensions, including that of covenantal curse. I referred you to Joshua 7 and the story of Achan. Who can read these words without a chill up and down the spine:

> Then Joshua, together with all Israel, took Achan son of Zerah, the silver, the robe, the gold wedge, his sons and daughters, his cattle, donkeys and sheep, his tent and all that he had, to the Valley of Achor...Then all Israel stoned him, and after they had stoned the rest, they burned them...Then the LORD turned from his fierce anger (vv. 24-26).

Sadly, in today's theological world, the concept of covenant is virtually dead. Oh to be sure, there are those who study and discuss "covenant theology," as if it were a particular brand of Reformed thinking unique to the Puritans or the Dutch in the last few hundred years. But as a living and functioning key to their own daily faith, covenant is non-existent.

One reason for which the doctrine of the covenant is non-functioning in the faith of many believers today is their reaction to the theology described above in the story of George and Tena. I recall watching an episode of *All in the Family* in which Archie Bunker decides to get his new grandson baptized, against the explicit wishes of his son-in-law, who is agnostic. He sneaks down to the local church, is unable to find a priest, but performs the ceremony himself in the baptistry of the empty building. Then finally, he can rest secure. That episode spoke volumes about a wrong view of the doctrine of covenant. And many genuine believers today recognize the misplaced reliance on a ritual, and flee from it in practice and in their theology. To separate it from faith and obedience makes a mockery of both. That's what Archie did; that's why so many are opposed to covenant theology and its practices *as they understand it.*

Sadly, these folks miss the powerful truth of covenant in their own lives, in their approach to their children, and in the pastoral life of the church. Fact is, God *does* make promises to us and our children. Those promises do not cancel all the Scriptural calls to personal and genuine faith; neither do the calls to faith and response negate the promises of God.

Key to understanding covenant as both a Scriptural doctrine and as a practical life principle is to understand it as a *legal relationship*. The best analogy I can think of is the relationship of marriage. When my wife and I were married, we were *legally* married. I don't mean that flippantly, either, despite the fact that the pastor who officiated was deposed from the gospel ministry not long after our ceremony. The wedding ceremony established a legal relationship, a formal covenant, which is no less spiritual for the fact of its formality. During the establishing of that legal covenant, both of us took oaths, pledged vows, and exchanged signs of the covenant promises we made—wedding rings.

That we were now legally married in no way guaranteed that we would live faithfully in that covenant. In fact, living covenantally in marriage required daily responsibilities each one of us would have to bear. I had to give leadership like Christ did; sacrificial, soft-hearted, unconditional. My wife would have duties as a Christian wife, too, and they would obligate her to respond to my love as the church does to her Lord Jesus. *The covenant promises did not render the covenant obligations unnecessary; the covenant obligations did not negate the validity of the promises.* When I look at my wedding ring, a simple band of white and yellow gold, I remember her promise. That gives me great comfort and provides a background against which I deal lovingly with my dear wife each day. Likewise, when she looks at the ring I gave her, she recalls my vow. I know it comforts her with the solid foundation upon which she can build her life with me in our home. Neither of us is spiritually naive; each knows the other is a sinner. Yet, neither of us fears speaking truthfully to the other, and if necessary, holding the other accountable if a sin is committed. We are not afraid the other will turn and run from the marriage. We bank on the solid base of the legal relationship known as the wedding covenant. We *stand on the promises made.*

So it must be with our understanding of covenant with God. He has made wonderful promises to His people, breathtaking in their scope and generosity. (Read Deut. 28:1-14; it's awesome!) But those promises do not negate the call to faith and obedience; in fact, they come along with terrifying warnings and a list of curses for disobedience and unfaithfulness (vv. 15-68).

So it must be with our approach to our children. If we fail to view them legally, in covenant with God by virtue of the fact that they are the children of believers, we miss a most wonderful blessing and a solid foundation that rests upon the security of God's truthfulness. We also miss the solid ground on the basis of which we approach them with rebuke, correction and demands for obedience. They belong to God; they must respond. Both are true.

- Read once again the promise to Abraham, the father of believers throughout the generations, in Gen. 12 and 17.
- Read also Acts 2:39, which links parent and child together in covenant, yet without denying the dynamic of repentance and faith.
- And finally, read I Cor. 7:14, where it is declared by the Apostle that the children of believers are holy. The point there is not that they are without sin, or somehow immune to temptation and unbelief. Rather, it is that they are included by God in His covenant people, considered to be "within the circle" and therefore recipients of His special grace. That legal position, that covenant status, does not negate the call to faith. Quite the opposite, it demands it!

Now, without reducing these paragraphs to being a polemic for infant baptism (the "wedding band" of God's promise applied to believers and their children, demanding the "wedding obedience" of their faithful and obedient lives), do allow me to quote from a form for baptism used in the church I serve. My point is not polemic but pastoral. I hope and pray you will grasp the parental and the pastoral comfort that belongs to those who believe in and stand firm on the Scriptural doctrine of covenant. It affects the way you view your children—both your children by blood as a parent, and the children of the faith for those of you who are pastoral elders. Notice the two-sided covenant dynamic inherent in the following:

> Our baptism into the name of God the Father is his assurance to us that he makes an everlasting covenant of grace with us and adopts us as his children and heirs. Therefore, he surrounds us with his goodness and protects us from evil or turns it to our profit....(B)ecause all covenants have two sides, baptism also places us under obligation to live in obedience to God. We must cling to this one God, Father, Son, and Holy Spirit. We must trust him and love him with all our heart, soul, mind, and strength. We must abandon the sinful way of life, put to death our old nature, and show by our lives that

we belong to God. If we through weakness should fall into sin, we must not despair of God's grace, nor use our weakness as an excuse to keep on sinning.[1]

Another form puts it into a bit simpler language:

> Thus in baptism God seals the promises he gave when he made his covenant with us, calling us and our children to put our trust for life and death in Christ our Savior, deny ourselves, take up our cross, and follow him in obedience and love....We are therefore always to teach our little ones that they have been set apart by baptism as God's own children.[2]

I trust you grasp the point. Confessing the Scriptural doctrine of covenant gives us solid ground to stand on as we look at our children—both as parents and as pastors. The children of believers, the children of the church, belong to God; He has placed His mark on them. We must let them know of His claim, and lead them in the only appropriate way for them to respond.

The Danger of Presuming Regeneration

At the same time, and on the other end of the spectrum from those who ignore or deny the covenant promises of God, stands another theological problem that has generated difficulty for parent and pastor alike. It is *presumptive regeneration*, and it affects those who take the dynamic of the covenant and twist it into something it is not.

Reformed Christians have always believed that believers and their children are to be baptized. But in explaining why infants or children are to be baptized, our answers were not always consistent. Some simply stated that we baptize children because of the command and promise of God, because they are in the covenant, with all its promises and with all its obligations. Baptism is a sign of his promise. Others argued that we are to baptize because we may *presume that children of believers are regenerate*. Baptism is a sign of their presumed regeneration.

Now, without entering into the details of this theological debate, allow me to cut to the chase and make my point. The problem with

---

[1] From the Form for the Baptism of Children used in the Christian Reformed Church in North America. *Psalter Hymnal* (Grand Rapids: CRC Publications, 1987), p. 957. This form is a translation of one first written in 1566 in German in Heidelberg, and used throughout the Reformed world yet today.

[2] From an alternate Form for the Baptism of Children, *Psalter Hymnal*, p. 961.

presumptive regeneration is that, in many Reformed churches today, many parents, and with them many elders, seem to cruise through life with a false sense of security about the spiritual well-being of the children entrusted to them (George and Tena in the story above). The idea of presumed regeneration has been stretched beyond bounds of Biblical covenant teaching, petrified as if in stone, and now paralyzes parents and elders into inactivity when faced with disobedient and unbelieving children long past infancy. When presumptive regeneration dominates one's approach to children, be it as parent or as pastor, the Biblical call to repentance and conversion seems to drift into irrelevancy.

In the passage with which we began this chapter, Job recognized that, if children show evidence of sin and rebellion (and each one will!), it is unrighteous and dangerous to assume, on the one hand, that all will work out in the end, and therefore to do nothing, or on the other hand to wring one's hands while hopefully waiting for some "experience" to bring about the conversion of the children entrusted to you. Children of every age sin; God has established ways to deal with sin. Those ways always include repentance and conversion. The covenant of God, and baptism as a sign of that covenant, does not nullify such heart-and-life responses; rather, it demands them. It demands that parents and pastors pray for soft hearts in their children; it demands that parents and pastors alike teach and show their children by example just what a soft heart acts like in the presence of sin. It demands that parents and pastors confront their children with their sin, plead with them to repent, hold before them the call to be converted to Christ, and remind them that such is demanded precisely because they were baptized. It demands that parents and pastors serve as the self-conscious pattern of godliness, showing clearly their own desire to know Scripture and to do what it says, evidencing in their own lives the urgency of daily prayers of confession, repentance, intercession, thanksgiving, and adoration.

The Apostle Paul stressed just the same things in his farewell address to the elders in Ephesus. When summarizing his own ministry, to serve as the pattern for theirs, he states: "I have declared to both Jews and Greeks that they must turn to God in repentance and have faith in our Lord Jesus" (Acts 20:21). There is no justification for restricting such a description (and by implication, such a *prescription*) to adults alone. In fact, to fail to call children to repentance and faith is a grievous sin! And to fail to live the same in your own lives as parents or elders is hypocritical!

In Practice...

What's the point? I'd like to make several:

1. *First*, I challenge you to view the children of the church with the eye of Job, possessing a realistic understanding of the power and presence of sin. Know that the youth under your care can sin, and will fall under sin's power at some time in their lives. Don't be shocked by it, but don't ignore it as insignificant, either. Above all, don't cut the kids off from your care and love just because they have "disappointed" you! What if God did the same to you?

2. *Second*, remember—and teach—the significance of baptism. It is like a wedding ring, signifying both the *promise* of love and faithfulness, and *obligating* each member of the covenant to keep faith with the other. Neither baptism nor a wedding ring provides guaranteed security without the obligations of faithfulness. Nor may you presume regeneration in someone who is living in calloused disregard of sin, any more than a spouse may take the health of his or her marriage for granted in the face of overwhelming evidence of neglect, cruelty, or infidelity.

3. *Third*, keep in mind that it is parents to whom God assigns primary responsibility for the nurture of their children. (Notice that word, *nurture*. It suggests careful and balanced attention to a young, growing plant in a greenhouse. Neglect of spiritual instruction and encouragement is just as deadly to the young plant as is the sudden shock of 50 pounds of fresh manure.) At the same time, a pastoral elder can and must develop a long term relationship with children under his care. Take them out for a coke; visit with them personally and privately about their faith and its struggles; pray for them diligently—*by name*, and make sure you recognize them and speak words of encouragement and love to them regularly when you see them in church. At the same time, always recognize that your care for them depends on your encouragement and challenge to their parents. You can help the kids a bit, maybe even teach them a Bible class from time to time, but a few minutes of your time isn't likely to overcome the many hours of contact with parents who fail to nurture, pray, encourage, or strengthen their children. That fact doesn't excuse you from pastoral duties with the kids. Rather, it simply demands that as you deal with families, you must seek to encourage parents to nurture their children to faith, and that, with prayer, urgency, and a healthy sense of Biblical realism.

13

POLISHING YOUR LENS - HOMEWORK ON MINISTRY TO FAMILIES

In this part of the training book you hold in your hand my intent has been to sharpen your shepherding eye, to help you see people and situations like a pastor must, to develop discernment about the spiritual enemies that the sheep face in today's pastures, and to suggest a strategic blueprint to guide you in planning both the attack and the defense against those enemies. We spent quite some time on the shape and dimensions of family ministry. In the next chapter, we'll turn our attention to senior citizens, and develop a ministry plan for pastoral care of these people.

In this chapter, it is time for you to be active in your own analysis of the church family in which you live and minister. Whether you are an elder now, have been for years, or hope someday to be, the shepherd's eye must be evident. I Tim. 3 and Titus 1 both require the evidence of such spiritual perspective, discernment and ability to "manage" the family of God.

There are several resources in these pages: *First*, some individual Scripture studies, designed to keep clear the connection between your own "listening to the voice of the Good Shepherd" and providing care for His sheep and lambs. *Second*, some group discussion materials for use within a group of existing elders or in training potential elders. Feel free to adapt it to your unique situation. Finally, *Case Studies* (which appear in the appendix to this volume) that can be used in a variety of settings, including discussion material for monthly elder's meetings. The key to all this material is flexibility; use it as your needs and situations dictate.

Part One: The Marriage Relationship

Read the following Bible passages carefully, and write your answers to the questions listed.

Genesis 2:18-24 What can you learn from this passage about the *reason* God ordained marriage?

Adam "named" the animals. This isn't a reference to calling dogs "Fido" or "Spot," or lions "Rex" or "Elsa"; rather it has to do with studying, classifying, understanding them so as to be able to exercise stewardship and dominion over them. Then he "named" his wife (v. 23). What's the point? What's the significance of the "application" of this story in v. 24?

Psalm 127-128 (read as a unit) The first of this couplet of Psalms addresses the "building" of a house. The psalmist isn't thinking of two by fours and sheetrock, but of the establishing of a family line, a dynasty like the "house of David." What lessons do vv. 1-2 teach you about your family line?

What can you learn from *Ps. 128:3-4*? To what kind of people does God promise such blessings?

Polishing Your Lens / 117

What does v. 5 suggest about the link between the Christian home and the church of the Lord?

Proverbs 5:15-20 What does this graphic and vivid imagery teach about marital fidelity?

Proverbs 12:4; 14:1; 18:22; 19:14 In what way can a wife be the making or the undoing of her husband?

Proverbs 31:10ff. List some of the specific responsibilities and gifts which the Lord honors and grants to the "wife of noble character." How would this list enable you to answer a man or woman who had been affected by the influences of feminism, and who consequently looked down on "just being a housewife and homemaker"?

Proverbs 5; 6:20 - 7:27 From this extensive passage, explain why sexual sin is such a grievous ill. Make a list of the various consequences of such sin.

Matt. 5:27-32 How did Jesus expand on and deepen the traditional Pharisaic understanding of adultery?

How do the shocking "remedies" of vv. 29-30 relate to the subject of adultery and lust? Are we to take these literally?

Compare vv. 31-32 with **Matt. 19:1-12** and summarize your findings on the subject of divorce. Who may divorce? When is it scripturally permissible? In such a case, is it scripturally commanded? Why is it so dangerous to treat divorce lightly? What is the point of Jesus' teaching in Matt. 19:12?

I Cor. 7 The chapter opens with the statement: "Now for the matters you wrote about." Make a list of what some of those questions apparently were, and note how the inspired Apostle answered them. From that list of questions and answers (drawn only from I Cor. 7), derive some applications to the current crisis in marriages in our generation.

Polishing Your Lens / 119

Eph. 5:21-33 How does v. 21 influence the entire section to follow (vv. 22 - 6:9)?

What is the *essence* of the duty Christ assigns to wives (vv. 22-24)?

What is the *essence* of the duty Christ assigns to husbands (vv. 25-33)?

What common practices and understandings of the "common" view of marriage in your community might not pass Biblical muster, when compared with this passage?

What attitudes expressive of *feminism* would run into trouble with this passage?

Part Two: Family Relationships:

Deuteronomy 6 Make a list of the specific teaching assignments given to parents in this chapter. According to verses 4-9, are all these assignments to be carried out verbally?

Spend an evening reading through *Proverbs*. In your reading, make a careful list of those passages that suggest *constructive* parental assignments (chief among them is communicating carefully the "law" of God, providing direction and fostering wise habits of thought and action in all of life). Jot down notes about the assignments and the blessings that obedience provides.

Likewise, make a list from *Proverbs* of the important passages regarding *corrective discipline*, the negative but necessary corollary of the above. Note especially why discipline is important, how it is to be applied, and what character issues discipline seeks to shape.

Focus your attention on *Proverbs 17* for a few minutes. Answer the following:

- What *urgency* does v. 1 give a pastoral elder about dealing with family problems among the congregation?

- What is the point of v. 2? What wisdom could such a passage provide to a pastoral elder to help him deal with siblings fighting viciously over their deceased parents' estate?

- Is verse 6 an instruction, a command, an observation, or a goal? Explain.

- Explain why verse 9 (compare 10:12 and I Peter 4:8) is a critical passage for use by pastoral elders when dealing with marital strife or with family conflict. Does it justify the behavior of one member of a family whom you believe has committed grievous sins against another but never confessed? How about family members who haven't spoken in years and who justify their behavior with an appeal to this verse, saying, "we don't get along and Prov. 17:9 tells me it is better not to dredge up the past than it would be to deal with the original problems?"

Matthew 10:34-39 Read this passage carefully, and in context (note especially v. 21). Is the passage teaching us that it is Jesus' intent to break up families? What do you understand to be the point of the passage?

Matthew 12:46-50 Read this passage carefully. Can you think of pastoral situations in which such a passage would be of comfort? Can you think of some in which it would a difficult truth to face?

Part Three: Group Exercises

1. Which of the passages you studied in this section dealing with the family (Deut. 6, Prov. 17, Matt. 10:34-39 and Matt. 12:46-50) would you use in the following situations? (Don't limit yourself to these, of course. If you think of other passages you'd rather use, list them and note why.) While reflecting on the appropriate passage to use, discuss these cases with others in a group setting, and try to develop a comprehensive pastoral strategy for each case. Include in your strategy plans for first steps, long-term ministry plans, other Scriptural truths to be conveyed, utilization of other resources in the church and how you would involve other members.

- A young man who recently became a Christian is preparing to marry a girl from your congregation. His mother, a traditionalistic Catholic, threatens to disown him if he goes through with the marriage. This is no idle threat. She owns several large manufacturing plants, and he was slated to become the next CEO. Her threatened action could cost him millions.

- A family from your congregation recently witnessed the "defection" of a young mother. Announcing that she was "tired of the hassles of life with 3 young children who demanded more than I could give," she hit the road. You are faced with tear-streaked eyes and broken hearts when you go to visit the young husband and the children; when you arrive, you also have to answer the question the 9 year old asks you: "Is God angry with my mummy?" You answer:

- Marsha, 18, ran away from home. Her family found her, after 3 months of police work (and many sleepless nights and dozens of hours of your pastoral support, prayers and tears) in New York city, where she is working as a lingerie model and, the police suspect, as a prostitute. Marsha won't come home. The entire family are members of your congregation.

2. Use, perhaps in a series of elder's meetings, or in a series of potential elder training sessions, several of the *case studies* that appear in the appendix to this volume. (The leader or trainer may select ones appropriate to the local situation, or you may use one or two per month for "continuing education.")

THE SHEPHERD'S EYE

Section Three:
A STRATEGIC BLUEPRINT FOR PASTORING SENIORS

Retirement — Vacation or Vocation?

- Mickey Mouse is 65 years old.
- Over 12% of the US population is 65 or older—that's over 30 million people.
- The US Federal Government spends nearly 30% of its annual budget on people age 65 and older. By 2025, that amount could well be 50% or over.
- The fastest growing age group in the US is the 85+ generation. There are nearly 3 million in this group. By the turn of the century, there will be 5.4 million. By 2050 this group will comprise 5% of the US population. At that time, people over 65 will make up 22% of the population. By contrast, in 1900 people age 65 and older made up only 4% of the population.[1]

We turn our attention next to the elderly. The statistics above are striking, and suggest that a comprehensive strategy for pastoral care on the local church level would be a wise investment in time and prayer.

Count Noses

Where to begin? First, assess your congregation. How many old people are there in your church? It might be a harder question to answer than you think. Teenagers think anyone over 30 is ancient; retirees have a different perspective. Once I had an invitation to pastor a congregation in Wisconsin. On the phone, a younger member told me that theirs was "an old congregation" requiring much pastoral work with the aged. Another member, an elder in his 80s, told me it was a "young church" with pastoral needs that seldom

---

1 From *Report of the Committee on Senior Ministry*, (Grand Rapids: Christian Reformed Home Missions, 1984) p. 2.

included visiting older people. When you're a kid, most people are old. When you're in your 80s, most people are young, still "wet behind the ears."

CHECK YOUR ATTITUDES

Having recently served as pastor of a large Midwestern congregation with a sizeable population of seniors, I have witnessed many attitudes toward these folks. I've been struck, in recent years, about the simplistic approach many take to seniors. There seem to be two. *First*, aging is universally a negative phenomenon; with it comes health problems, financial limitations due to fixed incomes and rising health expenditures, loneliness and nursing home care. *Second*, aging is primarily a positive experience; with it comes the freedom from work obligations, allowing the retiree to travel, "spend the grandchildren's inheritance" (surely you've seen the bumper stickers), winter in Florida or Arizona and do whatever you wish.

Neither attitude is entirely accurate, of course. There are problems unique to the aging process. Certainly the things noted above are very real, like financial considerations, decreasing quality of physical health and mental acuity[2] and increasing health care concerns and costs. In addition, I've seen over the years of my ministry a great amount of stress on the marriages of older folks, due in no small part to the significant adjustments of retirement schedules; add to that the emotional frustrations of loneliness, fear of death, and the very real problems that come with the death of a spouse or the loss of one's freedom to live in one's own home. Finally, don't overlook the spiritual temptations that seem to hit some older folks harder than they would have some years earlier. For some, a degree of financial security brings the temptation to materialism, in place of life-long stewardship. For others, the freedom of their schedule and their lifestyle brings with it a kind of hedonism, a disproportionate love of pleasure that replaces the balance of life's priorities. Still others become remarkably individualistic and selfish, downloading the family and church priorities that have occupied a central place in their lives for years, replacing them with hobbies and habits that their children find strange. And in not a

---

2 The wonderfully descriptive passage of Ecclesiastes 12 portrays in picturesque words the limitations of age, calling God's people, in light of that fact, to "remember your Creator in the days of your youth." Clearly, the loss of physical strength and mental sharpness affects opportunity for spiritual celebration in the delights of God and His Creation.

few cases, seniors begin to exhibit symptoms of a growing distance from life-long patterns of careful attention to the Word and prayer, to worship and Christian service. And this all at a time when such patterns should be deepening.

But it's important for pastoral elders in the body of Christ to have a more balanced view; focusing only on the problems brings a skewed perspective. Listen:

> Much has been written about the elderly, about their physical, mental, and spiritual problems, about their need for a good home, good work and a good friend. Much has been said about the sad situation in which many older people find themselves, and much has been done to try to change this. There is, however, one real danger with this emphasis on the sufferings of the elderly. We might start thinking that becoming old is the same as becoming a problem....[3]

There are some joys unique to seniors as well. Their mature love and balanced comfort with a dear mate is enviable to many young couples who are struggling with the pressures of this fast-paced life. Their reduced scheduling demands do allow for more freedom for enjoyment and travel to be sure, but also for Christian service, for devotion to the Word and prayer, to involvement with their church, their children and grandchildren and other Kingdom priorities. Nouwen and Gaffney describe the blessing of aged folks coming to enjoy a kind of detachment, "a gentle letting-go, that allows the elderly to break through illusions of immortality and smile at all the urgencies and emergencies of their past life. When everything is put in its proper place, there is time to greet the true reasons for living."[4]

In the next pages we'll look at your duty to provide pastoral care for people in their "golden years." As we do, I will suggest several foundational Biblical principles that must guide your approach to older people as you seek to provide pastoral care to them.

THE RETIREMENT YEARS: VOCATION, NOT VACATION

Let's begin by noting the fact that "retirement" is a rather recent invention, a fact surprising to most people today who believe it is the ultimate goal of one's work-life to hit 65 (more often 62 or even

---

[3] Henri Nouwen and Walter Gaffney, *Aging: The Fulfillment of Life* (Garden City, NY: Image Books 1976), p. 16.

[4] Ibid, p. 77.

earlier, these days!), draw one's pension, start collecting Social Security and join AARP. When God created man in His image, He installed him in creation as God's own steward, an agent of dominion over creation in God's Name and for God's purposes. Such is the clear message of the early chapters of Genesis (esp. 1:26) and Psalm 8. Nowhere in Scripture does one read of God releasing man from his assignment. We do read about people becoming too old to fulfill their duty, but never in the strength of life. Work *is* the meaning of life, properly understood.[5]

It took the influence of dualistic views of man, most notably from the Greeks, to change mankind's attitude about work. No longer was it viewed Biblically as of the essence of one's life, that which gives him purpose and dignity, but now it was viewed as something low, degrading, perhaps necessary but certainly not desirable. The ideal was to think, to contemplate, to philosophize, not to work.[6] In modern times, under the influence of the Enlightenment, such attitudes live on. The mean necessity may require one to labor, but the ideal is the life of leisure.[7]

When American culture developed the Social Security system as a retirement fund, and when it was coupled with individual pension payments from employers, the merger of secular notions of work and modern financial prosperity made the *need* to work beyond a certain age unnecessary. Just as modern young America endures the work-week to get to the play of the weekends,[8] so modern Americans endure the career to get to retirement. It's advertised as nothing but an extended vacation.

---

5 See Lester De Koster, *Work, the Meaning of Your Life* (Grand Rapids: Christian's Library Press).

6 See Acts 17:21 for a description of the Athenians in the days of the Apostle Paul. Also note Paul's description of the Greeks whose passion is to "look for wisdom" in human philosophy, in I Cor. 1:22.

7 Add to these ideas the rapidly changing world, from the grinding labor-intensive lives of every inhabitant for the first 1900 years of the Christian age, to the life-changing impact of the industrial revolution, to the even more radical changes of our modern transportation - easy and computerized world, and you will understand why attitudes toward work have changed and are changing. Man doesn't have to do as much as he once did every day; in fact, the next decade will witness even more radical changes, as offices will relocate to people's homes, and the fax machine and modem will replace the conference table and the water cooler. In Dallas, the first waves of this "revolution" have already hit; the changes to be apparent in lifestyles will be remarkable.

8 The Voit athletic equipment company even markets its products that way: "We Make Weekends!"

Such ought not to be the case. God's people are always called to lives of service. When they retire from the factory or business or farm, the address in which their service is rendered to the Lord might change. What does not change is the fact that they, with all their gifts, experience, wisdom and time belong to the Lord. They are His. Remember the goal of Eph. 4:16... "the whole body, joined and held together by every supporting ligament, grows and builds itself up in love, *as each part does its work.*" No age limit is mentioned.

SENIORS: CHURCH ASSETS, NOT LIABILITIES

Against this background, it's no wonder many have unbiblical notions about the elderly and about the goals of retirement. Over against it, I offer a thesis that I believe to be both Biblical and important. It is that *seniors provide unique assets to the church body.* Remember that one of the central themes of this volume is that one of the most important duties of pastoral elders is to equip the members of the body of believers to fulfill their own ministries (Eph. 4:11-12). That doesn't change just because some of those members happen to be elderly!

Consider some of these ministry uses for godly senior citizens *within the church family.*[9]

- Discipling younger or less mature members of the body of believers. Look up Titus 2:1-8. Note there the duties laid upon the hearts and minds of "older men" and "older women" with regard to the younger men and younger women. Fact is, the experiences and wisdom gathered through years of life before the face of God are invaluable assets to the church of Christ.

- In the education ministry of the church, remember the assignment given us in Col. 3:16: "Let the Word of Christ dwell in you richly as you teach and admonish one another..." That assignment has no age statute of limitations. Older saints are

---

[9] While I have tried to be as comprehensive as this brief training volume will allow, I also know that some may wish much wider reference material. I have been most blessed by the 29 page manual referred to in footnote 1 above. This report includes 4 pages of annotated bibliographical entries, as well as an excellent survey checklist written by well-known sociologist David O. Moberg of Marquette University in Milwaukee. The checklist can be effectively used to assess attitudes, to evaluate structures, facilities and programs, and to develop ministries to senior citizens. To obtain the *Report of the Committee on Senior Ministry,* call Christian Reformed Home Missions at 1-616-241-1691.

excellent teachers for Sunday School, as High School Youth Group Leaders (OK, perhaps they won't be the best sponsors for a white-water rafting expedition, but they might just surprise you. And they will most certainly give added wisdom and insight to the kids!), as Bible Study leaders for men's groups, women's groups and the like. You name it, they probably can be effectively utilized.

- In the fellowship ministries of the local church, elderly members can provide great help as visitation teams, drafted to assist pastoral elders or to follow-up on evangelistic contacts to the church.

- They can be used as assistants to the deacons. Read carefully I Tim. 5:9-10. It seems clear that the "list of widows" was not a list of those *needing* care (that set of qualifications appear in vv. 3ff.), but of those *providing* assistance and ministry to others (requisite spiritual qualifications are listed distinct from those listed a few verses earlier). Such godly men or women would coordinate a ministry of compassionate care among the needy, the sick, the bereaved; and what a wonderful treasure to find wise counsel in the tender support retirees could provide for the myriad single parents with their special hurts and problems that are dotting the church's landscape.

In addition, let's recognize wonderful ministry opportunities for seniors *outside the boundaries of the local church*.

- Take a lesson from the world's playbook, and establish something akin to the Service Corps of Retired Executives (SCORE), which provides retired businessmen and women as advisors to young start-up companies, minority-owned companies without leadership experience, or small businesses needing experienced counsel. The local church, or perhaps a group of churches in consultation with one another, could provide such a service for the people of the Kingdom, using the gifts, experiences and wisdom of senior citizens. Applications could include:

    1. Retired businessmen and women could provide analysis and consultation for Christian business men and women.
    2. Retired farmers could provide similar consultation, evaluation, and assistance for Christian farmers struggling to make a go of it in a rapidly changing agribusiness environment.

3. Retired medical personnel could serve as first-level advisors for young families, especially in the day of changing medical care routines, where even getting advice about whether or not one needs a doctor can take up to half a day's wait in an office waiting room.
4. Seniors could provide some greatly needed day care for children in an emergency, or even for other seniors, to give full-time care givers in the family a break.
5. Retired attorneys, school teachers, and even ministers can be valuable resources to provide consultation and advice to members of the flock.

I trust you get the point. To fail to make use of the unique assets the senior members of the congregation can and do provide is folly. To fail to apply those God-given gifts to the needs of the flock is a sin of another kind; pastoral neglect.

PASTORAL MINISTRY IN NURSING HOMES

We cannot close this special look at the pastoral needs of the aged without a careful look at the 5% of the senior population that call nursing homes "home."[1] Is it fair to say that the needs of those institutionalized during their elderly years place special demands on officebearers? No doubt. Consider the following struggles typical to such residents.

- One is *depression* and its attendant *hopelessness*. An old saint once perceptively observed to me, "When you move in here, you know you're going to die here. There's only one way out—a gurney, feet-first. It's depressing." He was right.

- Another is *loneliness*. Some elderly people live in facilities where many of their friends live, more like an apartment "neighborhood." But not all nursing homes are like that, and not all older people have access to them. Many are so lonely that they cry for hours each day; a visit cheers them up immeasurably; it can hardly ever be "long enough" to satisfy them.

- A third is *helplessness*. Often, the elderly and infirm are placed (note the passive verb "are placed;" it's significant) in available care facilities that are less than ideal, and often against their wishes. Sadly, many are institutionalized without valid reasons beyond that of the "convenience" of the children and grandchildren. Not only do such old folks feel helpless in such situations; they also sense rejection and a genuine lack of love.

---

[1] That number may surprise many; the attitude of most is that the percentages are much higher. Such is simply not the case, but the attitude fuels the misperception that the aging process always results in problems. See *Generations*, Vol. 8, No. 1, Fall, 1983.

- And, let's not forget a sense of *worthlessness* that pervades the atmosphere of some nursing homes. I've visited folks in places that smelled like urine, where the food was "predictable" at best, often inedible, and certainly not always served up appealingly and with dignity; where the day was spent sitting by a window, wistfully thinking and remembering, always brought back to the reality that there is nothing else to do (except, if it's Thursday, Bingo at 10:00 AM. Wow). Dignified gentlemen and career women, having identified their reason for living with their life-long careers, they are suddenly faced not only with nothing to do with their time, but with the sense of a loss of identity. Likewise lifelong fastidious housewives are disgusted by their new environment with its sounds and smells. They kept their own home spic and span for years, and would never have thought to entertain guests without presenting their "best foot forward." That they are deposited into such a distasteful situation, and that they can't do anything to improve conditions, makes them feel frustrated and worthless.

It is clear that even strong believers require *encouragement* in such settings. Spiritual discouragement sets in all too easily. Perhaps, facing their advancing years and the prospect of "lingering" (often more frightening to many than death itself), these dear folks need to hear the Bible read to them. Often their eyes are weak, and they cannot read for themselves. Still, they desperately require the comfort of God's Word to assure them that they belong to Him (or to challenge them if they do not!). Another important aspect of pastoring such people is to *challenge* them to be busy in service to Christ where they are. Again, they must know you pray for and with them, including regular prayers for their loved ones whom they don't see as often as they'd like. Occasionally, they must be gently rebuked when they become so full of self-pity as to drive away those who love them most. And these pastoral considerations are just the beginning; how about the financial needs, or the difficult and major decisions that people must make about selling the family home, dealing with the family pet, or (a terrifying thought) a spouse who can't live with her mate because one requires care in one kind of facility, while the other has different needs. It's like death before you die!

Does the elder have to provide all this care himself? Absolutely not! In a former congregation, we had one retired elder (some congregations call them "sabbatical elders," men once ordained but now between terms of active service or no longer able to serve) who was unable to serve in office because of some physical limitations. We drafted him to coordinate nursing home visits. He selected several other older gentlemen, and they covered these homes for us, reporting to the elders when they thought special circumstances required special attention. It was wonderful for these brothers who now had a vital ministry, for the nursing home residents who now received needed attention and care, and for the elders who were relieved of a heavy burden of time and responsibility. Were I to do it over again, I'd be even more aggressive. I'd encourage older women to do such visiting to other women, couples to do such visiting with other couples, and so forth. I'd also give the visiting teams some specific training, helping them to learn how to focus their visits on more than just social calls.

Ministering to the elderly in nursing homes must be specific to the situation. That is, you must not, by your visits, continually send the message that you are the care-giver and they the recipient. Rather, as members of the body, they have a duty to care for each other.[2] Try to get them to commit to visiting 2 or 3 other people within their nursing home each day. It may be difficult, since people often become very self-centered as they age. Their health becomes a concern; things they once did without thought now require much effort and planning. They think of themselves all day long and must be challenged to think of others. Encourage them to read Scripture to those who cannot read, to become involved in Bible Studies (even to lead, where abilities exist), to pray with each other. Try to arrange for a group to gather together to listen to a sermon tape, or to a broadcast of your church's worship service.[3] Call them to be a community of faith; don't allow them to be just a community of individual old people with mental or physical infirmities. In other words, pastor them with purpose!

A Pipe Smoker's Evangelism Club?

The above suggestions emphasize pastoral strategy for the care of believers. But not all people in nursing homes are converted to

---

2 Reread I Cor. 12. The notion of every member belonging to the body applies in nursing homes as well.

3 Technological advances in recent years make it easy to do. In our local congregation, we have the microphones wired to the phone lines; from there a simple conference call connects several invalid people live to the worship service. It's wonderful!

Christ. I vividly recall one old codger named Dick who was a foul-mouthed 92 year old. He drooled tobacco juice on his shirt, hissed and spat at visitors, cursed continually, and literally chased people out of his room. No one liked to visit him. Repeated visits over a span of more than a year (I can be stubborn) softened him to me. (It took serious softening; on my first visit, he threw an ashtray, called me a name I hadn't heard since working summers as a student in the steel mills, and accused me of being a "false prophet"!) I learned that he had one son living 200 miles away who never visited. He had no other family. He chewed tobacco only because he could not light his beloved pipe any more (his arthritic fingers wouldn't work). When I offered to buy him some good tobacco, fill his pipe once in a while, and enjoy a good pipe with him, his eyes teared, his heart softened and we began to talk about sin, our Savior and repentance. (OK, I can hear you now, scolding me for smoking and for leading him to that sin. In the first place, I was young then; since then I've quit. In the second place, he was 92; what was I going to do, shorten his life expectancy?) I am not quite sure whether or not he ever was converted. There seemed to be evidence of real faith, but at 92, he was not always cogent. Of this I am sure; had I not been diligent, faithful, persistent, and somewhat creative (to my knowledge, Mouton-Cadet blend pipe tobacco has never been suggested as an evangelism tool before!), I never would have had opportunity to speak of Christ with the crusty fellow.

The point is not to encourage a "pipe smoker's evangelism club for nursing home visitation." It is rather, to suggest to you who visit such homes, to be sensitive to the many old people there who face the end of their lives without the comfort of belonging to Christ. Eternal punishment within sight of people who will die soon; what a fearful thought. If ever evangelism was not only important but urgent, it is here. Make yourself available to them. Challenge other believers who live in the home to be evangelistically sensitive, too.

AND THE DEACONS...?

While this volume focuses on the work of the elders of the church, nothing of what I've described above belongs exclusively to them. They are to, be sure, primarily responsible for the spiritual care of the aging saints as they are for all other members of the church. They, most likely, will be active themselves in a visiting ministry. But all of God's people are commanded to "love one another," and the special place of the weak and the powerless in the heart of the Father demands that our mutual love not overlook the needs of the elderly who may be "out of sight." We must not allow them to be "out of mind." Elders can make wise and profitable use of other members of the church to fulfill aspects of this ministry.

Of particular value are the deacons. Deacons are charged with managing all of the God-given resources of the church, cultivating stewardship of time, talents and treasures in service to Christ. Deploying such resources is critical in the care of the elderly. When a church member is faced with the cost of a nursing home stay for a parent or spouse, they often go into some sort of emotional tailspin. Such costs can be, and usually are, astronomical. It is not always appropriate to assume the deacons will be there, checkbook in hand. But it is fair to suggest that the diaconate be the resource within the church able to counsel with families in this situation, knowledgeable about the laws, the local, state and federal agency provisions, the tax implications of such arrangements, etc. In today's climate, just as a good and proper Last Will and Testament is an exercise in Biblical stewardship, so is wise planning for nursing home care. The deacons must be prepared and willing to provide such guidance and counsel. In so doing, they will serve God's people well.

Polishing Your Lens — Homework on Ministry To Seniors

Once again it's your turn to do more than just read what I have written. Below appear a series of assignments that will have you searching the Scriptures, writing your answers to questions posed, and spending time with others in group exercises that aim to develop both pastoral insights and strategic discernment and skills.

Part One: Individual Scripture Studies

Read *Job 12:12*. Is this an iron-clad truism, applicable in every situation? (Consult a commentary or two, as well as footnotes in e.g. the NIV Study Bible).

Read *Prov. 17:6*. What's the point of this proverb?

Read *Ecclesiastes 12:1-7*. With the help of a commentary, if you have access to one, try to identify some of the imagery of physical aging contained in this long litany. I'll get you started:

v. 2 may well be referring to the loss of mental sharpness and the beginnings of senility. What do the following images refer to?

- "keepers of the house tremble"
- "strong men stoop"

140 / With A Shepherd's Heart

- "grinders cease because they are few"
- "those looking through the windows grow dim"
- "the doors to the street are closed and the sound of grinding fades"
- "when men rise up at the sound of birds..."
- "when men are afraid..."

After you note the physical imagery used, go back to read verse 1, and then read verses 6 and 7. What is the point of the passage as a whole? Is aging a process that *prohibits* conversion? Is it only young people who are able to "remember their Creator"?

Read *Zechariah 8:3-5*. How do the aged fit into God's promise of the future blessings Messiah will bring to the people of God? What is the point? Can you think of pastoral uses of this passage?

Read *Acts 2:17-18* (quoting the prophecy of *Joel 2:28-32*). What is the implication of this prophecy to the age in which we now live, the age of the out-poured Holy Spirit who is active within the life of the body of believers? May we deduce from it that older believers are still to be used actively within the church?

Read *I Cor. 12:27-31*. Assume that the first-listed gifts of "apostles" and "prophets" were only given by the Lord to the first generation of the NT church (I know; that point is contested heatedly by charismatic and Pentacostal communions. But for the sake of argument, agree with me here!), can you *identify within your local church fellowship elderly people who possess clearly the following spiritual gifts:* (yes, write their names down)

- teachers

- those with medical skills and knowledge

- those able to help others

- administratively gifted individuals

- translators to/from various languages

Now add the list of spiritual gifts from *Romans 12:6-8*, and do the same thing:
- servant-spirited folks

- encouragers

- generous contributors

- leaders among men (leadership skills)

- folks with skills in compassionate ministry

Now, can you think of ministry needs within the local body of believers that could benefit from the exercise of those gifts and those gifted individuals? *Do something* about it: speak to someone who can invite their participation, or speak to them about volunteering!

What ought to be the attitude of the church toward older members, as taught in the following:

- Lev. 19:32

- I Tim. 5:1

PART TWO: GROUP STUDY EXERCISES

Discuss the following situations, and identify how you would handle each in regard to the following: *Scriptural passages you would use, specific steps you would take to minister to the individuals or families, other resources of the church you would involve or apply, immediate pastoral goals, long-term pastoral goals.*

1. Joe and Marge retired at 58. He had made quite a bit of money in his own business, and they've looked forward to full-time RV travel. They planned to live in a motor home, and on the road, for several years before coming back "home." When you inquire about their plans for church, for spiritual nurture, for ministry involvement in Christ's name, you are told: "We haven't a clue. We may worship at churches in areas we visit; we may not. Don't worry about us. We'll be in touch periodically. If you need to reach us, our kids will talk with us once a week when we call. We're looking forward to being 'footloose and fancy free'!

- Pete and Wilma are in their 80s and are very bitter. Life had been hard; Pete had worked as a laborer for 50+ years, had never made much money, and now they were living on a meager fixed income. Rising costs were eating much of their stipend monthly pension, and they were faced with having to sell their home to move into a small and inexpensive apartment. Wilma, especially, expressed visible bitterness toward God. Their children are in the area, but don't visit the folks much.

- Charlotte had never married, and was now a spry and lively 71. She had taken an apartment in a retirement village, and came to you to ask for advice on how she could serve Christ and His church within that village of elderly folks. The village is a couple of miles from your church, and no other church members live nearby.

4. Annie is dying. She's been in the hospital for several months battling cancer and struggling with the side effects of chemotherapy. The doctor has told her children that their 76 year old widowed mother would die soon and they should bring her home and seek hospice care to make her final days more pleasant. Annie is a godly woman, a long-time member of your congregation and you are her pastoral elder. Several issues come up during your visit with the children, prior to your entering her room for prayer. They ask your advice on the following:

   - "The doctor suggested we not tell Mom she's going to die soon. Do you agree?" (What do you tell them?)

   - "If we do have to tell Mom that she doesn't have long to live, will you help us?" (What do you say to them? What would you say to her?)

Homework on Ministry to Seniors / 145

- "We don't know much about hospice care. Is it a good idea?" (Find out, if you don't know, about hospice care in your area: costs, availability, testimonies from some who have used this ministry to the dying.) From your newfound knowledge, what would you say to Annie's children?

- "Mom sometimes gets confused at night and begins to swear and cuss horribly. She has never in her life talked like that! Do you think it means she's not a believer in Jesus?" You answer:

- "Mom doesn't have a last will and testament. Since Dad died a couple of years ago, she just couldn't bring herself to get to a lawyer. What should we do?" How would you advise the children? Would you apply other resources from the church to assist them? Which?

Part Three
THE SHEPHERD'S HAND
Developing Pastoral Skills

THE SHEPHERD'S HAND

Section One:
THE ELDER AND TEACHING

"Apt To Teach"

Summary Review: In the first section of this volume, I sought to awaken in the reader the "heart of the shepherd"— that love for the sheep of the flock which is patterned after the love of Christ, the Good Shepherd. In the second, I emphasized the need for the cultivation of a pastoral eye— developing the keen vision that sees both the wolfish fangs of the Enemy and of the pastoral strategies necessary to care for the flock effectively. I suggested some blueprint strategies for family ministry and for the care of the aged as examples. With this chapter, we begin the third part of this book, a section offering practical assistance for several of the specific duties assigned to pastoral elders in the Bible. As in the earlier sections, we return to the dominant image of the sheep-herder in Biblical times to understand the tools in the shepherd's *hand* in our day and age. They are the shepherd's *voice,* his *rod* and his *staff.* The voice of the shepherd is the tool with which he leads and directs the sheep; in elder parlance, he must be "apt to teach." The rod of the shepherd is that clublike weapon he uses to defend against specific enemies, a lion one time, a bear another, or a wolf at another time and place; in elder parlance, the specific skills of visiting the individual sheep and lambs of the flock and calling them to faithfulness. The staff of the shepherd is a tool of rescue, of retrieval. The large crook draws the lost back, pulls the fallen out of the crevices in the mountainous terrain; in elder terms, the ministry of discipline, of holding the flock accountable to obey the voice of the Good Shepherd.

The Elder As Teacher

Over the years of my ministry, I have taught a great deal. I guess that's expected of those like me who were trained, called and ordained to be a "preacher" or "teaching elder."[1] Believing it to be within the scope of my principal duty, in previous fields of service, I was grateful to have been able to teach most, if not all, the doctrinal instruction ("catechism classes") for the students spanning the range from Grade 3 through Grade 12 and beyond. I was grateful for the opportunity to help establish good and solid doctrinal foundations in an entire generation of God's people, and I was grateful because of the *pastoral contact* with the children of the church such teaching responsibilities gave me.

But, with all that teaching, I neglected one very important thing, which I now am able to see in retrospect. By teaching all the classes, *I kept other elders from teaching*. I'm sure some of the elders were pleased by the arrangement; after all, they had plenty of other things to do. Yet, by keeping them from teaching in the church, I effectively hindered one of Christ's own mandates, and hampered the use of one of the precious gifts the Ascended Lord gave His church; a teaching eldership.

First, a brief review of several key passages. Read these carefully:

> ...*go and make disciples of all nations, baptizing them...and teaching them to obey everything I have commanded you (Matt 28:19,20).*

> *Now the overseer (elder) must be...able to teach... (I Tim. 3:2).*

> *And the things you have heard me say in the presence of many witnesses entrust to reliable men who will also be qualified to teach others (II Tim. 2:2).*

> *And the Lord's servant must not quarrel; instead, he must be kind to everyone, able to teach...(II Tim. 2:24).*

> *You must teach what is in accord with sound doctrine (Titus 2:1).*

I know that these instructions were given to various groups and individuals in the early church, and not all were addressed to el-

---

[1] In the church in which I serve, the understanding is that there are *three* offices in Christ's church: minister, elder and deacon. In many others, it is understood that there are *two*: minister (pastor) and elder are considered to be aspects of the one office of elder, and thus are referred to as preaching or teaching elder on the one hand, and ruling or pastoral elder on the other.

ders as we know the office today. Indeed, the first listed passage was spoken by Christ to the apostles, and the last three to pastors in the early church named Timothy and Titus. Yet, the critical requirement of the I Tim. 3:2 passage—that elders must be "able (or "apt") to teach"—ties the elder's office in with the gifts of Christ to the church, given to "equip the saints for their ministry" (Eph. 4:11-12). Simply put, if you are an elder, you must be involved with the work of teaching.

THE FOCUS: MAKING DISCIPLES

That means *discipleship*! That's the overarching point of Jesus' words in Matt. 28:19-20. The church, especially but not exclusively involving the elders, must be busy every day with the responsibility of making and developing disciples who follow our Lord. That involves both the careful instruction and nurture of the youth of the church, and the well-planned instruction of the mature members of the church.

What do I mean by discipleship? Discipleship, simply put, means *reproducing yourself and your faith* in the lives of others. Allow me to explain what I mean.

The Greek word for disciple is *"mathatas,"* a close cousin of the word for "lesson or instruction." In the verbal form, it refers not only to learning lessons but to the *relationship* that exists between the mentor and the disciple. One *"becomes* a disciple"; one does not merely "learn lesson material." One is an "apprentice," not merely a student.

The importance of all of this is made clear by Jesus' words in Matt. 28:19 when he commands the church to "make disciples." Obviously, Jesus wants the disciples the church makes to be *His disciples*, not ours. Yet, just as obviously, the process of disciple-making will require more than just instruction in predetermined lessons; it demands the development of a relationship of trust, of modeling, of revealing the heart of your faith to another who must pattern his faith after yours. Remember Jesus' definition of a "follower" (a disciple)? "If anyone would come after me, he must deny himself and take up his cross and follow me" (Mk. 8:34). No, Jesus is not minimizing the importance of doctrinal content; His command to "teach them to observe all I have commanded you" makes that clear. But He is reminding us that discipleship is a living relationship with the Master. Such a thing cannot be taught as a series of lessons; it must be taught by apprenticeship, by modeling, by one disciple opening his heart and life to another.

That's the image you must have in your mind as you contemplate your duty to teach. Scripture never requires that you be competent to stand in front of a hall full of graduate students and deliver a wonderfully challenging and informative lecture without anyone nodding off. Nor does it require that you must be able to manage 36 squirmy first graders without help, and actually teach them something in the process. What it *does* require, however, is that you be able to communicate to a youngster or to a mature adult just what is involved in following Jesus Christ. You show that by "teaching them to observe" His commandments; you show that by revealing your own struggle of self-sacrifice; you do so by exposing the pain of self-denial, while at the same time, celebrating the joy of such commitment, because "faith is the victory that overcomes the world."

AIM FOR WISDOM

What must you do to accomplish this assignment? To be sure, you must be deeply rooted in Biblical teaching. But that, too, involves more than you think. Remember the phrase "sound doctrine" in Titus 2:1? It refers not merely to a mastery of the nuances of creeds and their structure, but refers to Biblical teaching that provides health. Un-sound doctrine is like an unhealthy diet that is heavy in fats. It feeds of course, but only makes the flock fat and unhealthy. Like malnourished sheep lose the sheen of their coat, and are no longer contented but wander and fight, such a spiritual diet only provides verbal weapons that God's people will use against each other in divisiveness and argumentation (see II Tim. 2:14). Instead, "sound doctrine" is balanced teaching; it is God-honoring, and it makes for healthy believers; it promotes Christlike living in the day-to-day faith of the man of God. To teach this way, in other words, requires the elder to be a *master of application*, one who is able to make clear to his students just what the point of a particular Biblical truth is. Your students must become disciples who are not only *smart* in the knowledge of Scripture, but who are Biblically *wise* in walking in the ways of the faith.[2]

---

2 A look at any good Bible dictionary will reveal that the word "wisdom" in Scripture always refers to the practical living out of the faith. One teacher aptly called it "applied knowledge."

That kind of teaching, that kind of disciple-making, takes time and a significant investment of personal commitment on your part. It's not done only by leading a class; you must involve yourself with your apprentices. That can and should be done in the relationships you have with those in your elder-district as you shepherd the flock; it can and should be done as you get to know the children of the flock well so that you can shepherd the lambs. And, it can and should be done more formally as well, if you are asked to teach Sunday School, catechism, or an adult course in the local church. Good teachers offer more than information; they offer themselves. No one can teach another to follow the Master who is not already following Him; no one can make disciples who is not already a disciple.

18

Teaching the Lambs of the Flock

Once Upon A Time

Years ago, in many Reformed and evangelical churches in this land, there was Sunday School and there was catechism. The former taught Bible stories and Bible songs thought to be important for the children of the church. The latter taught doctrine. Men and women from the church taught Sunday School. Seminary-trained ministers taught most of the children's catechism classes. A good friend of mine, Dr. P.Y. De Jong, once told me he instructed over 500 catechism students *per week* while serving in a large church in Grand Rapids, Michigan, in the 1940s. The practice of such a two track curriculum developed for several reasons. *First*, such ministers were, in many cases, some of the most well-educated people in the church, certainly the most thoroughly equipped to teach Biblical doctrine. *Second*, it had become an expected part of the work of the preacher. *Third*, in many areas, all the kids came for catechism after school or on Saturday mornings, so it was physically possible within the limits of the pastor's schedule. There were some benefits, too. The kids got to know the preacher, and he them. That simple fact provided more *pastoral* benefits than we'd care to admit, maybe even more than the *educational* benefits.

Times Have Changed!

But times have changed. No longer is such a thing physically possible. In the church I serve, for example, there is no way I could gather the kids together after school for catechism; students in this church attend about 25 different schools all around the Dallas metroplex. Furthermore, during the Sunday school hour, the pastor can only teach one class, and he is often involved in adult education. Additionally, such a dependence on one man isn't educationally wise. The kids we deal with today come from an extraordinarily wide diversity of backgrounds, both familial and educational. Some know little if anything about the Bible. Many don't know the books of the Bible; few know more than a handful of Bible stories. The church's educational ministry is, by definition, much more challenging in our "post-Christian era" than it was in times when our culture was "Christianized." In some cases, training requires a 1 to 1 student to teacher ratio. It certainly requires teachers who can do more than ask the students if they memorized their assigned homework.

And let's face it, having the preacher do it all wasn't such a good idea. Sure, some did a wonderful job, and the churches were blessed because of it. But some were simply horrible teachers, and generations of kids learned to loathe catechism because of it. (Folks have said to me "my worst memory of church as a kid was catechism class with the preacher. I don't want to do that to my children.")

What must we offer if we are going to reach, train, *disciple* the children of today's world as they fall under our shepherding care? Certainly, as believers we are committed to God's Word as foundation material for our educational ministry. It, and it alone, can be said to be the "voice of the Good Shepherd" which calls the sheep and the lambs to follow Jesus (John 10:3-4). But how do we teach God's Word effectively today? If old-style pedagogy won't cut it today, what will? Remember, this is the age of kids raised on TV with 10 minute attention-span requirements before a commercial break, on programs like Sesame Street and Barney, and on fast-paced video games like Nintendo and Sega-Genesis. How can we compete? How can we prepare today's children for service to Christ? If you are an elder, you are charged with *oversight* of this ministry. Here are some ways you can oversee the educational ministry to the children of the church.

A LAMB-TRAINER'S CHECKLIST

1. Assess the local situation. Before anything else, you must know what training your local church is providing. Is the curriculum consistent? It is high-quality? Do the teachers know what they're doing? Do they know their place in the larger curriculum goals? Look over the student body you are called to train. Are they from widely diverse backgrounds? Do some have good knowledge of the Bible, while others are intimidated and shy because of their lack of knowledge. Are some classes boring, so that students aren't challenged? Are others more like baby-sitting services for coffee-drinking parents? Look back over the testimonials of the most recent dozen or so young people who professed their faith. Have the students revealed a superficial understanding of Biblical faith, or have they revealed deep, thoughtful and articulate faith? *Do the hard work of honestly assessing the kind and caliber of training your church is currently providing to the lambs of the flock. If you are unable to do such an assessment yourself, bring the issue to the board of elders of the church and challenge them to do it as a body.*

2. *Identify your educational goals*. This may be scary because many churches don't have any, at least none that are clear and that function to shape their educational process. But such goals are absolutely crucial! Allow me to offer an idea of what I mean, hoping that it will prod you to ask the difficult questions in your setting.

I believe that the nurture of today's children must provide at least three kinds of Scriptural knowledge—distinct, yet interdependent—by the time a student completes the normal church training regimen at the end of High School. Ask yourself whether your church is providing some, most, or all of the following:

A. ***Bible knowledge of both Old and New Testaments.*** By this I mean a thorough grounding in the stories, broad knowledge of the major books, themes and teachings of the Bible, memorization of key passages, *and demonstrated ability to work with Scripture*—to conduct or even to lead a Bible study, to explain the outline of the Gospel in an evangelistic setting, to use resources like concordances, commentaries, etc. *Every* believer must be sufficiently trained in these things to be considered "equipped" for ministry (which is what Eph. 4:12 tells us our goal must be).

B. ***Doctrinal knowledge.*** By this I mean a thorough grounding in the major doctrines of Biblical truth so that each knows what he believes, can answer those who challenge him, and is able to withstand the blowing winds of doctrine that shift rapidly in new directions each day.[1] We must still teach the

---

1 I referred to this earlier as catechism instruction; the term may be unfamiliar to some readers. It refers to the old practice in many reformation churches to use secondary (to the Bible) documents called "catechisms" for the instruction of the children and new believers of the church. Among the most popular ones was the *Heidelberg Catechism*, still in active use in many churches. It is based on an experiential sequence; the believer's knowledge of his *sin*, his *salvation* in Christ, and his call and duty to Christian *service*. It makes use of three other documents: the *Apostles' Creed* as a summary of doctrinal truth, the 10 Commandments as the foundation for Christian ethics, and the Lord's Prayer as the source document for Christian piety. Another popular catechism is the *Westminster Shorter Catechism*.

old truths, but we must do a much better job of it than churches have recently done, so that the lambs of the flock know Biblical doctrine better, and are better able to articulate and use it effectively against the errors that seem so much more aggressive today.

C. A *world-view perspective* that enables each student to think Christianly about God, church, world and their place in it, including personal issues of vocation. By this, I plead for a training regimen that equips students to be ready to "think Christianly." Such is precisely what writers like Chuck Colson, R.C. Sproul, Herbert Schlossberg, and Francis Schaeffer have called for.[2] Kids today need to be ready for the aggressive worldliness they will face in their future. They must be able to read the daily newspaper or watch the TV news and identify, for example, the sinful powers of secularism, materialism, relativism, pragmatism and feminism. They must know what is wrong with each of these "isms." They must know that the Christian faith is bigger than "getting saved, and getting to heaven"; that it also embraces a way of living each day on earth as before the face of God. They must understand the concept of *office*,[3] that rich Biblical theme that teaches us that each believer has a calling—a vocation—and not just a job.

D. **Practical Christian Living Skills.** Having said all this about world-views and Biblical perspectives, I would be remiss if I did not quickly acknowledge that such is worthless unless the students know how to live their faith *practically*. When I plead for world-view perspectives, I mean the ability to live day-to-day with *wisdom*, that "applied knowledge" that enables believers to "walk their talk." Your curriculum must provide *specifics*. You can flap your gums for hours about "*materialism, the modern evil of covetousness,*" but if you don't teach people *how* to manage their money—how to establish a

---

[2] The constant theme of the writings of these Christian authors, many of which have been cited earlier in this volume, is the shaping of a "weltanschauung," a world-and-life-view; a self-conscious way of viewing self, the world around one's self and all relationships within that world, from a known perspective. It is precisely the point the Apostle Paul made in II Cor. 10:5 when he declared his purpose to be to "take captive every thought to make it obedient to Christ," a thought itself undergirded by the truth of Psalm 24:1: "The earth is the Lord's and everything in it."

[3] Referred to above in chapter 10; see K. Sietsma, *The Idea of Office*, op. cit.

personal or family budget, and all about tithing, investing, and the dangers of debt—you won't honor the Master, they won't overcome materialism, and you won't have helped very much.

3. ***Assess Your Curriculum.*** Most churches buy a curriculum either from their church's publishing division or from someone else's.[4] Irrespective of the source of your material, here's the question you must face. *Is the curriculum material we use achieving our goals?* Are the children learning the Scriptures thoroughly? The doctrines of the faith? A Biblical world-and-life view? Practical Christian living?

4. ***Back to Basics.*** I know that if you do the work I suggest above, you may well be a bit frustrated, if not fit to be tied. Every church I've seen, including several I've served, needs help in these areas. I'm not asking you to fire all your teachers, pitch out your curricular materials, wring your hands, and sit outside your church's main entry in sackcloth and ashes crying, "woe is me." I *do* suggest that the *first thing you* do, before you do anything else in regard to the training of the lambs of the flock, is to challenge the local elders to come to agreement on and to state specifically *just what kind of disciples you believe the Lord wants you to make.* Many boards of elders have never thought that far, never begun to think in terms of such far-reaching goals. Let's be clear; unless you must come to clarity on this question, you will never develop a program of nurture that trains and equips the lambs of the flock so that they grow unto health and service.

Assignment for Further Work:

1. Make sure you work through the checklist suggested above, either individually or through discussion in a group setting with others.

2. In addition, write a paragraph or two about "what kind of disciples Christ asks us to make." Make sure you base your thinking and writing on Scriptural teaching. Share your paragraph with other elders, and solicit their reaction.

3. Pray this week for the teachers and the students in your church's education ministry.

---

4 The Christian Reformed Church in North America, the Presbyterian Church in America, and the Orthodox Presbyterian Church all offer consistent, well-developed curricula.

19

A Catechism on Sex - Helping Parents Establish Biblical Values

My wife and I recently led an Adult Education seminar in our congregation on the subject of *Sex Nurture: the Responsibility of Parents*. Because our society is so gung-ho on the subject that it has become a mandatory part of the public school curriculum, and because so many parents feel overwhelmed about the subject when faced with the idea of giving moral direction to the mass of information their children come home with, we came up with this little "catechism." I include it here as a separate chapter in the section dealing with elders and teaching because the pastoral elders of the church bear a great responsibility in this increasingly sexualized age. It is an age possessing vast amounts of information about sex, yet one without solid values despite its heightened awareness. In such a time elders must be active in sexual nurture, not so much to teach children details about sex and sex-related material as to equip parents to do a better job of instilling Biblical values in these things.[1] After all, as we've seen in previous chapters, it is clear that confusion about Biblical values in this area of life will have grave consequences in the marriages and families of the flock under your pastoral care.

A Catechism on Sex

Question 1: Why bother?

("After all, they learn about sex in Sex Education class at school, and what they don't learn there, they'll learn on the street. My generation never even had those classes, and we turned out OK. Besides, we're not qualified instructors.")

---
1 See James Dobson, *Preparing for Adolescence* (Ventura, CA: Regal Books, 1978).

Answer: First, let's be clear about what we mean by "sex nurture." Teaching God's children Biblical values about sex and sexuality is not the same as communicating a bunch of facts about sex organs and techniques for intercourse or masturbation. In the same way, teaching a 15 year old about carburetors, pistons, brake rotors and clutch mechanisms, is not the same as training him/her to drive safely and responsibly. Teaching an adolescent about sperm, eggs and birth control, is not the same as training a child in the ways of the Lord about sexuality, marriage, physical purity and holiness. Second, *not* teaching God's children about the remarkable and sometimes shocking changes in their bodies and emotions is to fail to equip them to handle the rocky road of adolescence ahead. That borders on cruelty, and almost certainly will result in serious problems with their fragile and developing self-image during these difficult years. Finally, to fail to shape their thinking with *Biblical* teaching about physical holiness in relationships is to expose their tender bellies to worldly thinking and the sharp tearing fangs of the devil in this wicked age. Such failure has contributed greatly to the increase of premarital sex, teen pregnancies and venereal disease among God's people and their children.

Question 2: Why must elders get involved and why must they equip parents?

("After all, neither elders nor parents are expert in reproductive matters. Our knowledge is limited to their own experiences; it's not scientific. As an elder, what would I say? Besides, it's embarrassing and I'm scared!")

Answers: The primary responsibility for the nurture of the children of the church is assigned to parents, not to teachers at school. In Deut. 6, the Lord tells parents to "impress them (the commandments just given in Deut. 5) upon your children. Talk about them when you sit at home and when you walk along the road, when you lie down and when you get up...." As you well know, one of those commandments is the 7th, forbidding adultery and calling God's people to honor marriage and the marriage bed (Heb. 13:4). For parents to raise God's children without teaching them about serving their Lord in matters of marital fidelity and sexual purity is to neglect the 7th commandment. Besides, training children about sex and their sexuality is not exclusively a scientific enterprise. What they learn from watching Daddy and Mommy hug, hold hands and kiss, from knowing that the bedroom door is closed sometimes, from seeing pregnant ladies, is some of the most profound "sex education" parents can offer. And it is training by lifestyle rather than by words. And because elders are charged with oversight of the entire flock, and with defense of that flock against the corrupting values of this perverted generation, they must help parents fulfill their responsibility to prepare the children of the church to think Biblically instead of thinking like pagans.

Question 3: How much should parents tell their children about sex?

("Maybe I'll mess up some of the facts. I'd just die if I found out they knew more than I do. What if they corrected me? Besides, do 8 year olds really need to know about condoms, AIDS, and menstruation?")

Answers: Corrie Ten Boom's father was right. Remember the scene from *The Hiding Place*, when little Corrie asked a question about God's will, the answer to which was too difficult and deep for her to understand? Her father pointed to his suitcase, and asked his daughter if she could carry his heavy suitcase from the train. She replied, "No, Papa, you always let me carry the lighter bag." He answered, "That's because you can't handle the heavy one yet."[2] So it is with knowledge about sex. Children can't always handle the heavy stuff. That doesn't mean they shouldn't carry the knowledge they are able to handle. Generally, the best rule of thumb is that if parents have a good relationship with their children and talk about all kinds of things regularly (the importance of dinnertime devotions and discussions is incredibly underestimated), they will ask what they need to know. And your answers should aim to provide only as much information as they need to carry with them.[3]

Question 4: When should parents start training children about sex?

("Do I wait till they are 10, 12, or 16? Should I talk with my 5 year old about 'the birds and the bees'?")

Answers: Begin as soon as they are able to open their eyes! But remember what we said above; sexual nurture is not "a talk" with

---

2 Corrie Ten Boom, *The Hiding Place* (Washington Depot, CT: Chosen Books, 1971)

3 My wife and I had decided that it was time I had a formal talk with one of our young children about sexual matters. The perfect occasion came up unexpectedly; the child was riding with me in the car, and while looking out the window at the country scene began to describe what he had learned in Science class about the reproductive life of plants. I seized upon the moment, of course, and delivered myself of a careful "application" to human love, sexuality and intimacy within marriage. The child listened politely, waited until I finished, and then matter-of-factly said, "Like I was saying about plants, Dad...." Fact is, the child wasn't ready yet, even though I was.

God's children. They will communicate more about Biblical values from marital hugs, kisses and playful tickles in the kitchen, having parents turn off certain TV programs (yes, in the middle of the show if necessary!), discussing others with them to make Biblical points about the behavior of the characters, and showing discretion and demanding respect for privacy (a good lock on the bedroom door), than they ever will with a single, anxious "speech" on the subject. Kids learn about marriage from watching their parents, both the good lessons and the bad. Know that, and parents are already on the road to educating their children Biblically in sexuality.

Question 5: What content must be taught?

("I hear 'experts' on TV talk about birth control devices and usage, about 'positions' for 'creative sex,' about the 'alternative lifestyle' of homosexuality. How must I cover all that?")

Answer: Packing "facts" into children without providing a moral framework for understanding and evaluating them is cruelty, not education or nurture. And teaching so much information about sex that a young couple has nothing left to discover about each other when they marry is robbery! Instead, we suggest you emphasize the following major Biblical principles as you equip parents:

1. Stress the precious *nature of the marriage relationship*. Begin to teach your children early that marriage is a gift of God. Respect your own marriage-partner; insist that your children respect your spouse. Make clear that marriage must be "in Christ," so that when the hormones of growing adolescents explode, there will be a background of understanding that provides a measure of spiritual discernment.
2. Stress the *permanence of marriage*. Not enough parents these days remind their children that, though the world believes marriage may legitimately and easily be broken, God says marriage is for life. You take care of the marriage you have; you don't throw it away and start over again. Unless you teach this, how will they understand that sex is not merely "physical recreation for consenting adults," but belongs appropriately, and delightfully, only within the marriage relationship?
3. Teach your children that *sex before or outside of marriage is sin*; it is self-centered and leads to abuse, exploitation and pornography. You do that throughout their childhood, when you comment on TV programs,[4] or answer questions about "Bill's

---

4 Perhaps it's overly obvious, but I think it needs to be said that one of the reasons kids get a skewed view of sex even in Christian homes is that many

dad who gets *Playboy* magazine." You also do that when they are about to begin their dating lives, and you remind them of how you (and God) expect them to treat their date and themselves, with dignity and respect.[5]

4. Of course, you may well have to *teach some details*, to transmit information about intercourse, "where babies come from,"[6] or even to discuss openly with older children matters pertaining to homosexuality or other sinful perversions. Sadly but surely they will be exposed to these things in a world that flaunts such things on TV and in every newspaper. When asked, answer honestly, on a level appropriate to their age and understanding.

The key Biblical concepts to be taught can be easily remembered by using the mnemonic **CHILD**:

C for *Chastity:* God desires chastity and purity (Eph. 5:3f.).

H for *Holiness:* Your body is God's temple; sex within a godly marriage is a holy activity (I Cor. 6:18-19).

I for *Intimacy:* Sex is private, intimate; to function only in a godly marriage; not for public talk or viewing. Also, telling children too much sexual information will ruin intimate discovery later (I Cor. 7:3f.).

L for *Loyalty:* God desires marital faithfulness and loyalty (Gen. 2:24f.; Matt. 19:6).

D for *Demonstration:* It is important for parents to demonstrate loving, respectful and tender relationships within their marriages. Children learn best when they see Mom and Dad live out a wonderful marriage. One cannot with words alone correct a lesson modeled over the years of your own life. Tend your own garden first!

Christian parents uncritically consume worldly TV programming without ever making a comment. How do we expect our children to be sexually holy when we watch sexual perversion ourselves, even angrily defending the practice with statements like, "I'm mature enough to handle it. It won't affect me!" Consistency is demanded here.

5 I read once of a couple who developed the practice of giving each of their children a "promise ring": a rather precious reminder of the vow each was asked to take to remain a virgin until marriage. A beautiful practice!

6 A handy little book on this subject for younger children is Margaret Clarkson, *Susie's Babies* (Grand Rapids: Wm. B. Eerdman's Publishing Co., 1960). See also Lenore Buth, *The Facts of Life: Teaching Your Children About Sex* (A Focus on the Family pamphlet. Call 1-800-A FAMILY to order; a wonderful resource. For older children, I refer you to Dobson, *Preparing for Adolescence* op. cit., and Josh McDowell's bestseller for teens *Why Wait Until Marriage?*

"OLD DOGS, NEW TRICKS"
- TRAINING ADULTS IN CHRIST

After church was over, the routine was predictable. The adults went outside, stood on the sidewalk surrounding the church on the corner, and talked. The kids ran off energy, chasing around the church lot, slowing down periodically when scolded by a watchful parent or other adult concerned about skinned knees and torn "Sunday clothes." Then the bell rang, and Sunday School began. The kids filed back into the building, sat in pews for the "singing time." Soon, they divided into classes appropriate to their age groups. Meanwhile, the parents either went home, or, as in our family's case, walked to Grandma's house for coffee, homemade bread and jam, and conversation. Adult Sunday School? What's that?

Sound familiar? Perhaps not, if your experience is in a Baptist or other evangelical church where adult Sunday School was stressed. But if you grew up like I did, in one of the many churches that did not emphasize Sunday School to a high degree, the description is probably accurate. The few notable exceptions were the churches who were doing a fine job of evangelism, in which many were coming to worship who had never had the benefit of good discipling and nurture as children. But even then, adult Sunday School was not a very popular educational tool. More typical was individualized instruction by the pastor or an elder, and that only "kicked in" when an individual wanted to make a personal profession of faith and needed to be prepared for the interview. "Adult education" meant reading the Bible, meeting with the pastor and going to church; it was finished when an articulate profession of faith was made. The goal was simple; knowledgeable faith.

GOALS FOR ADULT EDUCATION

Scripture teaches us a different set of goals. Knowledge of God and His Word is important, of course. In fact, it is crucial. Yet it should never be an end in itself; its goal is mature service and obedience to Christ. To say it in slightly different language, the goal of adult education is not knowledgeable-faith but *serviceable-faith;* equipped for *ministry*, every believer offering him/herself in obedient service to Christ. That's the point of Eph. 4:11-12. Remember that passage? It is the seminal text that establishes the different role of the office-bearer in the church from that of the office of believer. Apostles, prophets, evangelists, pastors (and here shepherding-elders also fit) and teachers are all given to the church by Christ "to prepare God's people for *works of service*." (I don't particularly like the NIV translation "works of service"; the word is *diakonias*, and refers to the *various ministries God's people offer to Him in response to His grace in their lives*). The roots of the idea were priestly. In the Old Testament, the priests offered themselves in temple service before the face of God. In the New Testament, that temple service isn't limited to a few Levites, a single building or one location; in fact, Rom. 12:1-2 makes it clear that all believers are priests of God and offer priestly service wherever they live and move and have their being. Now here's the point: You as elders (and deacons, and preachers) have a job to do in the life of the church. That job in its most basic statement is *you serve the Word so well that God's people can serve before Him in the living of their lives*. Let me be specific:

- Your task is not just to teach Bible doctrine so that people know it enough to profess faith. It is to teach the doctrine of God's Word so that people can *use* it; defend it, teach it to others, be so strong in it that they will not be uprooted by the struggles of life. Interestingly, Heb. 5:14 refers to "solid food" (as opposed to the "milk of the Word"), and is *not* referring merely to doctrine. "Solid food" involves both the "teaching about righteousness" and the "constant use" that results in training folks to distinguish good from evil. In short, a practical Christian ethic is inseparably connected to solid doctrinal training. Mature Christians are not just those who know more, but those who can live out their faith more discerningly. That must be the goal of doctrinal instruction.

- Adult education involves more than just pastoral-elders; it surely embraces the teaching-elders or preachers. And if this is your calling, your task isn't finished when you preach sermons that are *merely* Biblically accurate, and correct in form and style. Rather, it is to open texts so clearly, so directly and so *practically*, that God's people are gripped by the truth, the grace, the power, and ultimately the duty laid upon them to respond in heart, soul and life. The powerful, timely and Biblically-appropriate sermon application is perhaps the hardest thing about preaching; yet to fail to do it well is to gut your preaching. Here lies the difference between a dry theological lecture and living and vital preaching!

And that's where Adult Education comes in. The debate ought not to be on the level of *whether* to have education available to adults. Rather, the debate ought to be on the level of *what kind of training* the adult education courses provide. It is the *goals* I want you to think about. You must develop mature, practicing disciples for Jesus Christ. You must train people to serve in ways that make them uncomfortable (evangelism), as the claims of Christ usually do. You must equip people to defend the faith in an increasingly hostile world. That takes knowledge, of course, but also skills. You must cultivate in your people a distinctively Scriptural view of God and the world (in a previous chapter I called it a world-view; it is that Biblical perspective that sees Jesus Christ as the Lord and Master of all dimensions and facets of life).

A Curriculum Proposal

Allow me to share with you a peek at a curriculum plan we have developed here in Dallas. Understand clearly; I'm not suggesting you adopt ours. I do not believe it is the curriculum plan to end all curriculum plans. But it is working; it is effective. Look at it closely. Observe the goals. Note the underlying assumptions. Watch to see how the goals are worked into the course progression. And adapt it as you will to fit your circumstances.

You will, of course, have to determine your own adult education goals yourself, within the context of Biblical instruction (Eph. 4:11-12, e.g.). You know your schedule; we know ours. We can't do much mid-week, due to distance and the spread of the parish we serve; you might be able to. We have two morning services, with Sunday School for all ages between services. We are able to offer 3 adult courses each Sunday morning and 2 on Wednesday evenings *at all times throughout the year* (no lengthy break in the summer). You might not be able to pull that off in your schedule, but you can learn some lessons from our experiences. Some details:

1. The calendar is divided into 5 quarters of 8 weeks each, beginning with September.

Each Sunday school course is 1 quarter (8 weeks) in length. That allows for the use of various qualified and competent teachers who would be unable to commit to an entire year. Quarters are divided from each other by a week designated for special purposes; friend day (evangelism), special fellowship time for the diverse congregation we serve, a video or film of high quality for the entire church, etc. In the summer, we have a special focus; with different teachers and a different format, but with the same goals.

2. Each quarter, at least 3 courses are offered *at the same time* on Sunday mornings as electives for adults. These 3 course offerings reflect 3 separate curriculum tracks:

> A. **Membership Track**: Course 1- *nature and commitments of local church membership;* Course 2- *basics of Biblical doctrine;* Course 3- *personal evangelism training;* Course 4- *training in personal and family stewardship.* (Because of the unique demands of ministry in Dallas, and the demands of living as believers in this area, we ask all who seek membership in this church, including transfers, to take all 4 courses.)
>
> B. **Maturing Track**: Biblical and/or creedal studies (for example, intense study in a book of the Bible, or the use of one of the fine books by R.C. Sproul or another classic or contemporary author, the use of audio or video tape studies, or doctrinal studies like *Heidelberg Catechism* training described earlier). Five different courses per year provide much diversity. Here the emphasis is on the defense of the faith, the explaining of the truths of God's Word to a world that no longer knows nor believes. Skills in apologetics are intentionally developed. Distinctly Christian world-view is targeted.
>
> C. **Practical Track**: Biblical application courses, including *Worship Music* training (developing both an understanding of the nature of true worship, and skill in singing praise appropriately), *Parenting Principles and Skills* (including the sharing by older parents of discipline tactics and methods so that younger parents can learn from them), *Financial Stewardship* (including the development of a budget plan), *Biblical Foundations for Christian Marriage* (including assignments for couples to work through in their own marriages), *Biblical Counseling Seminars* (including assignments and homework), *How to Study the Bible* (including

reading, research, outlining and lesson-plan assignments), *Developing a Dynamic Prayer Life* (including the radical practice of praying together!). I trust these examples reveal the heart of what it is we try to do and stimulate you to think and plan wisely.

3. On Wednesday nights, two courses are offered to adults on alternating weeks (1st and 3rd, 2nd and 4th). Currently, we are offering a course in *Church History*, since so few have ever traced the faithfulness of God through the centuries of the past, and a survey of the Old Testament called *Promise and Deliverance* (from the book of the same title by S.G. De Graaf [1]). It aims to establish a consistent and working hermeneutic (method of interpreting Scripture) by tracing the mighty acts of God revealed in the Old Testament. We find that few believers today are conversant with the Old Testament; this course is a crucial component of our answer to this observation.

4. Each summer, the courses vary to accommodate vacations and to allow Sunday School teachers to take courses for their own growth and nurture. We typically offer courses that include challenging films or videos, or that teach each class as a stand-alone unit that doesn't depend as much on previous weeks' material. Also, every summer, we offer a Sunday afternoon (2 hours preceding evening worship) course for several weeks to train and develop *potential officebearers*. We use materials like the present volume, which actually grew out of these classes. Our nominations to the offices of the church are made exclusively from the group of those trained each summer.

I trust you will be gracious as you examine the curriculum described above. It isn't perfect, as any elder or teacher in this congregation will readily attest. We make constant adjustments, seeking better Biblical coverage and more appropriate applications for each student. Though it is a bit risky "exposing" one's work in print, I did it for a reason. I want you to examine your own train-

---

[1] S.G. De Graaf, *Promise and Deliverance* (St. Catharines, Ontario, Canada: Paideia Press, 1981). Four volumes. This is an excellent overview of the Scriptures; not a verse-by-verse commentary, it was written by the author, a pastor, to equip his church's teachers to tell the stories of the Bible without reducing them to mere moralism or superficiality. Especially helpful is its approach to Old Testament narrative. The author's introduction to volume one is worth the price of the set. *Available only from:* Westminster Discount Book Service, PO Box 125 H, Scarsdale, NY, 10583.

ing regimen, to compare your church's curriculum offerings with the Biblical goals set before you in the passages we've studied together. No matter what the past practices in your congregation, you can change, improve, and begin today to beef up the program.

You may be "old dogs," and so may your people, but both you and they can learn new tricks!

Assignment for further work:

Secure an adult curriculum plan from your pastor or one of the education committee members in your church. Compare it to that presented above. If this one is lacking in any area, write me to tell me. If the curriculum of your church is deficient, decide specifically what you plan to do about it.

The Shepherd's Hand

Section Two:
The Elder and Member Visiting

Visiting To Encourage

When the Apostle Paul establishes his pastoral *"bona fides"* in Acts 20:20, just before he hands out instructions to the Ephesian elders, he refers to a practice central to his work. The practice was *pastoral visiting in the homes of God's people*. He says, "You know that I have not hesitated to preach anything that would be helpful to you but have taught you publicly and from house to house."

Several churches have long practiced such visiting; in fact, in some the practice is carefully prescribed and regulated with great detail.[1] Sadly, the practice is not popular today, certainly not like it was in Paul's day. (An elder once told me "I'll go to meetings, but I don't do visiting. I'm just not a 'people-person'." I bristled, frustrated and angry with the inroads made by the administrative model that supplants the shepherding model for elders. Then I said to him, "You're an unfaithful shepherd, and you ought to be scared to death of God's warnings to unfaithful shepherds!" He didn't understand.) Yet, even among those churches where the practice of visiting in homes is regular, it's not always effective. Far too often, the visit becomes irrelevant (a discussion about the weather, the job, or the kids, around coffee and a slice of pie), remains spiritually superficial ("how are you getting along in church?"), or worse, becomes a gripe session ("anything about our church you don't like?"). Sadly, the *Biblical purpose* for pastoral visits to members of the flock in their homes is not always clear either to the pastors or to the flock. In the following pages, I propose to do something about that. My concern is not just *that* you visit, but that you visit *Biblically and effectively*. So, we start with what the Bible says about visiting.

---

1 In the Christian Reformed Churches and other denominations and congregations which embrace the legacy of the church order of the Synod of Dort, 1618-1619, the practice requires *annual* home visits to the members of the church by the pastors and elders of the church.

Several New Testament verbs shape pastoral visiting. The first of them is "encouragement."

ENCOURAGEMENT: THE SPIRIT'S "HANDS AND FEET"

The command to encourage appears frequently on the pages of the New Testament. Before reading further in this volume, take up your Bible and read I Thess. 5:11,14; II Tim. 4:2; and especially Titus 1:9 and 2:15, addressed specifically to officeholders. An elder is to "hold firmly to the trustworthy message as it has been taught, so that he can encourage others..." And, a pastor[2] is to "encourage... with all authority."

Now, as with most translations from ancient languages like Greek, the original word has many shades of meaning. The original word here is "parakaleo," and is the root word for the Holy Spirit's Name "Paraclete," "Comforter" or "Counselor" (depending on your english translation) in John 16:7. From those translational options, you will readily see that the modern understanding of "encouragement" doesn't begin to cover the meaning of the Biblical term. Encouragement as the Bible describes it links the work of the Holy Spirit to the work of the shepherds of the flock who care for Christ's Church. To say it bluntly; God assigns to the elders of the church the awesome task of giving human shape to the comforting and encouraging work of the Holy Spirit. Pastoral elders become the Spirit's hands and feet and voice to do that work.

Why such an assignment? Because the church of the Lord Jesus is a battling, oppressed, suffering church. She is *militant*, in the sense that she is ever engaged in the battle of the ages against the Prince of Darkness, waging war with the "sword of the Spirit which is the Word of God" (Eph. 6:17). And because she is militant, she ought to expect that the Devil will not leave her alone. Dad warned the sons he raised on the South side of Chicago; "if you get in a fight, expect to get hit!" So Jesus warns all of us that when we are faithful to Him we will be identified with Him, and will "take the heat" He took. Remember His words? "If the world hates you, keep in mind that it hated me first...If they persecuted me, they will persecute you also" (Jn. 15:18,20). If you are in the fight, you can expect to get hit! Throughout history the church has witnessed the oppression the world heaps on the church when she is faithful; it's

---

2 As a reminder, "pastor" and "elder" are both words Scripture uses for the shepherding care of the flock. I use them interchangeably throughout this volume.

no different today. When the people of the Lord are faithful to Him, the world hates them because their existence is a painful and irritating reminder that life outside of Christ is empty and lost.

Jesus also knew that, while engaged in such struggles, believers could weaken. In Jn. 16:1 He says, "All this I have told you so that you will not go astray." And, because He knows the Devil won't leave us alone, He promises that He won't either. That's why He sends the Holy Spirit, the "encourager" [Jn. 15:26]; that's also why, throughout the New Testament, He commands His shepherds to carry on the same work of "encouraging" His church. In the original, the word "paraklete" suggests the idea of "coming to someone's aid; standing by to urge them on." God himself does that by His Spirit; how appropriate that He calls elders to do the same among the flock. It's desperately needed.

Look at some of the passages I asked you to read: In I Thess. 5:11, Paul's call to "encourage one another" has in view those grieving and hurt and confused because of the final enemy of *death*; in v. 14, his concern is the *timid* (the frightened); in II Tim. 4:2 he has in mind the treacherous danger of *false doctrine* that saps the church's strength; in Titus 1:9, he calls for defense for those battling *false teachers*. Does anyone doubt the need? Haven't you run across believers who love the Lord deeply, but who are crushed because of a tragic death? Haven't you seen believers so timid in the face of this ungodly world as to be virtually paralyzed when it comes time to speak a word for the Lord or to be active in Christian service? Haven't we all seen what false teachers and false doctrine can do to well-meaning Christian people? Look around you — they're right in front of your nose!

You see, this is a world that is "no friend to grace," as the old hymn said it. It's a tough place, with seductive temptations that hit below the belt with blows struck by the Evil One who doesn't play by the rules. You know it in your life; I know it in mine. You and I, as shepherds of Christ's flock, had better be aware of the wolves, bears, and lions attacking the sheep. The flock needs to hear the soothing voice of the Shepherd who promises always to be there for his people and never to leave them nor forsake them. Then they can make it through the night. That's *encouragement*.[3]

---

[3] Reminds me of Louis L'amour western novels. (Yes, I actually read that cowboy stuff; I'm a Texan now.) In them, the author often comments on the origin of all the cowboy songs; they're developed during night rides, when the cowboys circling the cattle in the open range would sing softly just so their voices would reassure the herd, keep it together, keep it from "spooking."

An Encouraging Word

It's one thing to tell you that you must be encouraging to a weary, hurting, frightened and confused body of believers. It's quite another thing, however, to know how to do that. The Bible is clear on that too. Encouragement is *Word-based*. Not only is the Word to be preached publicly (remember Acts 20:20), but from *house to house*. The shepherds of the flock are to "bring the message home." They are to carry the encouraging voice to the specific lambs and sheep, and never let it become merely generic sound.

Let's focus for a minute on the II Timothy and Titus passages. First, notice Paul's inspired command to young pastor Timothy (II Tim. 4:2): "Preach the Word...correct, rebuke and encourage" (or "exhort" — the same Greek word lies behind both English words). Clearly, encouragement is linked directly to the "Word" Timothy must preach; in fact, it is the selfsame "Scripture" that Paul has just finished describing as "God-breathed and profitable...so that the man of God may be thoroughly equipped for every good work" (II Tim. 3:16-17).

Next, look at Titus 1:9. "He (an elder) must hold firmly to the trustworthy message as it has been taught, so that he can encourage others by sound doctrine." Again, note the method; encouragement is given through the Scriptural message, the Biblical doctrine, the Word of God. No one would argue that good preaching isn't encouraging. But good preaching isn't enough; shepherds must apply Biblical truth directly and personally to individuals in the daily grind of their lives.

Now look at Titus 2:15. Here Paul tells pastor Titus to "encourage and rebuke with all authority." In other words, as shepherds minister the Word of the Lord, they must take care not to let anyone treat it as if it comes just from a man. Make it clear that your teaching is God's teaching, from God's Word, with God's authority.[4] That, in the final analysis, is what makes it encouraging!

None of this ought to be surprising. After all, we started this study by defining the task of encouragement as the human application of the Holy Spirit's work as "Paraclete" or "Comforter." It is consistent then that the comforting and encouraging we do is to be done with the very Word the Holy Spirit inspired!

---

4 When a shepherd begins to doubt his authority and his commission to speak with that kind of voice, or when he begins to lose sight of his duty to God when speaking, he ought to read carefully and with trembling hands the words contained in I Thess. 2:4-6 and v. 13.

PRACTICALLY...

Let's get specific. The work of an elder or deacon to encourage the flock is not merely emotional support, a "being-there-when-they-need-you" kind of thing. To be sure, your presence is a witness to the Lord Jesus' promise not to leave or forsake His own; yet encouragement and comfort in the fullest sense of the term is given only when you open the Paraclete's Book. That's when you are doing what God commissions you to do.

You get the point, I trust. You work for, and with, the Holy Spirit. You must use His words to assure His people of His comforting and encouraging presence; thus you renew their faith, invigorate their zeal, and rekindle their commitment to Jesus Christ. It works just like He said it would:

> ...the sheep listen to his (the shepherd's) voice. He calls his own sheep by name and leads them out...his sheep follow him because they know his voice" (Jn. 10:3-4).

Homework assignment:

Carefully examine the following representative situations. Develop, on paper, a pastoral action plan for a *visit to encourage* for each situation. Include in your action plan the specific Scripture passage(s) you would read, and a one sentence goal statement describing concretely what you hope to accomplish during the visit.

1. You are preparing for a pastoral follow-up visit one year after the death of a 45 year old head of household who left behind a wife and 3 teenagers.

2. You are asked to visit a woman in her early 90s who is extremely weak and frail physically, and is confined to her bed most of the day. She cries daily for the Lord to "deliver her" from this body of death and take her to heaven; she has prayed that prayer for 10 years, and can't understand why she is still alive and languishing.

3. You are preparing a visit to an eager young Christian doctor who recently was unjustly sued for malpractice by a money-hungry patient and a gold-digging attorney. His entire practice is at stake and he is profoundly depressed because of the injustice of it all.

4. A mature Christian woman of your congregation just lost her job. Although no one said anything official, she's convinced

it is due to a "youth movement" in the company. She despairs of finding another position at the age of 58. Finances are a large problem.

5. You visit a fellow believer who is frustrated because a close friend, an unbeliever for whom he had been praying and seeking opportunities to witness to the Gospel of Christ, just joined a Muslim group in town, proclaiming loudly that he loved and needed the discipline Islam provides.

VISITING TO REBUKE

Pete is the son of one of the elders of your church. He was always a bit of a rough character, right on the edge of being a real rebel, but his training at home and church had given the elders reason to hope. Now he had gone off the deep end. While at college, he'd moved in with his girlfriend and didn't seem to be at all conscience-stricken by his sin nor worried about consequences. Pete's folks, well known and respected believers, are understandably crushed. The burden of shame and sorrow they carry is a heavy load; you can tell the strain from their faces. Since the flock you serve is spread out over a large geographical area, Pete's situation is not commonly known among the membership. After all, they generally only see one another on Sunday, and college kids are out of the loop of congregational life anyway. As a result, the "urgency" brought on by public knowledge and opinion is lacking, and the eldership, anxious to avoid intensifying parental grief, "drags its feet" on the matter of confronting Pete.

Alice lives 750 miles away from her home town and home church, having moved to Mississippi to take a job after college. After relocating, the church that her home pastor had recommended to her, saw her at worship once or twice, and never again. Her home church wrote her once, six months later, encouraging her to find Christian fellowship within the family of God (courtesy copy to the Mississippi church consistory). The church in Mississippi is genuinely interested in her, but feels no warrant to challenge her non-attendance and apparent spiritual apathy; the home church is simply too far away. She receives no visits.

That the Bible charges the believing community to "rebuke" one another comes as no surprise. Open your Bible to the book of *Proverbs* to read Scriptural wisdom about "rebukes"; mull over the following passages: 3:11; 9:8; 15:31; 29:1. Look next at the NT passages in which Christ commissions the church to "rebuke": Luke 17:3; I Tim. 5:1 & 20, II Tim. 4:2; Titus 1:13; 2:15. Go ahead, do it. I'll wait for you....

Problems arise, of course, in our relativistic age of "live and let live,"[1] when the church tries to honor Christ's command to rebuke. She is accused of operating with a "self-righteous judgmental spirit." In such an age, it's important to have clear answers to a few basic questions. What distinguishes Biblical "rebuke" from self-righteous judging? How can a rebuke be done properly? Is it worth it? How important is rebuking to the life of the church?

Let's be honest. All of us face the danger of self-righteousness. But the ministry of rebuking is no more a function of a self-righteous spirit than parental discipline is automatically physical abuse. To be sure, some would argue that every rebuke proceeds from self-righteousness, and that every spanking is abusive (my kids tried that one on me...once!). The presence of temptation does not always mean the presence of sin. The temptation toward self-righteousness on the part of the pastoral elder must be diligently resisted; such resistance is possible only when frail and sinful men who are elders remember their own weakness and frailty. Remember the words of Galatians 6:1: "...if someone is caught in a sin, you who are spiritual should restore him gently. But watch yourself, or you also may be tempted."

What keeps a rebuke righteous is a combination of two things; righteous motivation and a righteous standard of judgment. The motive is righteous only when it reflects God's intent. The Galatians 6;1 passage cited above reminds us what that motive must always be; *restoration!* I must never rebuke someone merely to prove him wrong, to make him pay, or to punish because I (or even "we") believe punishment is warranted. I can and may rebuke a brother or sister only with a view to restoration. That's the point of the instruction about "redeemed communication style" in Ephesians 4:29. My words must be uttered to "build up," and never to "tear down" my brother. Likewise, I must avoid any rebuke delivered because someone violates *my* standards of behavior; I can rebuke a brother only because he violates God's. The only way to assure myself that I am within bounds, that my rebuke is not self-righteous but Biblically righteous, is to *link my rebuke to a specific Scripture passage.*

---

1 Cf. chapter 7 above for an extensive discussion of relativism.

Specifically, when you make a visit to Pete or Alice from our examples above, seek to restore, not to enforce. Bear the Word of rebuke because you care deeply for them and about their walk with Christ. Don't try to enforce certain accepted standards of behavior, even if those standards have long precedence and widespread religious acceptance. Come with the Bible open, held in hands trembling with the fear that you yourself are not far from sin. Enter their home with a specific passage in mind. Make it clear that you are as much bound by the claims of Scripture as they are; that every one of God's people is always under discipline of the Law of the King.

REBUKE WITH AUTHORITY

It is important to note that the Scriptural charge to "rebuke one another" is one that applies to all believers. God calls all who have been redeemed in Christ to care for one another in such a way so as to protect the holiness of Christ and to restore His people to holy living. Jesus' words to His disciples in Luke 17:3 apply broadly to all Christians who must deal with the sins of their "brother"; rebuke him, and, if he repents (!), forgive him.

But the charge to rebuke is especially directed at the leaders, the pastoral elders of the church, the shepherds of the flock. Titus, told by Paul to straighten things out in the church on Crete, is also to correct false doctrines and root out unholy living on the island. He is told, in sum; "These, then are the things you should teach. Encourage and rebuke with all authority. Do not let anyone despise you" (Titus 2:15). Note the sense of the commission. Not only is Titus to teach and to rebuke, but he is to do it with real and visible authority. (One leading Greek lexicon suggests a better translation might even be "with all impressiveness."[2] The point is that the authority is transparent and is to be acknowledged by the people.) So important is the idea to Paul that he follows it up with the reminder: "do not let anyone despise you."

The authority, the commission, to speak the very Word of God is so crucial to the life of the church that it is to be exercised even at personal cost. There is always the risk, when teaching and especially when rebuking, that someone will become angry with you, even despise you. There is always the risk that they'll take your words "with a grain of salt," ignoring you as irrelevant. There's

---

[2] Bauer, Arndt, and Gingrich, *A Greek-English Lexicon of the New Testament*, s.v. "epitagas."

even the risk that they'll "turn it back" on you, suggesting that you ought to "practice what you preach," that "you're a fine one to talk." *Don't be deterred.* Let them know you speak for God, from His Word, and that He must be answered. Let them hear that message with all the seriousness and urgency you can muster.

A Function of Loving Rescue

I can just see some of you bristle. "Here's that same old talk about authority again. What happened to love? That's the primary command to the NT church, after all." Indeed! Authority deals with issues like one's commissioned *right* to speak or one's *manner* of speaking. But all of our rebuking, indeed, all shepherding of God's precious people, must precede from love for the sheep. Remember, John 10 distinguishes between the shepherd and the hireling on that issue alone; the shepherd loves, the hireling does not.

How can *love* be the *motive* for a rebuke? After all, receiving a rebuke is hard. It hurts deeply. It doesn't *feel* like you're being loved! To understand how a rebuke can be loving, you must understand that failing to rebuke someone is to consign them to death, speaking spiritually. That is so often forgotten. It is thought to be "easier" to lament Pete's sin with his folks, even share their grief, than it is to confront Pete. It is believed to be "easier" to decide that someone else is responsible for Alice than to make the call yourself. However, what is "easy" falls by the wayside when you remember that unless Pete repents, Pete is lost! Unless Alice finds life in Christ and His body, she is outside of Him! Death has such a person in its grip, and God has called you to rescue them. Proverbs 15:31 calls a rebuke that is heeded "life-giving." Jude 23 graphically challenges us to "snatch (sinners) from the fire and save them." Such is the function, the purpose, and ultimately must be the motive, behind a rebuke.

I once watched an emergency rescue team rescue a woman from the raging waters of a flood plain after a torrential rainstorm had washed away her vehicle. She was clinging to a tree limb; when the rescuers reached her, she transferred her "death grip" to the neck of one of them. He wasn't particularly kind and understanding as he dealt with this woman; frankly, he was hard-nosed and authoritative as he shouted to her to "let go" of his neck and to hold on to a rope secured to a rescue boat. He shouted loudly at her, trying to pierce through the fog of her terror. He needed authority to effect her rescue. So does an elder. Kind and soft words of persuasion would have cost her life, and could have taken him down with her. Sometimes kind and soft words don't awaken an individual sinner to the reality of his dangerous spiritual circumstances, either. A firm rebuke, authoritatively delivered, is the only hope for rescue!

And, if you still aren't persuaded to do the difficult but important work of pastoral rebuke, remember one other thing. *The elders of the church are answerable to God for whether or not they do the work of rebuking.* If a believer falls into sin, and you do not rebuke, you are responsible for your inaction. Ezekiel 33 makes it frighteningly plain; the "watchman" appointed by God to care for His people is responsible for their blood if he fails to "blow the trumpet" of alarm. Such is the nature of a rebuke; it is the trumpet call of God warning the believer of the danger of sin. You and I dare not fail to sound the alarm!

Assignment for further reflection:

1. Read carefully the following Proverbs: 9:8; 15:31; 17:10; 19:25; 25:12. Prayerfully analyze your own response to rebukes you've received in the past. How must you grow in regard to *receiving* rebukes? What obstacles lie in your heart or life that hinder you from this blessed gift of God.

2. Write up an action plan for a *visit to rebuke* to each of the two cases described at the top of this chapter. Include the specific Biblical passages you would refer to, and describe clearly your goals for the visit(s).

Visiting To Admonish

We proclaim him, admonishing and teaching everyone with all wisdom, so that we may present everyone perfect in Christ (Col. 1:28).

Let the word of Christ dwell in you richly as you teach and admonish one another with all wisdom... (Col. 3:16).

Now I myself am confident concerning you, by brethren, that you also are full of goodness, filled with all knowledge, able also to admonish one another (Rom. 15:14, NKJV).

Now we ask you, brothers, to respect those who work hard among you, who are over you in the Lord and who admonish you (I Thess. 5:12).

One of the duties God assigns to believers as they live together in the family of God is mutual admonition. Ranked right up there with the other "one another" commands ("love one another," "encourage one another," "pray for one another"), "admonish one another" is a crucial practice within the life of the church. And, from the verses printed above, it is clear that it is not only to the community at large, but in a special way to the pastoral elders of the church that the responsibility to admonish is assigned.

"Admonish" means "Counsel"

For most of my life, I understood the word "admonish" to mean "scold," and with good reason. I had much experience, having been scolded often in my childhood and more than a few times since (some think I still need it frequently!). Among the several definitions of the word in the English language, "to reprove or scold" is one of the more popular usages.[1] I've always preferred the word

---

[1] *Webster's Encyclopedic Unabridged Dictionary of the English Language* (New York: Portland House, 1983).

"admonish" to "scold," however, to describe the experience. I thought it had a bit more class—a more genteel expression for a good old-fashioned chewing out.

In the New Testament, which often defines and uses words quite differently than we do in late 20th Century North America, "admonition" is a much richer idea than scolding. It aims at the activity of "giving counsel" or "advising" someone, and picks up a lesser-used meaning of the word in English dictionaries.[2] This notion implies that "admonishing" involves the work of applying the truths of the Bible to the living out of someone's life. "To admonish" is to call a believer to his or her duty, to help a fellow believer give shape to his or her faith in this hostile and tempting world. Sometimes this may involve confrontation with a person who is drifting away from Biblical principles (a scolding!), but often it is more gentle, involving a kind of heart-sensitive listening and the giving of advice and direction to a hurting, frustrated, naughty, lonely, or confused believer.

"Wait a minute!" you say. "That sounds like `counseling'. If you're suggesting that every pastoral elder and deacon is supposed to be a counselor, you're off base! We have professionals for that. Ministers are trained in clinical counseling, and there are psychologists—even Christians—available in many areas these days. No way am I trained and equipped to be a counselor."

You're dead right, of course, if by "counseling" is meant something embracing secular psychological approaches and methods. But when I say that the Biblical command to "admonish one another" means "to counsel," secular psychology has little to do with what I am describing. For some reason, too many folks automatically assume that "counseling" means "psychological counseling," and the result of that tragic assumption is that little Biblical admonition is being done, either by believers or by elders.

It's time for re-education in the churches of the Lord about this important work Christ has assigned to us. A quarter century ago, Jay Adams (then of Westminster Seminary) started a counseling revolution with the publication of his book, *Competent To Counsel*.[3] In it, he argued (based on Romans 15:14) that *every believer* is com-

---

[2] *Webster's* lists as a third meaning for "admonish," the definition "to urge to duty." This is much closer to the primary meaning of the term in the Greek.

[3] Jay E. Adams, *Competent To Counsel* (Grand Rapids: Baker Book House, 1970).

petent to do that which God commands him to do, and "counseling" ("admonishing," from the Greek word "noutheo," is unfortunately translated "instructing" by the NIV) is no exception. Adams asserted that the church had gotten off track by adopting the worldly model of counseling—a strictly psychological one—that places far too much emphasis on sickness as the origin of all sorts of mental, emotional and relational ills. Adams' work was a cry in the wilderness to return to Biblical diagnosis and terminology, including a reintroduction of the Biblical notion of *sin*. He called for a return to Scriptural "counseling" that involves confrontation, direction and advising, even suggesting a new name to distinguish it from its worldly counterpart: *nouthetic counseling*.

Adams' books[4] were not warmly received by the psychological establishment (even and maybe especially the Christian psychological establishment). However, few if any of his critics have attempted—much less succeeded—to deal as comprehensively as he with the clear command of the texts quoted at the beginning of this article; "to admonish" one another. The Lord Jesus knew nothing of the modern methods of psychology, and yet His Spirit charged us all, and the elders in particular, to "counsel/admonish." Could it be He knows something we don't?

The Requirement: Spiritual Wisdom

"OK," you grudgingly admit. "I'll accept the notion that admonishing is counseling, and that especially the shepherding offices of the church have a great responsibility in this regard. That still doesn't tell me exactly what it is I'm supposed to do!"

Let's get specific. *Admonishing is the work of Bible application*, the work of calling a brother or sister to live out in practice what Christ has made them to be in Him. What the faithful preacher ought to be doing in every sermon—practically applying the truths of God's Word to the lives of God's people—is precisely what the shepherding elder (especially) must be doing personally with every one of the members in his assigned pastoral care district. When a person leaves church having heard God's Word preached, he or she must take it home and live it out. "Hearers" must become "doers." And elders must help them do just that. They must insist on

---

4 See also his books *How to Help People Change*, (Grand Rapids: Zondervan Publishing Co., 1986); *Ready To Restore, (a layman's guide to Christian counseling)*, (Phillipsburg, NJ: Presbyterian and Reformed Publishing., 1981); *A Christian Counselor's Casebook*, (Phillipsburg, NJ: Presbyterian and Reformed., 1974).

Scriptural living; they must help the saints understand what that means, and how to do it no matter how complicated it may seem or how great the world's pressures may be to sin. That work of specific, personal application, helping believers live out their faith in all the situations of their lives, is "admonition."

To do that requires *wisdom*. I find it striking that in both of the Colossians passages quoted at the beginning of this chapter, the inspired Apostle speaks of "admonishing with all wisdom." In the Bible, "wisdom" has to do with living practically according to God's ways. It is "applied knowledge." The wise person is the person who understands how all of life fits together in God's world, and that all of life is holy to the Lord.

Remember when you were a youngster and you had a problem? Maybe it was a boyfriend/girlfriend problem, or perhaps an early "cash flow" problem—you spent more than your paper-route earned. Remember talking to Mom or Dad? Remember how calm they were, knowing that it wasn't the end of the world? They saw the big picture; they saw beyond the immediate crisis. That's why their advice always seemed to be so right, so wise, even though you hated to admit it or even accept it.

Transfer that notion to the church and you get a handle on the ministry of "admonition." Imagine a young family that is financially strapped, as so many seem to be these days. Dad takes on a second job to try to make ends meet. Since he's seldom home, the kids begin to be a real handful for Mom. They start being more and more independent and rebellious, and begin to hang around with troublemakers. Mom becomes frustrated and resentful, naturally, and more than a little jealous of her friends who don't have such problems.

"Discipline" folks like that? Not in the usual, hard-nosed sense. Dad is doing his best, and the wife and kids are responding rather naturally to the vacuum created by his actions and absence. Instead "admonish"! Now is the time for a wise elder to visit in the home with the parents to point to priorities—financial, family and time priorities—established by Scripture. Now is the time to talk about the "cost of discipleship," and the greater cost of failing to give Biblical leadership in the home. Now is the time for elders blessed with wisdom to teach the family Biblical budgeting (a most appropriate ministry of the deacons); now is the time to involve the believing community to "bear one another's burdens" prayerfully, if not financially. If this is done, and done well, such people of God will develop increasing maturity in their own lives as they grow through the struggles of the day. No psychologist is needed here, nor in most similar family crises. What is needed are elders (and deacons) who are blessed with wisdom and who are willing to get involved, personally and intimately, in the work of admonition with Biblical insight and according to Biblical principles.

I'm not naive. There are some cases, obviously, where psychological help will be required. A wise pastoral elder will not be so brazen as to think he can counsel wisely when he is out of his depth! Yet, most of the pastoral difficulties we face do not require referral. The Bible is true; God's people *are* competent to counsel! My experience is that the majority of cases you will deal with have to do with people's relationship with God (the need for confession, repentance, forgiveness, dealing with guilt, etc.) and their relationships within the family unit (marriages, parent-child, etc.). Clearly, Scripture speaks much about these relationships, and speaks clearly, and a wise elder will be able to apply its truths to the concrete situations he faces.

To do the work of admonition among people with sinful and proud hearts requires spiritually mature pastoral elders. That's one of the reasons Paul warns the church against ordaining anyone to office too soon—before sufficient examination, before they give evidence of such spiritual maturity and wisdom, before they show aptitude to provide "counsel."

SPECIFICALLY...

What does all this mean? Allow me to suggest several specific implications.

1. Before nominating a man for office, make sure he has a "track-record" of "counsel/admonition" among the flock as a loving believer. Far too seldom do potential elders undergo careful scrutiny on the basis of the ministry they are already performing among the flock. Far too often they are nominated or proposed for service based upon what those nominating them think or believe they will do.

2. Again, before nominating someone for the office of pastoral elder, make sure he is faithful in worship and in the study of Scripture. To give counsel from the Word, a wise elder or deacon must be constantly receiving counsel from the Word!

Men who do not faithfully attend the preaching of the Word and who do not faithfully immerse themselves in Scripture study and prayer are unqualified for office and cannot perform their duties!

3. Those of you who are preachers (teaching elders), make sure you help the elders in their pastoral work by suggesting specific passages to apply to specific cases. Never send them on a visit without specific instructions, if you know the case at all in advance.

4. In your meetings, consider using some of the case studies listed in the Appendix to this volume, or use some from Jay Adams' book *The Christian Counselor's Casebook*. Both of these are only resources, but in your discussions, you will have ample opportunity to analyze issues, strategy, examine procedure, advice, etc. That process prepares you for future ministry.

5. How about a new Sunday School class at your church? Led by an elder or two, it could be called "doing the Word," and should have no other goal than to identify specific ways to put into practice what the sermon of that morning laid on the hearts of God's people. Think about it!

Assignment for further work:

Write a one or two page paper distinguishing the character and goals of Biblical *rebuke* from the character and goals of Biblical *admonition*. Make sure you weight your paper heavily with Scriptural references. Share it with your preacher and/or with (other) elders from your church, and discuss with them their reactions.

Visiting To Guard

The year was 1960. I belonged to the YMCA and had signed up to tour Joliet Stateville Federal Penitentiary outside of Chicago with a Father-Son group from our local "Y." Dad and I were eager to see this "dark side" of life, before only imagined. The thirty mile bus ride seemed like it took forever, of course, but finally we rode up the long drive to the front gate. Immediately, excitement was replaced by a foreboding chill. "What must it be like to be locked, to live, behind these gates?"

The tour commenced. We walked through administration buildings, saw the warden's office, the officer's quarters and then entered Blockhouse A. An enormous concrete and steel structure, it was cold, it smelled and it echoed. I didn't like it, and I don't think any of us on the tour, men or boys, enjoyed walking past the rows of cells that later would suggest pet store dog cages. The faces behind the bars were all different, some angry, some sad, some empty. Most—in the eyes of a 10 year old—were ominous. I had bad dreams for weeks.

Only one part of that tour gave me any comfort. Despite the bars separating criminals from tourists, despite all the security measures we passed through, only the visible, seemingly omnipresent guards provided any sense of protection. I found myself looking for the guards, secure in the knowledge that if they were around, we were OK. They made us feel safe. Bars might fail, hands might reach through, but a guard right there...well, it made you breathe easier. I'm sure the inmates viewed them differently, but we all felt better because they were there. The church of Jesus Christ does not face an enemy who is locked behind bars. In fact, Scripture makes clear that our foe possesses fearsome spiritual powers and attacks the believing community both from the outside, using the principalities and powers of the world as his tools, and from the inside, employing false doctrine and unholy life-styles to erode the faith (Eph. 6).

Yet, God has set guards in place for His church, guards whose task is so difficult because the Enemy is so dangerous. Those guards are the elders of the church. They are the God-appointed protectors, the "watchers," the security men whose task is to serve God by defending and protecting what is most precious to Him—the lambs and sheep of His flock. Unlike a first century shepherd, who could sit upon a hillside and observe at once any dangers that threatened the flock, today's elders have to defend the members of the flock much more personally. To be sure, certain spiritual dangers afflict God's people as a corporate body. Yet in the diversity of our age and our culture, many of the corrupting powers of the Evil One attack individual believers and individual families and so demand individual guardianship. That's why I include these pages in the section on pastoral visiting. Guarding is a function of intimate pastoral care and attention and mandates your visiting your people where they live.

GUARD YOURSELVES

In the first place, you must watch out for yourself! Sound strange? Only if you forget that the real difference between a guard and an inmate is that the inmate was caught. All have broken God's law; all deserve His judgment.[1] Listen to these specific Scriptural warnings about *yourself*:

- He who guards his lips guards his life, but he who speaks rashly will come to ruin (Prov. 13:3).

- Hold on to instruction, do not let it go; guard it well, for it is your life (Prov. 4:13).

- Be on your guard against the yeast of the Pharisees, which is hypocrisy (Lk. 12:1).

- Watch out! Be on your guard against all kinds of greed (Lk. 12:15).

- Above all else, guard your heart, for it is the wellspring of life (Prov. 4:23).

---

1 Romans 3:10, 23; see also Acts 20:28.

I don't suspect I need say much about any of those warnings from Scripture. They are all abundantly clear. Each of them identifies a very real danger to our weak flesh. There is not a believer alive, elders included, who is not faced daily with the temptation to sin by means of a mouth run wild, with a heart full of greed or perverse desires, in two-faced hypocrisy, or with a know-it-all stubbornness that refuses instruction. No elder can defend God's people from such foes without having battle experience! God tells you; brother, these are problem areas. Watch it! Guard yourself! Be aware of your weakness, and find protection in the spiritual armor that God provides (Eph. 6:10ff.). Take strength from a diligent searching of Scripture, from prayer and from active and devoted faith.

GUARD THE FLOCK

After dealing with yourself, the shepherds of the flock of Christ are assigned the duty to guard the sheep and especially the lambs. Jesus used a graphic picture to describe His own loving work as the Good Shepherd when He says, "The good shepherd lays down his life for the sheep" (John 10:11). Speaking to a culture familiar with sheep-herding, Jesus painted a graphic mental picture of the circular pen, often constructed of thorny bushes, within which the flock would find nighttime protection from both thieves and wolves. There was only one gap in the circle, a "gate," and the shepherd would make his bed in that gap. He would literally "lay down" his life.

Such is the image that must compel those whom Jesus Christ now calls to be shepherds of His flock in His Name. Whatever it takes, even at the cost of your very life, you must defend His flock. Remember Acts 20:28ff?

> Keep watch over yourselves and all the flock of which the Holy Spirit has made you overseers. Be shepherds of the church of God which he bought with his own blood....Savage wolves will come in among you and will not spare the flock. Even from your own number men will arise and distort the truth in order to draw away disciples after them. So be on your guard!

Notice the enemies identified; wolves from without, and false teachers (heretics!) "from your own number." You as elders must be on guard against *both* doctrinal perversion and worldliness. To say it a bit differently, be alert to Satan's ploys to seduce God's people with money, temporary pleasure through sex or drugs, fame or prestige; but also be painfully aware that the person sitting next to you in church may be Satan's undercover agent to chip away at the foundation by substituting pleasant-sounding falsehood for the truth of Scripture. Frightening thought, but it's God's point in the text!

This warning really only calls you to be Scripturally realistic. Recognize that the heart is desperately wicked—and that means *every* heart. None are outside of the corrupting reach of sin, and that includes every believer too. Don't be surprised at sin you uncover or discover during personal meetings with fellow believers, even those you regarded highly. Remember that David, the "man after God's own heart, committed adultery and murder, and that Solomon, the wisest man that ever lived, lost all his wisdom trying to satisfy 600 wives and the demands of an earthly kingdom. And if this is true regarding believers, don't naively trust the world to be gentle and kind in its seduction; neighbors may be nice people, but they are desperately wicked people too. Assume as a matter of course that people and institutions are profoundly corrupted by sin, and expect them to show it. Know that Satan is real, and that his stratagems are cleverly devised.

GUARD THE GOSPEL

But the warnings to guard yourselves and to guard the flock can never be separated from the charge to guard the gospel. Listen to Paul's challenge to young pastor Timothy:

> What you heard from me, keep as the pattern of sound teaching...Guard the good deposit that was entrusted to you— guard it with the help of the Holy Spirit who lives in us (II Tim. 1:13-14).

Notice how Paul views the apostolic teaching as the pattern, the type, the paradigm for the work of "sound teaching"? That apostolic teaching is the foundation for the New Testament, the written Scriptures. That Scriptural Word is the sacred "trust," the "deposit" that the Church is to guard. Doing that "sound teaching" is the task of the NT church—of your churches!

This doesn't mean, as some think, that the church's first order of business is to jump with both feet into every frivolous dispute over words, haranguing and arguing all points, small and great, as if they were all principial gospel-defense issues. In fact, such is not the case; that specific sin receives stern warning in 2 Tim. 2:14. To lose sight of this warning would turn us all into volunteer fire fighters, running around with apologetic buckets, watering down every bit of smoke we think we see. We would never preach, teach, evangelize or disciple the flock.

But it does suggest that the church, and specifically the eldership of the church, must never allow challenges to Biblical Christianity to erode the integrity of the Biblical message. For example, guarding the gospel means not only affirming Scriptural teaching about the sanctity and permanence of marriage, but also actively confronting those who violate it through fornication, adultery or sexual perversity. And that doesn't just mean the preacher in the pulpit preaching strong sermons; it means you in homes looking people in the eye! Again, guarding the gospel means not only loudly affirming that we have a "high view of Scripture" (I never met anyone who claims to be a Biblical Christian who would admit to having a "low view of Scripture," did you?), but rather, actively defending against any teaching that calls into question straightforward belief and obedience to the historical integrity and clear teaching of specific texts. In our day and age, feminism has brought about such a challenge to many Pauline passages, and the scientific community has brought a challenge against the historicity of early Genesis. And again, I'm not thinking of this "guarding" as taking place within the pulpit, first and foremost, but as the face to face ministry of the Word of elders who visit among the people of God.

Whether or not we all have a "stomach for" such debates, such struggles, within our various congregations or denominations, one thing is clear; our task is to "guard the deposit," never to apologize for it nor to seek ways to make it less offensive to an unbelieving and hostile world. To guard the gospel effectively requires that you who are elders must be knowledgeable about the issues, yes, the theological issues of the day. And I know of no way of gaining such knowledge than by reading. Read magazines, read books, but most importantly, read your Bible. Read large portions at one sitting, then go back over that portion more carefully during the following week or so. Take notes; think through the arguments the Spirit uses; analyze and reflect. Then, and then only, will you be prepared to "guard" the deposit, for only then will it be in your possession.

In Summary

Guard yourselves, guard the flock, guard the gospel. An enormous challenge, I'll admit, but not a very complicated one. You see, all of what I've said really boils down to one basic truth: God establishes faith and preserves it through the words of Scripture;[2] if Satan will attack the church anywhere, it is at that point. Personal obedience to Scripture will be challenged; a Scripturally-structured and directed church body will be mocked; Scriptural teaching will be opposed at every turn as inconsistent with life in our modern world. God knows that Satan hasn't changed his tactics since Eden: "Did God really say..." (Gen. 3:1)?

Assignments for further work:

- Individually, or in discussion with other elders, make a list of what you together perceive to be the greatest dangers facing your particular congregation of believers. Try to be as specific as possible; rather than just saying "family difficulties," try to isolate the range of sins that are causing those family problems; men not assuming their God ordained roles? women dabbling in worldly feminism? greed that is corrupting communal standards and thus making Biblical family goals fuzzy? such an addiction to TV that there is no time for family devotions?

- From that list, develop an "action plan" for guarding the flock under your care. Identify key Scripture passages you would use to alert the people to each of the specific sins you observe. Determine how you would involve the children of the church under such active guardianship.

---

2 Review the striking truth of Rom. 10:14-17 and of I Peter 1:23-25. In both of these passages, and in many others, the remarkable and inseparable link between the inscripturated gospel text and living faith is established. Apart from the Word, and that *preached*, there can be no faith at all!

PLOTTING A VISITING STRATEGY

In the last chapters, we looked carefully at a succession of Biblical verbs to discover your duty to teach, encourage, rebuke, admonish and guard. I hope the sheer number of words didn't cloud the simplest point of all; *being an elder demands that you visit the homes of your people.* Visiting face to face with the members of the flock of Christ is a critical component of shepherding.

Having told you what the Bible says ought to be the focus of your visiting, I have one more point to make, and it has to do with the question of *how.* How do you schedule visits to people in their homes? What do you say when you first arrive? How often should you call on your people? How do you phrase your questions?

I remember my first "family visit." I had all kinds of confidence, being a 3rd year seminarian. That, of course, rapidly evaporated and became a case of cotton-mouth within 5 minutes of the start of the visit. I ran out of questions, then ran out of ideas, and finally, ran out of words. I looked at the wise elder who had accompanied me, terror in my eyes, and saw him smile knowingly. He took over, and taught me more in the next half hour than I'd learned about visiting from years of study. Perhaps you know the feeling. Maybe you're a newly elected elder, dreading your first visit. Or perhaps you're a victim of the influence of the business-model of the eldership, believing that elders "attend meetings" to fulfill their duties. Such an emphasis on visiting people in their homes may be a shocking reality check for you. The following ideas might help you.

IN THE BEGINNING...

Let's begin at the beginning, the first visit you make as a pastoral elder among the flock. Sometimes, the nature, the timing, and the urgency of such a visit are all decided for you by the circumstances of life. A pastor friend of mine received a phone call the morning after he moved to a new city and a new church, informing him that one of the members of the body had just committed suicide while in a state of deep depression. The first visit to the home of the family was anything but routine!

However, most elders won't face such pastoral crises ordinarily and routinely. Instead, they will face the pressures and struggles of the "normal" Christian life as they care for their people. So they will make "normal" visits which, of course, are anything but normal, since every believer and every home is unique, gifted with unique spiritual gifts, and beset by specific satanic trials and temptations. Yet, there is a commonness to it all, one referred to in I Cor. 10:13 where the Apostle says "no temptation has seized you except what is common to man." In the routine pastoral care of the people of God, a "normal" first visit is one in which your purpose must be to get to know the people of God who live there in all their uniqueness. By that I mean the important work of *familiarization*. Like a shepherd walks among sheep, learning their individual characteristics, markings, personalities and letting them get used to his peculiar smell, so the pastoral elder visits among the members of the church, learning their characters, their unique life circumstances, their household habits and values, their problems and how they solve them. And he spends enough time with them so they can begin to identify his "smell"—his pastoral style, concerns, heart and character.

Familiarization is critical. The sheep must know the shepherd before they will trust him. The shepherd must know the sheep before he can care for them wisely and lovingly. Familiarization is the goal for the initial visit to the homes of the people of God. Here are a few practical thoughts.

Before the visit, make sure you know the names of everyone in the home, especially the children. Evidence that you have tried to learn names is evidence that you care about them as individual people. It's a great first step. Also, pray with your visiting partner, if you have one, before you go to the door. Make sure your attitude, your spirit, your heart, is right before God. Check notes with him about any known concerns you may have, based on information reported to you, whether financial, spiritual, individual or family habits, spiritual patterns, and the like. But be careful not to be so colored by what you've heard about people that you are unable to listen to them. Pastoral prejudice is a dangerous business!

During the visit, be transparent. Open up; let them get to know who you are as a person, allow them to hear about your family, your testimony of faith in Christ and what it means to you to walk with Him, what you believe the Bible says an elder is to be, what your plans are for pastoral care in your district, and how they might fit in as active participants in the body of believers. But don't talk more than a few minutes about yourself. Rather, listen carefully to get to know them. Ask each to relate his/her spiritual history. Learn about their job(s), hobbies, school, favorite toys, family history, how they came to your church. Try to see into their heart, to discern their deepest commitments from their description of what's important to them. Above all, be honest and don't be shocked. They must learn you are a real person; you must not act as if their real-life circumstances are somehow beneath you. Far too often people view elders as super-Christians, and feel they can't bring real problems to them. Dispel that myth up front.

After the visit, make notes on what you said and heard, and try to identify what subjects or issues you think need further attention, which areas of their lives reveal sensitivity or hurt, what strengths they show that should be utilized in the service of the Lord. That initial assessment will obviously be tested for accuracy throughout the time of your pastoral care of them and may well be proven inaccurate; but it probably will serve you as a foundation of knowledge, useful for future visits and pastoral care.

LIKE CLOCKWORK: RETURN VISITS TO EACH HOME

At least yearly (and in this impersonal and fast-paced world, I believe more frequent visits are needed; in some homes, monthly or even weekly visits may be called for), you must return to that home. Consider it the pastoral equivalent of the annual physical examination. For most people, going to the doctor for a physical once a year is fine, although for someone who had cancer surgery last month, the doctor will want much more careful supervision. So too believers. When great crises pressure their hearts and lives, or where their spiritual immaturity opens them up to greater temptation, more frequent pastoral attention may be indicated. I recall one young believer whose elder called every Saturday night in the early year of his walk with Christ. Unless he received that pastoral attention and encouragement, he wavered before the attraction of the party life-style, and he failed to attend worship the next morning, for obvious reasons. Did his elder "baby him"? Of course! He was a baby! As he grew, he needed less attention; just then, he needed a lot. Determining just how frequent, is where pastoral wisdom and judgment comes into play. A few suggestions:

Before routine visits, *check your notes* about previous visits and observations you made then. Refresh your knowledge about their involvement in ministries you may be aware of, so as to encourage them in such ministry or rebuke them for non-exercise of their gifts in Christ's service. (Remember Eph. 4:11-12.) Again, as always, be diligent in prayer about them and about your visit among them.

Keep a clear focus. Unless you know of a specific issue that needs attention (a wayward child who just moved out of the house, marital problems, a death in the family, etc.), your aim should be simple; to understand whether God's Word is alive and functioning in their home, and to encourage them to live in it. As before, listen carefully to what they say, and observe any cues you can gather from interpersonal communication style. If you ask a series of questions of the husband, and the wife answers them all, something may be afoot. Likewise, if the wife is eager to speak with you about the grace and will of the Lord, and the husband won't turn off the ball game, there are some serious problems!

Some practical suggestions you may find helpful include:

1. Have the visit at the kitchen table or in the family room—a place where conversation is normal.

2. Generally, use open-ended questions, questions that cannot be answered with a "yes" or "no" answer but require more comprehensive response.

3. Here are a few open-ended questions and important pastoral subjects you might cover in such a visit to get you started:

   - *Not* "Do you have personal/family devotions?" *but* "Can you describe your *pattern* for Scripture reading and study and prayer as an individual, or as a family." (Try to learn these sorts of things: Is he/she/they in the Word daily? Are they careful and organized about their reading and prayer, or is their custom haphazard. Do they read through a book of the Bible? Do they read aloud with their children? Do they stimulate family discussions about what has been read? Are they sensitive to prayer requests from other household members? Do they discuss *answers to prayer?* What do parents pray for in their children's lives? Do the children pray for their folks? How? When do they read Scripture and pray? Early AM? Mealtimes? Use devotional guide? Does the marriage couple read and pray together? At what age do the parents encourage the children to start an active devotional life?)

- *Not* "Does God's Word shape your life-style in this family?" *but* "How do you believe your home is different than a non-Christian home?" (Be prepared to listen and to talk!)

- *Not* "Are you making good use of the armor of God listed in Ephesians 6?" *but* "What do you as parents believe is the greatest spiritual danger facing your children, and why?" (Be prepared to talk about television!) "What do you do when your own personal struggles with sin and temptation reveal that you have failed the Lord?"

- *Not* "Are you evangelistically-minded?" *but* "Is it difficult to share your faith in your neighborhood or at work?" "Are your neighbors Christians?"

- *Not* "Do you have any problems in our church?" *but* "In what ways has the ministry of our church been a blessing to you and your family? How are you involved as part of our ministry? In what areas do you think we can improve our faithfulness, and how so? How can the elders better serve you in your walk with Christ?"

- *Not* "What is your view of Christian marriage?" *but* "Tell me what you think of the view of marriage that TV portrays in programs like *Cosby, Roseanne, Thirty Something* (or some such)?" "How does that portrayal compare with what Scripture says in Eph. 5:21f.?"

- *Not* "Do you consider yourself a Christian?" (I never ask that question, since so many counterfeit definitions of the word abound.) *but* "The Bible teaches that we know a tree by its fruit. What's the fruit of your life? Does your life, your family, your marriage produce evidence that you are rooted in Christ?"

Obviously these are seed-questions and are not meant to be exhaustive. But I trust you get the point. You must seek to discover how God's Word functions in their lives. You must accordingly try to encourage them to exalt Christ and His Word more and more. That demands that you get specific, as these questions imply.

How About The Thorny Visits?

How about those visits where you appear at the door of one of God's people with a specific and difficult subject in mind? For example, a call to rebuke or admonish a brother or sister involved in some public sin, or a call to discuss children's lack of attendance or participation at the classes offered by the church for their nurture. Any guidelines here? Here are a few.

1. *Get to the point.* Of course, you must always be pleasant and exhibit Christian grace, but don't beat around the bush discussing the weather for long. Tell them within the first few minutes of sitting down that you are here to talk with them about the specific topic or issue on your heart.

2. *Be positive.* Always keep the purpose of the visit clear in your mind. You're there to minister grace and bring about reconciliation, not to judge, no matter how they may feel about your presence at first. Keeping your positive Biblical purpose in mind helps you overcome their natural tendency to react negatively. They may need to be called on the Biblical carpet about some sin for which they must repent; that does not mean that there isn't a positive purpose for such repentance! Keep that clear in your mind; make it clear in your communication as well.

3. *Remember who you are.* You may not appear cocky, arrogant, or abrasive. Such attitudes or behavior are not fitting for a representative of Christ, and are certainly hypocritical for a man who is, like them, weak and sinful. At the same time, you must not be lacking in courage or boldness. You come in Christ's Name; you must speak a Word from Him addressed to the people in their life situation. You are there to encourage and shape their discipleship; let them see that you are also a disciple; don't fail to read from the Bible, and always try to have them read along in theirs.

4. *Pray before and after the visit.* Your humble prayer demonstrates your dependence upon the One who sent you; additionally, it communicates that you don't have all the

answers, but depend upon His Spirit for grace and wisdom. Above all, God's people must know you pray for them.

5. *Try to summarize each meeting verbally at the end of the visit.* This may sound strange, but I mean it. Each visit will have accomplished something, even if only revealing stubborn unbelief! Make sure they understand what you understand. At the end, draw together the strings: "Now, we have agreed that Scripture requires that you must begin showing love differently to your wife than you've been doing. You promised to do so beginning today, right?" Or, "Let me understand clearly. You know the Bible calls your behavior adultery, and says that God calls you to honor your marriage because that pleases Him. Yet, you say you won't give up seeing your boyfriend no matter what?" Matt. 18:15 requires that you "show him his fault." You cannot leave the home without being confident that you have done so. A summary of common understanding is helpful.

A Smorgasbord of Strategies

Though all visits you make are pastoral in purpose, aimed at caring for God's flock, defending it from the wolves of the world, and leading it according to the Good Shepherd's voice, we've seen that not all visits can be made with the same approach. Generally, the *first visit* you make to a home in your pastoral area of responsibility has an introductory aim. The *routine* and regular visits you make may target specific issues or subjects, but all aim to discover whether or not God's Word is functioning as the fountain of faith and life in that home. Only open-ended questions will reveal that information. The *special* visit is more formal, more narrow in scope, more pointed. Treat it accordingly.

As we've noted above, in some ways, each congregation is unique; in other ways all of God's people are alike. They face the same kinds of spiritual struggles, the same sinful weaknesses, the same worldly pressures. All need the encouragement of the elders; all will need admonition; all will require a rebuke, if not from an elder, then certainly from other believers. In light of this reality, it is wise for the elders of the local church to have an overall strategy for visiting the whole flock. Such a strategy allows for a *macro-assessment* of the well-being of the congregation as a whole, and enables pastoral elders to interact and advise the preacher and teachers about specific spiritual needs that should be addressed in the pulpit and in the classroom.

Without going into too much detail, allow me to identify several strategies I've encountered in my years of pastoral ministry. None of these, by itself, will secure good and effective visiting. They are only *approaches* or *schedules*. However, they provide the benefit of scheduling accountability to elders who themselves are busy, forgetful, timid and yes, sinful men.

If the elders of the local church are wise and experienced men of God who can and will function as self-starters, a list of the sheep assigned to their district will be sufficient to stimulate their pastoral care. They can then report to the other elders about their overall assessment of the pastoral status quo of these members; they can consult with a partner for visits where a Biblical witness is required, or where another's advice about a particularly thorny pastoral problem would be welcome.[1]

If the elders need a jump start, and most do, the church may be able to provide that with an overall schedule for visits that will cover the entire district or congregation on an annual basis (adjust accordingly if more frequent visits are necessary). Consider the following examples:

- Some schedule visits one or two evenings every month, during which all elders participate. It is simply another "meeting" to attend, but is attended in the homes of the people rather than in the church building.

- Other churches schedule a concentrated period of 2 or 3 evenings in a given week for announced visits to members of the church. Most who operate this way do so quarterly, thus securing coverage of the entire congregation yearly.

---

[1] A word is in order about the practice of visiting in *teams*. In many churches, *all* elder visits are expected to be team visits, that is, visits made by at least 2 elders. In others, both elders and deacons are assigned a district, and so elder-deacon teams visit together. I have often encouraged elders, on the contrary, to make visits alone, believing it much easier to coordinate two schedules than three. Further, I do not believe it Biblically required that all such visits are to be done by teams. The practice originated most likely from the Old Testament requirement that in judicial cases, things be settled at the testimony of two or three witnesses. That's the origin behind Jesus' instruction in Matt. 18:16 (referring to Deut. 19:15) to "take one or two others along" when visiting a sinner who will not repent upon first rebuke. But that specific situation is not the norm in every pastoral visit. When visiting to encourage, for example, no potential Biblical "judicial case" is involved, and so formal witnesses are not needed for every word. An elder must understand himself free, in such a situation, to visit alone.

- One church I know gives such visibility to its pastoral visiting ministry that they cancel all instructional classes and other church mid-week meetings for a two-week period, and schedule pastoral elder visits to the homes of the members during both afternoon and evening sessions every day of those two weeks. The elders go out two by two until the entire congregation is seen. At the end of the two weeks, several things are shown to be true. *First*, all the elders are bone-weary. *Second*, all the elders are spiritually refreshed by the evidence of the Spirit's work among the people of God. *Third*, the people of God have been reminded, once again, of God's wonderful and tender care provided them by the eldership of the church. *Finally*, the elders have gained insight into the spiritual condition of the flock and perspective on the health of all its members. They've learned where weaknesses exist, and where special attention is needed.

Any of these suggestions can be abused, or used, but with sterile administrative efficiency and without pastoral warmth. Such would be sad, for it would foster a formalistic attitude toward the urgent pastoral care Christ desires His flock receive. But the potential abuse does not make the ideas bad ones; the elders of each local church body best know the circumstances and needs of the flock under your care. Here's the point; *however* you do the work, make sure you visit all the sheep regularly and with pastoral purpose. The church will benefit immeasurably.

Point: however you do the work, make sure you visit all the sheep regularly and with pastoral purpose. The church will benefit immeasurably.

Of course, "sanctified common sense" dictates that there are certain situations in which a visiting partner is a wise addition, even where there is no formal judicial case requiring multiple witnesses. For example, an elder will be wise never to visit a single woman alone. Not only must he be aware of the potential damage to reputations (both hers and his) of wagging tongues, but he must also be aware of the danger of temptation to his and her flesh. No elder is beyond such temptation himself; any who thinks he is, is either naive or spiritually arrogant. I also believe it wise for elders ordinarily not to visit with children alone. Children are, by definition, immature; they may not understand the counsel given, may easily confuse what was said and may report the conversation inaccurately. Many real problems have risen because an elder's Biblical counsel to a child was twisted in the retelling, and the original problem escalated far beyond the immediate and threatened, in escalated form, to jeopardize the entire family, the elder and ultimately, the entire congregation.

The Shepherd's Hand

Section Three:
Biblical Discipline
The Ministry of Accountability

Church Membership - Committed to Follow A Recognized Voice

Items appearing on the elder's meeting agenda:

- *Bill and Carol White request we send their papers to Grace Church in Cleveland.*
- *Transfer papers of Mr. and Mrs. Wallace received from Christian Fellowship Church, Chandler, AZ.*
- *Herman Stijfkop demands we send his membership papers to his home on the grounds that he won't hold membership in any church that uses the NIV Bible.*

Do churches really send and receive "papers"? To be sure, churches use forms to "transfer" members, and those forms are printed on paper, but some churches do not believe in "memberships,"[1] and even in those churches that do, transfers to or from some churches in other denominations is often not permitted by denominational regulations. And how about that growing percentage of people who attend one church for its Sunday worship services, enjoy fellowship in a small group at another church, and take the kids to a regular Wednesday evening youth program at yet a third congregation? Are they "members" of any? According to several church growth experts and sociological-religious pundits, this phenomenon is on the increase; there appears to be a diminishing "brand loyalty"[2] with respect to local church membership, and it is joined

---

[1] A large and well-known congregation in Dallas with roots in the Plymouth Brethren movement distributes pamphlets in its "tract rack" that argue against the very *concept* of membership in local churches as being unbiblical. The pamphlet also speaks against local churches holding membership in denominations. Several people who attended that congregation for many years recently began to attend the church I serve; they wrestled for a long time with our understanding of membership. Quite a few have still not "joined."

[2] Among them is George Barna of the Barna Research Group, Ltd., in *The Barna Report 1992-93* (Ventura, CA: Regal Books, 1992) p. 94.

hand in hand with the decline of loyalty to denominational entities.

If you haven't faced these questions and their attendant problems yet in your local setting, hang on. You will. Such is the nature of our age, as the baby boomers—the independentistic, bottom-line oriented generation—continues to exert leadership. This age doesn't "join" things; it "grazes" from one pasture to another, enjoying the benefits of all without commitment to any. In the Dallas church I serve as pastor, we know this phenomenon well; fully 30% of our active and participating "members" are not members. We are working with them toward the *goal* of committed membership; we can not make formal membership a *prerequisite* for involvement.

In what follows I present some foundational principles about church membership to guide you in your local church discussion and practice concerning these matters. Being Biblical and clear about this matter of membership is important especially for pastoral reasons. If membership implies a level of commitment, membership is essential for effective pastoring to take place - both on the part of the elder and that of the "member." In fact, it will be my argument, that central to "membership" is this willing commitment of the individual believer to follow a "recognized voice"- elders whom he knows and can trust to minister faithfully and lovingly the Word of the Good Shepherd.

BIBLICAL PRINCIPLES OF MEMBERSHIP

Principle #1 *Membership in the local church is the visible expression of belonging to Christ; conversely, one cannot appropriately consider him/herself to belong to Christ if he/she does not belong to Christ's church in a formal way.*

Some of you who read this are probably sitting bug-eyed with indignation: "How dare you equate membership in a group of sinful people with the faith bond that unites me with my Savior? My relationship with Christ is direct, by faith. My relationship with a church is voluntary, a *result* of the relationship with Christ, not a component of it!" Indeed, if that is your position, you are in the majority of American Christendom. You are also wrong.

Now before you become incensed, let me explain. I know where you are coming from; most evangelical Christians today are more influenced *negatively* by the errors of the Roman Catholic view of the church than they are *positively* by Scripture. They are so determined to avoid the notion that the church *saves*, or even that the church *dispenses* salvation, that they fail to understand the church's role both in the Kingdom of God and in the life of the redeemed. Fact is, while Scripture doesn't use the word "member" very often to describe the relationship between the believer and the church, it does use a wide variety of word pictures that are most instructive.

Consider Luke 8:21. In it, Jesus identifies his "mother and brothers," his "family," as those who hear the Word and do it. From such a passage we appropriately refer to the church as the "family of God." But if the church is truly family, the implication is inescapable that there is no other way for fellowship with the Father than to be part of the Father's family, to sit at the Father's table, to hear and obey the Father's Word. Family privilege depends upon family membership.

Or consider John 10. In this extended metaphor, Jesus identifies His people as the "sheep of his pasture," the flock of the Good Shepherd. He makes clear that the flock will not follow a stranger's voice, but that they will follow His voice because they recognize it. Again, the implication is clear that the people of God, later in Scripture always called the "church," are the assembly of those who claim Jesus as their Shepherd and King. The point is unmistakable; you cannot, you may not, claim to follow Him without recognizing that by that very claim you identify yourself with His flock. If you have learned anything from this volume, you have learned that God Himself extends the analogy of shepherd and flock throughout the New Testament, and especially to the character of the office of elder. Bottom line? If you refuse to belong to a local church, submitting yourself to the care of Christ's shepherding elders, you deny that you are part of the flock, and thus in fact cut yourself off from contact with the Good Shepherd who leads His flock by that means.

Or again, consider I Cor. 12. In this extended metaphor, the church is clearly described as a "body" with the members identified as body "parts." Indeed, the passage is most instructive regarding the appropriate assessment and use of the gifts of God's people who are "members of the body." Yet one of the most significant implications of the word picture Christ uses in this passage is often completely ignored; one cannot be united to the Head, who is

Jesus Christ, unless he is part of the body! A finger severed from the hand may, for a while, be recognizable as a finger. But it certainly will not function, it will not take direction, it will not accomplish any active movement. In short, it won't *be* a finger, and it won't even look like one for long. So it is with a believer. Cut off from the Body known as the church and functioning with all the divine gifts given to her, the believer will make the sounds a believer makes, may even look like a Christian. But without the encouragement, the support, the interaction and sharing of all the gifts, without the mutual accountability the church fellowship provides, and without the nourishment of the preaching of the Word and the Sacraments, no individual believer can stand alone for long. Doctrinally he is too vulnerable to corrupting heresy; in his lifestyle he is too open to temptation. The enemy's power is too great to face alone. That's why Heb. 10:25 enjoins us, "Let us not give up meeting together, as some are in the habit of doing...."

There are several other New Testament images of the church; the temple of the Holy Spirit (I Cor. 3:16, where "you" is here a plural; distinct from I Cor. 6:19 where it is a singular form); the holy nation where God's people are "citizens," the "members of God's household," and the building whose component bricks are "built on the foundation of the apostles and prophets with Christ Jesus Himself as the chief cornerstone" (all of these are from Eph. 2:19-20). Without offering an extended analysis of these and many other images, I believe the point is clear. If it is unbiblical to view the church as savior, as the church of Rome does, it is equally as wrong to minimize her role in the life of the believer. It is simply a fact that in Scripture, the believer's relationship to Christ is inseparably connected with his relationship to Christ's church. To say it a bit differently, while salvation is not "by the church," it is Biblically true to say that "since this holy assembly and congregation is the gathering of those who are saved...there is no salvation apart from it.[3]"

In summary, membership in the local church is non-negotiable. On the one hand it is functionally crucial to the life of faith; on the other, failure to belong formally to it is disobedience to the pattern of the Lord.

---

3 So confess the Reformation churches in Art. 28 of the *Belgic Confession of Faith*, written in 1566 and embraced by many churches the world over since that time.

Principle #2 *The Scriptural notion of membership is that the individual/ family expresses willing submission to the spiritual authority of the local eldership* (Heb. 13:7,17; cf. Acts 20:28ff.).

While the Acts 20:28ff passage tells you a great deal about what elders are to be for the church, the Heb. 13:7 and 17 verses tell you a great deal about what and how the members are to think about their pastoral elders. God has established a pastoral "chain of command." Consider: When someone becomes a member, he acknowledges that Christ's authority over him is real, that it encompasses both the content of his faith (doctrine) and the living of his life (practice), and that the authority of Christ is visible and is entrusted to the men we call the elders of the local church. To *belong* is to surrender to the Head of the Church, Jesus Christ, Who is represented by the elders that shepherd or pastor the people of God. It is these men who will hold each member accountable in faith and life; God will, in turn, hold each of them accountable for that responsibility (Heb. 13:17). This is the Biblical way.

Principle #3 *Members belong to the local church; local churches (may) belong to a denomination.*

Sounds obvious, even simplistic, to some; sounds like heresy to others. Let me explain. No matter where I belong, if I leave to attend another church, even if it is within the same denominational federation, I must "request a transfer" to that church. It may sound a bit secretarial or perfunctory; it is most certainly not. The importance of this action is understood only in light of the previous principle. One is a member of a church when he or she has been taken under the pastoral care and responsibility of the local eldership. When that person relocates, he or she has an obligation to inform the elders, who must give account to God for their care. For example, as you read this, you are not under the care of the elders in Dallas but under the care of those local shepherds of God who are responsible for your pastoral care in the church you attend. Should you choose to move here, you will not automatically be a member of this church, even if you have been a member of another church in the same denomination. Instead, you must "transfer" from your home church to this new one. Such a principle is crucial to loyalty to the local church, and avoids the prevalent sin of looking at the local congregation merely as a "franchise" of the denomination. That in turn leads to principle four.

Principle #4 *"Transferring membership" means requesting release from the care of the elders of one church, and a self-conscious submission of the* *individual or family to the pastoral care and responsibility of the eldership of another church.*

"Papers" don't transfer, people do. Membership transfer is not a secretarial matter, it is a pastoral one. It is not superficial and unnecessary, but is profoundly significant for both church and individual to recognize the way Christ cares for and governs His people. Churches must take seriously the commitment they make when they receive members. They must also take seriously the duty to "release" people wisely, pastorally, and in such a way that the new body of elders understands the unique requirements that may exist for effective pastoral care of the individuals concerned.

Principle #5 *Membership involves doctrinal commitment.*

If I choose to submit myself to the care of the elders of a Baptist church, I ought to expect to be pastored according to their confession and practice, and challenged and rebuked if I chafe under their teaching. Likewise, if I place myself under the care of a body of Reformed or Presbyterian elders, I must expect them to pastor me in accordance with their understanding of Scripture and their commitments to the Reformed creeds. By definition, all churches believe something and thus embrace creedal standards; either those creeds are written and visible, or they are unwritten and assumed. In every case, they function to shape the beliefs and practice of the congregation. Membership with integrity involves both doctrinal awareness and a commitment to doctrinal standards.

Principle #6 *Membership is a visible testimony of commitment to other members.*

By this I mean, in light of Eph. 4:11-12 and I Cor. 12 (among other passages) that each believer is called to commit his/her gifts and talents to the service of the Lord. Membership in the local church is a visible pledge to use your gifts among that body of believers, to pray for them, to encourage them, to rebuke them, to forgive them, and to fulfill the rest of the "one another" commands of the Bible. Local membership also implies your promise to do all these things among this specific local community of believers. The member must know that he/she is part of *this* body of Jesus Christ, and pledge to function within it.

So What?

One task remains, and that is to explain what all this means for you practically on the local church level. I've already hinted at it in several points: *take membership very seriously.* Do not treat membership issues superficially, as mere "correspondence" to be relegated to that point in your agenda where it will be handled with all the passion of "received for information." Instead, make all membership decisions *pastoral ones.*

- When you *receive* someone into your church family, ask each person who requests membership, irrespective of their point of origin, to meet with your elders for conversation about their faith and life, their gifts and commitments, your church and its methods of pastoral care, its goals and vision, etc. Make sure you know them, and they know you. The pastoring required of you in I Peter 5:1-4 and Acts 20:28ff. demands no less.

- When you as elders deal with God's people, don't jeopardize their relationship with the local church by treating that relationship lightly. It is easy to say or do something that drives people away from a local body of believers, and implies that they ought to "go someplace else where they fit in." To be sure, a person's doctrinal differences with a local congregation may require that he or she affiliate with another congregation; integrity may demand such action. Yet, some elders seem to operate with a hardnosed and chilling ruthlessness: "You don't like the way we do things around here? Tough. Cork it or leave!" Sensitive pastoral care looks for ways to bring the sheep and lambs in, not to put them out of the fold. Remember that the Lord's church is not like an aisle in the supermarket where different brands provide taste options. Jeopardizing someone's relationship to the local church through pastoral insensitivity may well jeopardize significantly their relationship with the church's Head. That's something you don't want on your head.

- When you *release* someone from your care, do so with integrity. Write a letter to the next body of elders concerning the individual or the family you are releasing into their care. Inform them of spiritual gifts available for ministry, of special pastoral needs, of a history of difficulties. Moving from church to church has become for many the American way of avoiding spiritual accountability. We must not be part of that problem; we must seek instead to be part of the pastoral solution.

- When people join your congregation, make a big deal of it! Develop a "membership covenant" that states publicly the privileges and responsibilities of membership. Have folks sign it in front of the congregation. Introduce them to the congregation, talk of their gifts and willing service, and get them involved soon in congregational ministry. To fail to "kill the fatted calf" is to minimize the importance of local membership, and to flirt with a superficial "bean counter" approach to the flock of the Good Shepherd.[4] Don't ever forget the point of the Parable of the Prodigal (Lk. 15). The problem with the elder son was his refusal to celebrate! God rejoices in the finding of the lost. We must too!

---

4 Here in Dallas, a dear friend insisted upon such celebration, and so developed an annual Harvest Fest. Held in autumn each year, it celebrates the eternal harvest of new believers, new members and transformed lives over the last 12 months. We hear wonderful testimonies, introduce new people to the body, and thus encourage effective evangelists among the flock.

Church Discipline - Face To Face With the Word!

The great Reformation theologian, John Calvin, identified three "marks" by which one could identify a true and Biblical church from a false one. The first is that a Biblical church offers preaching that is faithful to the Bible. The second is that a true church celebrates sacraments according to what the Bible teaches about sacraments, both in terms of the number of them and in the manner of the celebration. Finally, said Calvin, a true church administers church discipline of its members according to the Bible.

I can almost hear the gaskets popping. "Discipline? You've got to be kidding. That's the antithesis of Christian love, the opposite of the gospel instead of the outworking of the gospel!"

It really isn't, you know. Jesus on several occasions spoke of the "keys of the kingdom," and no matter what you might think keys do, one thing is certain; they lock and unlock doors. For Jesus to entrust the "keys of the kingdom of heaven" to men like His disciples (in Matt. 16:19 Peter is specifically named; in John 20:22-23 the same sacred trust, albeit without the term "keys," is assigned to the eleven remaining disciples) *at the very least* implies that, in some way, their oversight of the flock of God involves an authoritative opening or closing of the door of entry. In John 20:23 and Matt. 18:18 this is further identified with "forgiving" or "retaining" sins. That, folks, implies authoritative discipline, no matter what else you may read into it.

Let me put it another way. If Jesus takes His own Word seriously, and of course He does, He also expects us to take it seriously. Any church that preaches the life-giving Word of God (what I Peter 1:23-25 actually calls the seed of regeneration) and then fails to follow up on that Word, fails to insist upon obedience and the doing of what was heard, doesn't really believe what it preaches, does it?

That's why Calvin called discipline an essential mark of Biblical vitality. The flip side of faithful preaching; it is nothing other than the ministry of accountability in which the elders hold the people of God accountable to put into practice in their own lives the Word they have heard and profess to believe.

I'm under no illusions about the ease of my task as I appeal in this chapter for a restoration of the practice of church discipline. There are several potholes in this road these days, real kidney busters at that. For one, we are living in relativistic times, when "live and let live" is the byword of our culture and when many believe any discipline—even parental—is arrogant interference with personal rights. In such times, applying discipline takes courage. For another thing, we live in litigious times; recent lawsuits have resulted in courts deciding against churches that disciplined their members, awarding large settlements to the litigants. Maybe you haven't faced it in your church, but I've heard those chilling words with my own ears: "Leave me alone or I'm going to sue." It's enough to give any elder the cold sweats.[1] Finally, we live in individualistic times, in which the sad truth is that other churches probably won't honor your process of discipline anyway, and members merely transfer from one church to another merely to dodge discipline. I repeat what I said earlier. The road isn't smooth; steering around these potholes we face two choices; drop discipline from our practice because it "won't work" in our age anyway, or review what the Bible says; crank up our faith and courage and get to work, trusting that it is the Lord's will to honor in heaven what His servants do in faith on earth. I propose the latter.

In this chapter, I take you on a brief tour of the responsibility of faithful churches to Biblical church discipline. My purposes are several; to review the Biblical *grounds* for discipline, to inquire into the Biblical *methods*, all while keeping in mind the Biblical *purpose*. Finally, the point is to help you, the elders of the local church, fulfill your pastoral task. So the chapter will conclude with suggestions to guide you in some of the practical aspects of a method for church discipline.

---

1 For a compelling and chilling tale of the cost of commitment to Biblical church discipline despite the cost of litigation see Chuck and Donna McIlhenny and Frank York: *When the Wicked Seize a City*, (Author's Choice Press: 2000).

FOR THE CHURCH'S SAKE

If you've been awake during the last hundred pages or so, you know I believe the office of elder is pastoral (shepherding) in character. Pastoral elders are told in Acts 20:28ff. to "keep watch over the flock," to defend it from wolves, and to be "on guard" against those who distort the truth. These pastoral duties articulated in the book of Acts present nothing new, but merely develop Jesus' earlier commission to Peter in Matt. 16:18f.:

> I tell you that you are Peter (petros), and on this rock (petra) I will build my church...I will give you the keys of the kingdom of heaven; whatever you bind on earth will be bound in heaven, and whatever you loose on earth will be loosed in heaven.

In an earlier chapter, I pointed out that the defense of the flock was to be carried out on two fronts. The Enemy would attack from outside the flock, as a wolf on the prowl. But the Enemy would also corrupt from within. Clearly such internal corruption involves doctrinal deviation—"teachers will rise up." Just as clearly, it can and often does involve the "yeast" of ethical failure. Defending the flock must involve protection on both fronts; in fact Scripture provides clear instructions concerning each. In Paul's first letter to pastor Timothy, he reminds him that he will face "deceiving spirits" who will corrupt good doctrine (4:1). Timothy's pastoral obligation in face of such error? He is to "command and teach" sound doctrine (4:11) and he is to carry out the difficult work of *discipline* among various groups of people (several groups are detailed in ch. 5). On the other front, Paul in I Cor. 5 addresses a grievous and public ethical sin in the body of believers. His apostolic solution is to exercise formal discipline, announced so sternly that it shocks the tender ears of modern readers: "...hand this man over to Satan, so that the sinful nature may be destroyed and his spirit saved on the day of the Lord" (I Cor. 5:5). Now, while I will leave for another time a more comprehensive analysis of what this verse means, I draw your attention to the next one, where Paul explains the reason for such a stern approach. *If discipline is not enforced, if public sin is not purged, the yeast will corrupt the whole body of believers!*

IN PURSUIT OF HOLINESS

> *You're not a bunch of holy freaks, are you? I'm not looking for a church that's full of holy freaks. I want to go to church with normal*

people, people kinda like me, people who know they gotta get right with God 'cause they messed up last weekend, drank too much, you know... I wouldn't feel at home with holy freaks. (The words of Ken, a drop-in visitor to a Sunday morning church service.)

The preservation of the church is not the only issue at stake in the matter of discipline. The holiness of God and the holiness of God's people are also in the crosshairs. I recently reread R. C. Sproul's *The Holiness of God*.[2] His treatment of the holy majesty of our God gripped me once again with the same sense of awe and humility that gripped me the first time I read it. But I was frustrated too. The world we live in simply doesn't have a clue. I guess we shouldn't expect that it would; the words of Ken, quoted above, express the world's notion of holiness rather accurately; it's weird, unnatural, out-of-the-ordinary and describes people who are spiritually arrogant, who think they're better than the rest of us.

Yet God makes abundantly clear that He expects, even *demands*, that His people be holy because He is holy.[3] In the Old Testament, *holiness* had two connotations; separation and purity. *Purity* is a concept most of us understand; God wanted His people to avoid moral defilement, not to be corrupted with sin. Sin was to be dealt with through cleansing sacrifice. But *separation* is a notion we tend to struggle with. Throughout the book of Leviticus, for example, you find strange (to our ears) commands like "do not mate different kinds of animals" and "do not plant your field with two kinds of seed" and "do not wear clothing woven of two kinds of material" (Lev. 19:19). In graphic and tangible ways, God was identifying His people as separate/holy, to be kept unmixed with the world. They were not to intermarry, to worship other gods, or otherwise to interweave their covenant lives with the practices, values and people of the cities and regions in which they would live. And to press home the point, specific "separateness" commands were articulated which applied to plants, animals and even cloth—dimensions of Israel's daily life that reflected the divine principle of holiness. Just as hybridization of animals could lead to the breeding of animals that were mutants or sterile, Israel would cease to be fruitful and productive in the service of the Lord were she to inter-

---

2 Sproul, RC, *The Holiness of God* (Wheaton, IL: Tyndale House Publishing, Inc., 1986)

3 I Peter 1:15; see also Leviticus 11:44-45; 19:2; 20:7. Holiness, not merely as a theological concept but as a mark of life, is the theme of the book of Leviticus.

weave her life with pagans around her. The "life principle" of each would be violated.[4]

Modern believers find the concept of separation difficult. After all, even though we are not to be "of the world," we are most certainly "in it," aren't we? Some may wonder if I'm advocating widespread acceptance of the Amish model. I'm not. Holy separation is neither that easy nor that clean. It's hard work that requires wisdom and discernment. Let me give you an example. I recall that, as a child, our "house rules" for Lord's Day observance (my parents' attempt to "Keep the Sabbath day *holy*") involved permission to watch little TV. The only exception: *Lassie*. Trivial and hairsplitting? Perhaps. One could argue for throwing TV sets in the dumpster. Yet even that doesn't insulate our eyes and ears from the world. No, my folk's answer may not have been faultless, but it was nonetheless a serious attempt to instill in four rambunctious boys a set of values, a practice of "separation" from the world, which, even then, was assaulting our eyes and ears through the TV. And we need more of the same today.

All the above leads me to a most practical and pastoral point. *Elders are men charged with the pursuit of holiness in the church on both fronts: purity and separation from the world!* If you don't have the holiness of God's people centered in the crosshairs of your ministry aim, you will never hit the target of your duties before the Lord. Read a couple of passages with me before going on.

> I urge, then, first of all, that requests, prayers, intercession, and thanksgiving be made for everyone—for kings and all those in authority, *that we may live peaceful and quiet lives in all godliness and holiness* (I Tim. 2:1-2, emphasis added).

> Our fathers disciplined us for a little while as they thought best; but God disciplines us for our good, *that we may share in his holiness*...Make every effort to live in peace with all men and to be holy; *without holiness no one will see the Lord*. See to it that no one misses the grace of God and that no bitter root grows up to cause trouble and defile many. See to it that no one is sexually immoral, or is godless like Esau... (Heb. 12:10, 14-16, emphasis added).

The first of these is from Paul's pastoral letter to Timothy. This little letter, along with its counterpart, comprises a masterful train-

---

[4] Noordtzij, A., *Bible Student's Commentary: Leviticus* (Grand Rapids: Zondervan Publishing House, 1982), p. 201.

ing course for pastoral elders. Already in the beginning of the first letter the Apostle makes clear to young pastor Timothy that the focus of his work as a pastor is to be on praying and laboring to shape a people marked by *godliness and holiness*.

That's also the point of the second passage. Holiness is marked by *discipline*. That is to say, elders who care about holiness will actively pursue it, correcting that which is worldly and calling the people of God to separate from that which is impure. Holiness is not merely a *nice* character trait, but it is a *necessity* for those who would see God. The inspired writer goes so far as to say "without holiness no one will see the Lord"! Think about that for yourself. Think about that for your people. Holiness is nonnegotiable!

How do elders pursue holiness? In general, of course, all discipleship, all correction, every rebuke, every admonition, is directly related to the pursuit of holiness. But in the Hebrews passage cited above, several specific principles are suggested that are worthy of your reflection.

- *Holiness is destroyed by the "bitter root" (v. 15).* Look closely at this verse. The author sets over against each other the *grace* of God on the one hand and the *bitter root* on the other. Using an agricultural metaphor, he paints the picture that just as a weed's root can spread far and wide and obstruct the good harvest, so the spirit of bitterness is an evil that will obstruct God's gracious work and undermine holiness. God's people must be *separated* from such a spirit, and they must be *pure* in their attitudes toward God and one another. In human life, a sin unresolved awakens bitterness. Bitterness takes root, and once deeply rooted opposes the working of grace. (The same principle appears in Eph. 4:26-27, where we are commanded not to "let the sun go down" on our anger, lest we "give the devil a foothold.") Do you know people who are bitter about their station in life, their finances or God's provision to them? Do you know folks who are jealous of the blessings of others, angry and bitter against the Lord because the pastors of the church have had to rebuke them (instead of letting sin "slide")? As elders, entrusted with the pursuit of holiness, you cannot afford to let such bitterness go unchecked. You must expose bitterness for what it is; the antithesis of grace, a root that will grow to "cause trouble and defile *many*." You must not wait for such folks to "settle down"; you must proactively confront such a spirit of wickedness. If you do not, you will have a much greater harvest of sinful weeds to deal with later on.

- *Sexual immorality is often the first evidence of a lack of holiness (v. 16).* You almost get the impression from reading the New Testament that it was directed specifically at our sex-crazed generation. Passages about sexual sin appear in virtually every NT book; so too in our society, implicit (if not explicit!) sex shows up everywhere you look. TV is sexualized in its content, and aggressively so; what was censored only a decade ago now appears without warning on prime time programming. Advertising uses sex to sell; clothing drapes (more accurately exposes) bodies suggestively. Restaurants use sex to beef up clientele (ever hear of the *Hooters* chain?). People who have no sense of the holiness of God or of holy living know something is wrong, but in their ignorance think the only way they can "help" is by pleading for "safe sex," instead of for holiness. Let's not be naive; in such a world, the people of God will face increasing temptation to sin sexually. That's what makes this passage so important; God's people must be marked by a *separation* from sexually sinful influences, and they must be sexually *pure*. Where sin has been committed, heartfelt repentance must be swift and genuine, and the sin must be stopped. Where someone is dabbling in titillating and tempting reading or viewing material, separation must be established. And it is the elders who are entrusted with accountability in these things, calling the youth clearly and frequently to sexual abstinence before marriage, calling those who are older to fidelity and purity within marriage, and calling all to separate from the world's fatal attraction with recreational sex.

- *Holiness involves heart-priorities (v. 16b).* The mention of Esau, who "for a single meal sold his birthright," is no accident. The presence or absence of holiness is revealed by the heart-priorities of the people of God. As Esau exposed his heart when he showed what meant most to him, so God's people reveal their hearts every time they make choices in life. The question is simple; do your choices reveal purity of heart and resistance to sin, or duplicity of heart and acceptance of sin? Unfortunately, elders often look in the wrong place, attempting to legislate holiness by micromanaging the exterior details of ethical obedience. It is easy to slip into a "moral policeman" mode, challenging people who drink a beer now and again, or chasing down rumors about "so and so" who was reputedly seen with "such and such." You would do better to spend your time and focus your energy on the heart, a much deeper quest. When you visit in the homes of your people, inquire about their goals and choices; observe from what is visible and infer from what is implied just where the individual or family puts the focus of their living. Look around you at what they have. Ask about their use of time. Talk about the TV and how it functions in their home and lives. Challenge them if it looks like they have misplaced priorities. Fight for God's people! Don't let people "sell out" like Esau did; don't let them grab for the here and now and lose sight of the eternal. Remember Jesus' words: "...where your treasure is, there will your heart be also" (Matt. 6:21).

AIMING AT REPENTANCE

If it is fair to speak of church (elder-applied) discipline as being for the sake of the church and for the honor of the Lord, it is incomplete to say only these things. Clearly (and for pastoral elders, *essentially*) discipline is, according to Scripture, intended to bring about repentance in the sinner, so that he/she will be reconciled to God and to God's church. Consider Matt. 18:15f. In this extraordinary passage, about which so much should be said, I will restrain myself (!) and make only a couple of observations.

First of all, the *procedure* commanded is so obvious as to need little comment beyond the observation that, should such a procedure be followed as a matter of course within the church, the vast majority of gossip and slander cases that undermine the unity of local churches would be substantially reduced.

Second, note the link between the formal process of discipline prescribed and the "binding" and "loosing" of sins described in verse 18. The point is clear; what the church forgives because of genuine repentance, God forgives (loosed; all legal claims are satisfied). Likewise, what the church declares not forgiven (still bound to the sinner, not satisfied by confession and repentance), God will not forgive. This is an extraordinary truth, one that those who resist the notion of church discipline ignore at great peril. It is God's very intention to bind Himself to the actions of those who speak in His name. To ignore this is to dismiss one of God's principal ways of dealing with sin among His people.

Third, please note that it is in regard to *this* issue - discipline through a process involving mutual responsibility and legal witnesses - and *not* in regard to small gatherings of worship or prayer, that Jesus says "where two or three come together in my name, there am I with them." In other words, He is not here promising His presence in worship services, but is granting instead His authorization to and approbation of the discipline work of the church!

In sum, Jesus authorized discipline, commands certain procedures for specific cases, and assured His church that He will "bind" Himself to their legal ("two or three witnesses" suggests nothing less) disciplinary pronouncements. But now, the point. Verse 17 is the key. At the "end" of the process of discipline, Jesus charges the church to treat the unrepentant sinner "as you would a pagan or a tax collector." What does He mean? Many interpret these words as establishing "the ban," the practice of the church to cut off all contact with the unrepentant in order to make them feel the pain of loneliness and the hurt of being shunned. Sorry to mess with such an interpretation, even if it is your understanding of "excommunication" or "disfellowshiping," but such a view of discipline is nonsense. What was Jesus' (and therefore His disciples') approach to pagans or tax collectors? Witness! Evangelism! He ate with them and associated with them so visibly that the religious leaders of the Jews blew a gasket (Matt. 9:10-11; 11:19). He told the Jews "I have not come to call the righteous, but sinners." His practice shows us precisely what it means to treat those under discipline as pagans and tax collectors. It is not to "ban" them, but to recognize that they are not part of the family of God, and thus cannot be expected to possess the grace and Spirit that the Father gives His children. Their sinful behavior, and especially their refusal to repent of their sins, has proven that they are really *not* "in the family circle" of faith. Therefore we change our approach because they have revealed their true stripes. We are to evangelize them, and employ Biblical strategies of evangelism, because we may no longer assume them to be among the redeemed. In fact, we are to assume that they are lost, desperately in need of the Savior.

You will find the same emphasis in I Cor. 5:5: "...hand this man over to Satan" sounds extraordinarily harsh, that is, until you read the next word, "so that the sinful nature may be destroyed *and his spirit saved on the day of the Lord.*" How in the world can one's spirit be saved if he has been "handed over to Satan"? You must understand that in the Bible, the church is viewed as the dominion, the realm or regime, of Christ. That which is outside of it Jesus calls "the realm of darkness." In John 16:11, He actually refers to Satan as "the prince of this world." This is what He had in mind. Jesus' entire earthly ministry was to declare "the kingdom is at hand," to announce a new regime, and then to reveal the dimensions of that regime as He cast out demons who represented the "old regime," and healed the sick from the effects of sin and its power. Make no mistake about it; Jesus' coming inaugurated a battle of kingdoms which His resurrection, ascension, and heavenly reign conclude with triumph; a victory already begun, but not yet finished.

Is such disciplinary work, such a firm assessment and radical declaration like "hand over to Satan," consistent with pastoral goals? Indeed, such work is important *precisely because* it is pastoral. The church is to exercise discipline so that no person may deceive himself into thinking that just because he is formally part of the church, he is thereby automatically at peace with God! In fact, one who is living in unrepentant sin, reveals by his very hardness of heart, that he truly belongs to, and operates according to the ways of, another kingdom—that of the Prince of Darkness. The church may never allow people to rest easy in sin, lest they never come to the awareness of their urgent need to repent. What pastoral insensitivity and neglect it would be for the church to allow her people to go to hell so happily deceived and without a fight! Indeed, what you don't know can kill you—eternally![5]

Here's the bottom line: if church discipline is applied with any other attitude and spirit than that of an urgent contending for the salvation of the individual who is right now outside of Christ, it is not Biblical discipline. If you, as a pastoral elder, apply discipline perfunctorily, merely to satisfy the requirements of your church's book of order, you are perilously close to the spirit of the Pharisees. If you apply it arrogantly, revealing a judgmental and authoritarian spirit, you are already in trouble with the Lord Jesus, who calls you to have a spirit of servanthood and love (Matt. 20:20-28). Biblical church discipline can only, and must only, be applied *in order to call sinners back*. Because that is the loving purpose, and because discipline is the only way that works to break through the crust that encases hard hearts, such discipline is absolutely necessary. There is no Biblical option. And that's true no matter whether our age understands, whether you are threatened with a lawsuit, or whether it's easier to ignore.

---

[5] Read Jude 23 for a perspective on how the Lord views discipline as rescue from the fire.

Thoughts on Methodology

Having said all that, I'd be remiss if I didn't address another dimension of the issue, namely the lack of a pastoral method of discipline so prevalent in today's evangelical churches. Most of the grievous failures I've witnessed in the realm of discipline in churches have occurred in this area. To be sure, some churches express hesitance to discipline at all; others speak often of discipline as a mark of the true church, but do precious little of it in the practice of their local church life. But usually where churches fail, is in the *process* of discipline as they carry it out.

Discipline as a Threat: "or else..."

Allow me to explain my last sentence. Far too often, church discipline is used as leverage. That is, it is not viewed as it is in Scripture; the careful, regular *discipleship* of individuals and families, including instruction, rebuke, admonition, and correction. Rather, it is used as a threat. Here's how it works:

> *Joe and Margaret are told by one of the elders that their son Bill ought to amend his life and return back to church more regularly "or else we'll have to begin discipline proceedings."*

Or this:

> *Pete and Anne have had marriage problems for years. Everyone knew about it; some even prayed for them and encouraged them during particularly bad spells. But now that they've announced that they'll be filing for divorce, an elder team arrives at the door to remind them that Scripture (I Cor. 7) forbids the divorce of believers from one another. During the course of the visit, a statement like the following is made: "You must not divorce, or else you will put yourself in jeopardy of the discipline of the church. And you wouldn't want that!"*

Now, I know you could argue that there is a deterrent value to punishment. That's long been the argument of the pro-capital punishment lobby in American politics. I've heard preachers and elders gush about the positively wonderful spiritual benefits of a church that is diligent to apply discipline. Yet, the above examples (which, by the way, are true; as they say, "only the names have been changed to protect the quasi-innocent") are not so much examples of deterrence as they are of sloth and dereliction of duty by the elders.

It might help to consider a parallel. Imagine that your teen-aged children are rebellious to the point of openly flaunting all your household rules. You watch them go from verbal rebellion to physical defiance (gestures, glaring eyes, and slamming doors), to blatant disobedience. Finally, when you can stand it no longer, you summon them to the family room and announce, "if you try that once more, I'll have to discipline you." What's wrong with this picture? Parental discipline is not thermostatically controlled to kick in only after parents notice that their children's hearts harden and their sinful practices become entrenched habits of disobedience. Discipline is a structure for life and an atmosphere within which life is lived; it should never be thought of merely as a "solution" to an immediate problem. It begins, in fact, the day your child comes home from the hospital wrapped in a receiving blanket. From that day on, with both word and example, you establish principles, teach values, demonstrate a method of dealing with sin and hold both yourself and your child accountable. The discipline established and demonstrated by parents aims at cultivating self-discipline within the individual child, a discipline which will function long after the parents are no longer looking over the child's shoulder every waking moment.

So too with the children of God in the family known as church. Many are immature in their faith (and that despite the number of years they've been members) and must be nurtured accordingly. You don't begin with threats only after sinful practices have calcified into habits of the heart. You begin with careful instruction, with a clear explanation of God's Word and will, with detailed descriptions of the painful consequences of sin on self, family, church, and on one's relationship with Christ. You hold them accountable within an atmosphere where it is evident that discipline is not punishment but accountability, where it is clear that *every* member of *every* age group is under the discipline and control of the living Word of God *every* day they live.

Specifically...

So, I offer the following practical suggestions for you to consider. Examine your pastoral relationship with your people in light of them and the related Scripture passages on which they are based.

1. Lay a foundation of trust long before problems arise. Parents who discipline effectively have established a relationship of love with their children, and it is that relationship which establishes the grounds and the purpose. That is true with elders too. You must make persistent efforts to know your people intimately. Visit in their homes frequently to pray for them and with them. Call them to rejoice in their happy times, to celebrate with them their children's accomplishments. Sit with them when life's sorrows bring tears. Make clear, in short, that you love them from the heart. Then later, if you must challenge, rebuke or admonish them, they'll know you mean it for their good. And that will certainly affect their response. Remember the truth of John 10:5. Sheep only follow a shepherd whose voice they recognize! If elders are to be shepherds in the spirit of the Good Shepherd, their flock must come to "know their voice," and through familiarity with theirs, to know His. Or consider I Thess. 2:7-8, 11-12. The apostolic model of care is to operate "like a mother" and "like a father." Read these verses carefully; the Spirit's similes make His point well.

2. Make clear just what repentance looks like. This may be so obvious to you as to be unnecessary, but I doubt it. Many elder visits with sinful members show the harsh edge of confrontation, even rebuke, without ever making clear that the purpose is repentance and restoration. Wise elders won't focus only on the sinful problem, but will explain carefully what God expects by way of response. Further, while you may tell people you want them to repent, you must ask yourself if you have communicated just what that means in real life. Consider Peter and Anne (discussed earlier). (An elder who had been involved right from the beginning according to suggestion #1 above would have caught the marital strain long before it had escalated, so this situation may well never had occurred. However, for discussion sake....) When you make the "discipline call" on them, what do you ask for? What will constitute repentance? Not going through with the divorce? Is that enough? How about asking for an agreement from each to work together on a specific plan designed to rebuild their marriage in God's Word. Propose specific steps you ask them to agree to and will hold them accountable for:

- a commitment to join together in daily Scripture study and prayer (passages you assign and will check up on)
- a promise to meet together with a pastoral counselor (one you select, and who shares your Biblical commitments)
- and/or an agreement to meet with an assigned mentor couple with Biblical wisdom borne of years of life's experience, or

perhaps one who had been rescued by God's grace from a failing marriage themselves.

The point? Before you go on such a visit, be clear just what you, representing Christ and His grace, will ask them to do, or to stop doing, or to change, or to believe, or whatever. *Don't just go to tell them that the status quo of their life is unacceptable.* Consider the patterns you find in Gal. 5:13-15 and Eph. 4:17ff. In these passages, which are only two examples of many contained in Scripture, you will notice the apostolic method - not only confronting sin, but offering specific instruction for the change to be made positively. In the words of one of the great Reformation Creeds, not only "the dying-away of the old self" but also the "coming to life of the new self."[6]

3. *Be persistent.* Again, discipline is not applied in a Biblical manner just because you have "followed the rules." You don't just make the requisite visits, warn the specified number of times and then report back that there is no repentance. Rather, you must demonstrate the heartfelt urgency that must be evident if you really love the individual as one of Christ's own. You must persist in calling, warning, and showing the hurt their sin causes both Christ and you, and in giving clear and visible testimony that you want them back in the fold and will receive them warmly when they repent. Consider Paul's statement in Acts 20:31 as a paradigm for your practice: "Remember that for three years I never stopped warning each of you night and day with tears." The point here is not the duration, but the relentless pastoral passion which the Apostle revealed in this declaration to the Ephesian elders, and which he holds up as the model for their work as elders - and yours.

4. *Finally, rejoice when repentance is granted by the Lord.* Obvious? Of course. But also so easily overlooked. Jesus thought the joyful reception of the repentant so urgent that He made very clear how distasteful it was to Him when His people acted like the older brother of the prodigal, instead of like the father who "killed the fatted calf." Crucial to understanding the parable is the context of the entire chapter. At issue in Luke 15, quite frankly, is God's desire to throw a party! The shepherd hosts one when he finds the lost sheep (v. 6); the woman calls one when she finds the lost coin (v. 9), and the father calls one when his lost son comes home repentant (vv. 23 and 32). But the older brother was jealous of all the

---

[6] From Lord's Day 33 of the *Heidelberg Catechism.*

attention. This is the rub, the sticking point of the whole chapter. Remember how it opened? The Pharisees and teachers of the law were bothered by all the attention Jesus was directing to tax collectors and "sinners" (vv. 1-2). The point is clear, and it hurts. Woe be to the church members who gripe about "all the time their pastors and elders are spending with the "new people." What about us?" You can almost hear God shouting "What's the matter with you? Throw a party! A lost one came home!"

How is it in your church? Do you convey an "it's about time" attitude? Do you treat miraculous repentance (is there any other kind?) as "business as usual"? Or do you wrap your arms around those who repent with tears in your eyes so that they know that they are truly welcomed home because of that repentance? Remember the church is not the community of the holy few, but the community of the forgiven who are now learning to follow the Master. It is the assembly of those to whom grace has already been shown who now can and do show that grace to others.

The Elder's Meeting - A Structure for Mutual Accountability

Elder's meetings—blessing or curse? Ask that question of most elders in the church of the Lord and they'll probably tell you that meetings are a necessary evil. Can't get along without them, but they don't rank up there with TCBY frozen yogurt on the top ten list of fun things to do. They take too many evenings away from the family, and usually accomplish far less than anyone would like. The only problem with changing them is that most elders are conscience stricken with the thought. After all, griping about an elder's meeting is a little like criticizing your wife's cooking - you just don't do it!

Well, listen to a lone voice in the wilderness. Elder's meetings in most churches are a waste of valuable time; in fact, such meetings usually are a pain in the neck. I'll let you in on a secret; one of the few times I grumble about the work of the ministry is when I am reminded that I will have to attend such meetings several evenings per week for the next 20 years or so.

I think I know why. Most meetings are held because it's time to hold a meeting. Either the church's book of order prescribes a certain frequency, or the local church is in the habit of holding meetings according to a set schedule. But in either case, meetings become a rigid requirement, a modern example of "the law of the Medes and Persians, which cannot be altered but abides forever." It's as if the Lord had added a verse to Acts 20. "Keep watch over yourselves and over all the flock over which the Lord has made you overseers. Above all, go to meetings. And make sure they run late."

It's easy to lose sight of the goal, to forget why we meet "the first Monday" of the month. Nowhere is it written, and few would dare even to suggest, that attending elder meetings is the only way, or even the best way, to shepherd a flock. Yet, I know of many local church situations so bound to structural traditions that the following would not be an unusual conversation:

> I nominate Bill for the office of elder. He is wonderfully qualified, has a shepherd's heart, has demonstrated a desire to care for God's people, and is a man of the Word and prayer.
>
> I agree, but Bill has a conflict on Monday evenings. He's on the hospital board, and it meets the same nights we do.
>
> Too bad. I withdraw my nomination.

A MODEST AGENDA PROPOSAL

Allow me to make a modest proposal about meetings; *make them worthwhile!* No, I don't mean that you should make sure that refreshments rival the local 5 star restaurant's dessert tray, complete with designer coffee (de-caf of course!). Rather, I suggest that elder's meetings ought to have a functional value; that is, they ought to serve practically to equip the elders to do the pastoral work they are called to do. Put another way, while shepherding elders don't do their work in meetings, the meetings ought to enable them spiritually and practically to do their work.

How is it possible to structure an elder's meeting so that it is productive and worthwhile? Let's start by considering what appears on a typical agenda. Yours probably looks something like this:

1. *Opening Devotions*
2. *Approval of Minutes*
3. *Correspondence*
4. *Old Business*
   - *reports of committees*
   - *disciplinary cases*

   Refreshment Break
5. *New Business*
   - *doctrinal or ethical issues*
   - *worship committee report*
   - *education committee report*
   - *building and grounds committee report*

- *fellowship committee report*
- *other matters*

6. *Adjournment*

Note how much of this kind of agenda is administrative in character, not pastoral in focus. Now let me remind you of one of the principle themes of this book. *The eldership is a pastoral office, not an administrative one.* The elders are to give themselves to the pastoral care of the flock, not function as a committee to decide when it is time to recharge the air-conditioner coils with freon. It's time our meetings reflected that understanding. For one thing, elder's meetings ought to equip the elders to pastor the flock. For another, they ought to encourage the elders in the ministry of their office, since any believer - including an elder - loses his zeal from time to time, particularly when dealing with some of the chronic sins of God's people. Finally, they ought to serve to link the pastoral elders with the Good Shepherd through prayer, the Source of all spiritual power, to transform life, restrain sin and bring about repentance and faith.

Allow me to suggest a new, all-purpose, agenda for elder's meetings. It's barebones, consisting of only 3 items each meeting. But don't be deceived. The three items identified are specifically and carefully recommended so as to achieve maximum value for the goals listed above. They are:

1. *Study/Training in Pastoral Skills*
2. *Pastoral Consultation*
3. *Prayer for the Flock*

In each case, the items that appear on the agenda have a specific purpose. In every case, they seek to answer the question: "How can this time together bless the elder in his work, and make him more effective for the care of the flock?" Let's look at each of them more closely.

Study/Training

The first item in our barebones agenda is study/training. It ought to be at the heart of every elder's meeting. I believe this agenda item is the principal way the preacher ministers to his elders, and the most effective way the elders encourage and build each other up. It is mandatory.

Obviously, "study/training" can cover a lot of territory. My own long-standing practice is to schedule 30 to 45 minutes for this item at the beginning of the meeting. I usually hand out a study sheet the previous weekend so the brothers have time to reflect on the topic in advance. Topics range from "the nature of the office of elder" (always the first study each church year, and always based on a Bible study of Acts 20:28f and I Peter 5) to "how to minister effectively to single women," from "tips for visiting in the home," to "the relationship between pastoral love and church discipline," from "ministering to children," to "caring for the dying."

In each case, I try to include several components.

1. First, a *case study*. By that I mean a written description of a pastoral situation I (or someone else) has encountered. Sometimes the case studies are fictional; usually they are not.[1]

2. Second, key *Scriptural passages* appropriate to the issue are suggested for review.

3. Finally, time is spent in *mutual discussion* of the pastoral questions: "What do you believe is the problem? What would you do in this situation? What would be your strategy for ministry? How many pastoral meetings would you anticipate? How would you apply the Scriptures? If a sin is involved, how would you work toward repentance, and what is the criterion for determining if repentance is evident?"

One side benefit of all this study material is that it becomes most useful for potential office-bearer training. Every summer, we in Dallas hold a series of training seminars for those we believe are potential candidates for the offices of the church. Observing them "in action," as a case study is presented and discussed, is a wonderful way for the current elders and deacons to assess future candidates for nomination. Another side benefit of this material is that you get to spend a year or so reworking it and editing it for a book like this one.

---

[1] Examples of case studies are available from a variety of sources. Jay E. Adams, *The Christian Counselor's Casebook* (Phillipsburg, New Jersey: Presbyterian and Reformed Publishing Co., 1974) is a treasure chest of resources for such a purpose. See also the *Appendix* to the current volume for examples of case studies written during my own ministry. Any experienced pastor can draft his own, changing the names for confidentiality.

Pastoral Consultation

This second element of the meeting is a face-to-face and hands-on consultation with the body of elders about specific cases in the life of your church. It is far from a free-for-all discussion, however. Rather, the attending elder (each elder has a district or care group for which he is responsible) seeks wisdom and advice from the brothers about a thorny problem. He sets the focus, presents the "case," asks the questions. Obviously, not every possible situation is discussed; in fact, only those are brought to the table that could not be handled by the elder alone, or by the elder in consultation with the preaching pastor. That keeps the focus sharp, and limits the meeting to a workable number of cases.

This is the category, as well, in which formal disciplinary action is to be raised. It is interesting, however, that within the context of a meeting agenda like this one, such discussions have a much more pastoral flavor, as opposed to an administrative, secretarial or perfunctory one.

Prayer

We conclude each meeting with a time of serious wrestling before the Lord for the flock in prayer. No elder, no body of elders, can do the work Scripture assigns unless they lay before the Lord the needs of the flock. Having spent much time in study about a particular subject, many individuals in similar circumstances come to the minds of their own district elders. Prayer is thus very personalized. Having consulted with one another about local pastoral cases, the burden the elder feels will lead him inexorably to his knees. In Dallas, we often spend as much time in prayer as we do in pastoral consultation.

I fear I'm about to step on a number of toes here, but I am burdened to cry out in great frustration at my firm belief, borne of experience, that many elders today simply are not men of prayer. Perhaps it is because a diligent prayer life is not preached nor promoted in many churches these days; perhaps it is due to the pressures of work and family life; perhaps because we look, at nomination time, for administrative and speaking skills rather than for pastoral hearts and pastoral patterns. Whatever is the cause, restoring prayer to its central place in pastoral care is crucial if the Lord's church is to be shepherded after the pattern of the Good Shepherd.

Now before you protest aloud that I'm being harsh with such an observation, be honest with yourself whether or not you really disagree with my analysis. Do you genuinely believe that the elders you know, regularly and diligently lift in prayer to the Sovereign throne of grace, the souls entrusted to their care? Do you believe that those elders pray specifically and urgently for the stubborn lambs or sheep in their district? Do you believe that the wounded marriages are held before the Sovereign God, as the elder pleads for His healing mercy? Do you believe that the elders you know pray as many minutes per day for their Pastor/Teacher as they talk about him over coffee?

Unless you know a remarkable group of elders in your experience and in your church, your testimony will parallel those of most Christians I know. And please understand, I raise this issue not in complaint that today's church has no good or pious elders, or in lament that I have served with such prayerless men that I have suffered in ministry. Quite the opposite is the case. God has preserved and equipped wonderful and godly men who love Him dearly; I have been remarkably blessed by the men with whom God has allowed me to serve. But the most godly among them themselves lament their own lack of prayer. I write these words with a sense of urgency and burden, in hopes that the godly men that God has called to the office of elder will become more Biblical in their understanding of their work, more humble in their approach to their people, more sensitive in their listening heart, and more bold in their prophetic address to the situations in the lives of the flock. And prayer is key to such maturing and growth.

If you are persuaded to dedicate a significant time in prayer to your meeting agenda, the obvious question arises; what should we pray for? Allow me to make several suggestions, all of which are derived from the pastoral prayer our Lord Jesus prays in John 17, (a very good place to learn how to pray for His people, I'm sure you'll agree!).

Pray for Spiritual Protection

The first lesson appears in verses 11-12 and 15:

> ...they are still in the world..., Holy Father, protect them by the power of your name - the name you gave me - so that they may be one as we are one. While I was with them, I protected them and kept them safe by that name you gave

me. None has been lost except the one doomed to destruction....My prayer is not that you take them out of the world but that you protect them from the evil one.

Notice what Jesus asks? *Protection*, that His flock will be kept safe after His ascension just as He was able to keep them safe while with them. To be sure, He speaks of more than physical safety; in fact in several Scripture passages (the preceding chapters in John's gospel, for example) He specifically predicts physical danger and hardship for His people. Now He prays here for *spiritual* safety; that His flock will be spared from the destructive powers of the Evil One. It is in connection with this concern that His prayer for unity is also most impressive. Unity must be understood to be one of the Sovereign God's gifts to His church for her spiritual protection; when the church is united in the Truth, it will be protected from the Evil One. Jesus' prayer in John 17 is reflected in the charge of St. Paul to the Ephesian elders in our oft-cited Acts 20:29f. He tells them that savage wolves will come in among the flock, so "be on your guard." Elders ought to understand that, expect it, and pray accordingly!

So, *lesson one*: Pray for the spiritual defense of those members of Christ's church because they live in a wicked world. Do so regularly. Do so with full and studied awareness of the spiritual struggles they face. Study the people, study their circumstances, study their weaknesses. Study all these things diligently...so that you can pray well!

Pray for Spiritual Joy

Jesus also prays for spiritual joy for His disciples. In v. 13 of the same chapter, He asks:

...that they may have the full measure of my joy within them.

Is the Savior asking here that His disciples will always have *fun*? Hardly. While many Biblical passages exult the wonderful joy that is ours in Christ (Philippians among them), none do so at the perilous cost of ignoring reality. Along side of all these celebrations of joy is the realistic awareness of suffering as the believer's lot in a wicked life. Read John 15:20 before you ever tell anyone (or mistakenly believe yourself) that the Christian life is roses without thorns. This verse and the one that precedes it warn us that the world will hate believers because it hated our Lord. 2 Tim. 3:12 boldly states that "everyone who wants to live a godly life in Christ

Jesus will be persecuted." And I Peter 4:12f. goes so far as to declare that we ought not to be surprised at persecution, but to be surprised if we do not suffer persecution!

Rather, Jesus asks the Father to give to His suffering, pressured, aliens-in-the-world-people the deep and abiding conviction that those who are in Christ are surely victorious, no matter what the world does to them! That brings joy, pure and unending, and provides a base of comfort enabling daily life without despair.[2] And so you must pray for your people. How do you pray for joy? For an easier road when the life they lead is difficult and painful? So, *lesson two*: Pray that God will grant your people the spiritual wisdom, strength, and conviction that life in Christ is more precious than anything this life brings. It is that perseverance that keeps God's people faithful no matter the obstacle; it is that perspective that provides hope which enables them to look beyond the temporary to the "eternal weight of glory beyond all comparison" (II Cor. 4:17); and it is that knowledge that assures them that no matter what they face, "…nothing can separate them from the love of God in Christ Jesus our Lord" (Rom. 8:39).

Pray for Effective Witness

Jesus not only prays for protection and joy for His disciples and for us, but also for effectiveness in the witness of the Christian life He calls us to live. Consider vv. 20-21:

> My prayer is not for them alone. I pray also for those who will believe in me through their message, that all of them may be one, Father, just as you are in me and I am in you. May they also be in us so that the world may believe that you have sent me."

---

[2] Once again, I refer you to the marvelous and encouraging confession of the reformation-age believers written down in Lord's Day 1, Question and Answer 1 of the *Heidelberg Catechism*:

Q. What is your only comfort in life and in death?

A. That I am not my own, but belong - body and soul, in life and in death - to my faithful Savior Jesus Christ. He has fully paid for all my sins with his precious blood, and has set me free from the tyranny of the devil. He also watches over me in such a way that not a hair can fall from my head without the will of my Father in heaven: in fact, all things must work together for my salvation. Because I belong to him, Christ, by his Holy Spirit, assures me of eternal life and makes me wholeheartedly willing and ready from now on to live for him.

Notice that? Jesus prays not only for His immediate disciples, but for us, who 2000 years later will believe because of the regenerating power of the Apostolic Word. And He prays that we will remain in Christ and in His Father (as branches in the vine) *so that* the world may believe! And of course, there is no way to remain in Him without remaining in His Word. Believers whose faith is firmly founded in the Scriptures are believers who will not falter.

Lesson three: Pray that God's people will remain in the Word so that they may be effective in advancing the reputation of our God. That is the best description I've heard yet of the Biblical call to "witness." So often we view "witness" as a canned, cold, memorized presentation. Better that we view it in a judicial sense; we are on the witness stand every day of our lives. On trial is the honor of God and the integrity of His believers. What witness do you bear by the life that you lead? That witness will be shaped most powerfully by the Word in which you are immersed; conversely, it will be compromised most severely if your Christian life is not grounded in the Word.

The point of all this is that the work of an elder is empty and vain unless it is grounded in the same soil as that of his Lord. Jesus built His entire ministry on prayer; we must too. The early Apostles appointed deacons so that they themselves could devote themselves more to the ministry of the Word *and prayer* (Acts 6:4); we must too. And our prayers must be specific; they must be pastoral, and they must seek the Father's blessing for the defense of the flock, for the empowering and comforting joy of their Christian service, and for the effectiveness of their Biblical witness for Him and His Name in this world.

Do you pray like that? Let me challenge each reader individually. If you are an elder in the church of our Lord Jesus Christ, set aside time every day for prayer on behalf of the flock. Be intentional; have the list of your district members before you. Reflect (even take notes if necessary) on their specific spiritual struggles and needs before you begin. If you cannot make it through the entire list, pray for one or two every day. And if that seems too much for you, listen to this story. I was told this anecdote many years ago - and believe it to be true - about the great preacher, professor, theologian, writer, editor and statesman (he became Prime Minister of the Netherlands around the turn of the century), Abraham Kuyper. It is reported that after he left a small, rural church to take pastoral charge of a large congregation in Amsterdam, during which time he was concurrently committed to editing a weekly magazine, writing for a daily Christian newspaper, serving as chancellor of and professor in a major university, all the while writing meditations, theological tomes, and many other projects, one old saint inquired of him: "Dr. Kuyper, how do you have time to do all these things and still pastor such a large congregation?" His answer revealed the source of his spiritual vigor and strength. "I don't. So, I increased my time in prayer to God from one hour per day to three!"

Let me challenge you as a group of elders as well. Keep the prayer priorities of our Lord before you as a body when you go before His throne in your meetings. Failure to do so weakens the church; but faithfulness in prayer will reap a wonderful harvest. Several things will happen immediately. First, you will be better elders when you visit among the flock; you will be more sensitive to their needs and struggles and will listen more attentively when they speak, for you will be listening in order to bring them before the King; you will be able to be more specific in your pastoral advice, rebukes, and/or challenges, since your focus will be the specific concerns raised above - protection from the Evil One, joy in their struggles, and effectiveness for their living witness. Above all, you will be given the wisdom of the Lord whose blessing and grace you have repeatedly sought.

In Dallas, our meetings have become something we actually look forward to. The blessing received more than compensates for the time spent, and that in itself is modest, usually about 2 hours. We seldom return home unable to sleep due to that common affliction known as "elder's meeting insomnia," for we have together placed our burdens before the Lord, and have His peace in our hearts. We have together become better pastors, because we are reminded each month that such is our calling, and because real help has been received and mutually shared. And because our meetings are viewed as tools to equip elders, rather than seen as the main component of the elder's work, there is less pressure on those gifted elders who may have a scheduling conflict. Most of the material is transferable to those unable to make the meeting by scheduling a brief breakfast or lunch with the chairman or the clerk.

I encourage you to take a look at your typical agenda. Determine whether it is sharply focused for pastoring, or whether unnecessary administrative matters have begun to eat up your time. Ask yourself the question: are our meetings worthwhile as tools to equip the elders of our church? If not, begin the process of restructuring!

Oh, and what do you do with all the myriad administrative details that such an agenda as the one proposed above will sweep off the table on to the floor? Frankly, you've got two choices. If you insist that the eldership must "govern" in the administration of church details (although the Biblical description for pastoral elders nowhere assigns such duties to them), you'll have to have a separate meeting strictly for administration, either on a separate night, or using modern telecommunications, using a conference call during a lunch hour. If, on the other hand, you are convinced of the pastoral model for the office I've been touting for quite a number of pages, you might be wonderfully freed by identifying those administrators within the body of believers (and in today's business-driven culture, such should not be difficult to find), and assigning to them all non-pastoral administrative functions within the body. They can (and probably should) still report regularly to the board of elders for oversight and accountability, but they will download from the pastors those pressing, but not high-priority agenda items, that hinder faithful pastoring.

APPENDICES

Case Studies for Pastoral Review

Case Study #1

You are visiting with a new couple in your church. Recently relocated to your area, they are describing their former church home, and how happy they are to be out of it.

> The elders and deacons were meddlers in our personal affairs! They tried to regulate what we believed; they even suggested that our life-style wasn't our private affair because it affected others! Can you imagine? What's worse, they wouldn't even send our papers to *us* when we told them we wanted out. Said something about only being permitted to entrust people to other elders. Who do those guys think they are? God?

Analyze the above.

- What are the central pastoral issues you must face? (including theological, interpersonal, ecclesiastical, etc.)

- What does Scripture say about those issues?

- What would be your *strategy* to deal with this situation? Be specific.

Case Study #2

Peter had been vice president of the church council for 2 years. He was pleased; the church members were 'toeing the line' rather well; no one was making any trouble. No one, that is, until the new elders were installed. They seemed to think there weren't enough Bible studies in the church and started several of them, right in people's homes. "Letting people study on their own is just an invitation to all kinds of trouble," thought Pete. He just couldn't remain in a church that was headed for such trouble. After all, didn't the Bible warn against "letting every man think he is king in his own eyes"? The more he thought about it, the more exercised he became. The more worked up Pete was, the less support he received from other elders he had expected would side with him. Pete decided to resign, both from the eldership and from the church, reasoning that he'd save everyone a bunch of grief by just "pulling the plug." He opted to quit altogether, rather than transferring to the Lutherans, the only other church in the neighborhood, because he'd heard they had similar problems with young upstarts causing trouble.

Analyze this case:

- What's the central issue here?

- What does Scripture say re. these issues? (Read I Cor. 12 and determine what application, if any, the passage has to this case.)

- What would be your strategy in dealing with Pete? Be specific and comprehensive.

- Do you believe Pete's attitude might have affected other members of the local church body? What would you propose as a pastoral strategy to deal with his influence?

Case Study #3

"Bob's a great guy, a successful salesman, with a personality to match. A good "giver" to church, he's proven that he's got the stuff to make a great elder. After all, he chaired the recent building campaign. Besides, everyone likes him." This was the nomination speech delivered by one of the elders of your church on behalf of a potential nominee.

Analyze the above:

- What's the pastoral issue the case study reveals?

- Do you agree with this man's conclusion about Bob's suitability for the eldership?

- How would you respond to someone who would speak these words? Identify specifically what you would say in such a meeting?

- What Scriptural passages apply to this pastoral situation?

Case Study #4

"Let's nominate Bill. He'd sure have a different attitude about church if he knew all the problems we face in Council. It would do him good to be an elder. Maybe he'd even come to church more often, and I'm sure he'd give more to the church!"

Analyze the above:

- How would you respond to such a nomination speech made in your church? What Biblical grounds would you give for your answer.

- Besides the issue of Bill's "qualifications for office," what other issues does this speech reveal might be pastoral concern in that local church?

- What Scripture passages would be applicable to this case?

Case Study #5

John had been a faithful elder, by all accounts. He was diligent, and his work had revealed a beautiful and mature heart of faith. He had cared for God's people with compassion and yet firmness. Even in the years since he'd been "on sabbatical" (no longer in active service), he continued to demonstrate a pastoral heart, visiting the elderly, praying regularly with widows, and discipling young men in a weekly Bible study in his home. He'd make an excellent nomination to be returned to active service *except*, that in his new job, he worked the second shift, and wouldn't be able to make council or elder's meetings on Monday evenings. Too bad...

- How would you identify the problem revealed in this paragraph?

- What would you do about it? (Would you be willing to discuss the possibility of changing meeting day or time? If not, why not? What other courses of action would be open to you?)

Case Study #6

James and Ann, a young member couple in their early 30's call to "inform" you, that despite trying hard for all 6 years of their marriage, they've had enough pain and suffering and are going to file for divorce. They inform you that they have "incompatible personalities," and think they made a mistake getting married in the first place. "Just thought you should know," says James as he concludes the conversation.

- What is the pastoral problem revealed in this case?

    Not seeing the institution of marriage as permanent

- What would you do about it if you were the elder? (Be specific: list planned visits, overall strategy and goals, etc.)

    - Rebuke, pray for repentance
    - Other visits for encouragement

- What are the relevant Scripture passages you would use?

    Matt 5:31-ff - institution of marriage
    Eph 5:22 - what wife-love looks like

- How would your approach change if, on your first visit, Ann were to reveal that she has fallen "out of love" with James and is "in love" with a man from work?

Case Study #7

Frieda, a single overweight woman in her mid-30's, is depressed. She tells you that she has thought of suicide, but is afraid of going to hell. She admits that she is very eager to be married, but is unhappy with the kind of men who ask her out. She thinks they're all "losers." She is thinking of joining a dating club she read about in the newspaper, and asks your advice.

- Identify the pastoral or spiritual problem(s) Frieda has.

- How would you pastor Frieda? (Again, be specific: identify plans and strategy.)

- What Scriptures would you read to/with Frieda, and why?

- Are there any unique problems you might face on a visit to a single woman like Frieda? How would you deal with them?

Case Study #8

Bill and Josephine's 21 year old son Bob has been spending a lot of time lately with a girl from the neighborhood. She is attractive, has a sweet personality, and practices yoga and meditation "to achieve inner peace." Her name is Moonchild (honestly), and she learned yoga from her parents, former hippies. Bob concedes that she's a bit odd, but sees nothing wrong with her practices. In fact, "she's unique, and that's what attracted me to her in the first place," he says. Bill and Josephine are concerned and very nervous about Bill's reputation as a former elder in the church. They call you for advice.

- List the issues you find in this case, and prioritize them in the order in which you think you should deal with them.

- How many elders would you involve? Why?

- What Scripture passages would you use on each dimension of the case?

Case Study #9

The youth group in your church requests the elders' permission to hold their meetings during worship services on Sunday morning. They argue that they have their own youth pastor, they have enough room in their youth room, and they are bored in the regular worship services anyway. Historically, you have taken the position that "God's people" as a corporate body ought to gather together before the face of God in worship without being split up into sub-groups divided by age.

- What is/are the pastoral issue(s) involved here?

- What Scripture passages inform your thinking about those issues?

- Their query of the elders raises a deeper issue. What is your church's understanding of the role and the format of worship in the light of Scripture? Write a few paragraphs on the subject, and discuss them with others.

Case Study #10

Mrs. Wilson is dying. She's 82, has been a member of the local church since she was a child, but is absolutely terrified of the possibility of going to hell. She declares without hesitation that she believes that Jesus died to atone for the sins of all who believe. She declares without hesitation that she believes He is the Son of God. You know from former visits with her that she has always been diligent in searching Scripture and in prayer. But she has absolutely no assurance of salvation. She is convinced she's not one of God's elect, and so lives in dread fear of eternal punishment. Her sister (also a member) tells you that their father used to call them "reprobates" when he caught them sinning. She admits that she, too, has a terrible fear of death.

- What *theological* issues are involved in this case? How would you deal with them? What Scriptures would be relevant?

- What *pastoral* concerns must you take into account while dealing with Mrs. Wilson? Any suggestions about the manner of approaching her or her sister? How does Scripture shape your approach?

- Of all the possible issues involved, which would you aim at first? Explain.

Case Study #11

Your co-worker at the office tells you over lunch that he believes Jesus is the Messiah, the *Son* of God, but that nowhere in the Bible does it teach that Jesus is *God*. Christian churches, says he, have *invented* the doctrine of the Trinity.

- How would you answer him? (Cite chapter and verse.)

- Can you identify his theological position as belonging to any church or cult you're familiar with?

- Would you expect him to raise other theological problems, knowing of this one?

- If you discovered that other people in your workplace held to his view, would it change your strategy of how you would deal with his question?

Case Study #12

Harold, a recent transfer to your church from another city, has a nasty habit of lying. He claims it stems from his childhood when he was abused. He says he lied then to avoid beatings and hasn't been able to break the habit since. He tells you that it really bothers him, but that years of prayer for strength to stop lying haven't been able to correct his habit. He concludes that he will have to live with this weakness. "It's my cross to bear," he explains.

- What are the pastoral issues in this case?

- What would you suggest as a pastoral strategy to help Harold? (Be specific! How many meetings would you anticipate? What Scriptures would you use? What goal would you establish for your pastoral work? How would you know if the goal was achieved?)

- One of Harold's former pastors tells you that he believes Harold's problems are "mental problems, and don't think you should waste your time. Harold belongs in long-term psychotherapy to deal with the unresolved abuse." How would you respond to the pastor?

Case Study #13

Bob and Gwen joined your church about a year ago. They say they really love it, are rather active in midweek Bible Studies and fellowship activities, give generously and actively witness to anyone they know who isn't a Christian. However, they don't attend worship services more than once or twice a month. When they do, they are quick to tell anyone around how much they've been blessed. They don't see a problem with their infrequent attendance. "After all, going to church doesn't save you," they say. Their background is Southern Baptist, but they seem genuinely thrilled with the doctrines of grace you preach and teach in your Reformed church.

- What so you see as the central problem? What theological doctrines does it involve?

- How would you deal pastorally with Bob and Gwen? That is, what would be the approach you'd take to them; what Scriptures would you refer to; how would you plan to deal with them?

- One of the former elders who has noticed their worship patterns suggests to you, rather forcefully, that you ought to "get tough with Sabbath breakers like Bob and Gwen." Do you agree with him? If so, how would you "get tough"?

- Let's change the scene a bit. Suppose Bob and Gwen had transferred to your church (one that confesses, as one of its creeds, the *Heidelberg Catechism*) from a Presbyterian congregation that confesses the *Westminster Catechisms and Confession of Faith*. In this scenario, Bob and Gwen *never* miss worship services at all. But early on in their tenure in your congregation you invite them to your home for Sunday dinner. They reply, "We don't socialize on Sabbath. We believe it's a day only for worship." You are confused, so read the Westminster Standards to compare them with the Heidelberg. You notice that the Westminster calls Sunday the "Christian Sabbath"; Lord's Day 38 of the Heidelberg does not, and seems to take a different approach to the 4th Commandment. How would you deal with *this* situation? As always, be specific.

Case Study #14

A new family (with parents in their 40s, 2 teenagers, and a 4th grader) appears in church one Sunday, guests of one of the members. They have been Roman Catholic all their lives, but have been displeased by the lack of spiritual nurture received in their parish. On the way out the door, they say to you: "We enjoy your church, Father. We'd like to join, but can't really leave the Catholic church. You understand, don't you? Can you come over for coffee to discuss how we can become involved in your church without leaving our church?"

- *Specifically*, what steps would you take to care pastorally for these folks in the *short term* and in the *long term*?

- Knowing their background, what other issues might you expect to crop up in the future? How would you pro-actively pastor them through these anticipated difficulties?

- Would you advise your pastor not to wear his pulpit robe any more, or in any other way to downplay the connotations of the clergy that might confuse an ex-Catholic?

Case Study #15

Emily, a college-aged girl from a broken, nominally-Catholic home, is staying with one of your church families for the summer, having met their daughter in school. Emily was overheard to express amazement at the strength of this family unit, loving the stability, the mutual affection shown, and the warmth with which she is received "like one of the family." But she also believes, and doesn't mind saying publicly, that the parents are incredibly "controlling" because of the household rules about church attendance, dating only within the faith, Scripture reading and devotions at mealtimes, etc. The parents come to you, their elder, for counsel about a strategy for effective witness without turning her off.

You tell them the following: (Be specific, and be Scriptural!)

Case Study #16

Todd is extremely gifted. He is an accountant by profession, but plays violin like a professional (which he was when he put himself through college and grad school by playing in a small orchestra). He possesses a quality soloist voice. His hobby, when he has time to indulge it, is woodworking. He's built several beautiful pieces of furniture in the large home he shares with his physician wife, Jill. During the course of a conversation with one of the deacons, Todd said; "Frankly, I don't have time to be active in church. Jill and I don't have children, really don't want to bring children into our lives at this point, and expect to do a lot of weekend traveling. Maybe in a few years...."

- Identify the pastoral problems you see in this situation.

    Selfism
    — antithetical to humility
    & heart to serve

- What would be your pastoral strategy as an elder (include relevant Scripture passages, number of planned visits and purpose of each, etc.)?

    Do nothing from selfish... in his own eyes

    Phil 2:3-4 — emptied himself...
    — rescue

    Matt 20-28
    Son of Man came
    not to be served
    but to serve...

    follow up studies on Service, loving God

Case Study #17

Jorge and Estrella grew up in a barrio, poor as church mice. They worked their fingers to the bone to build up their business, and recently it was acquired for millions by a large conglomerate. They are suddenly wealthy. As somewhat frequent attenders of your congregation (not members) they have been asking various members for advice about what to do with their new wealth. Several situations are described. Be specific about how you would handle each.

Situation 1: They come to you to ask whether the Bible has anything to say about financial priorities. You tell them:

Situation 2: They tell you, in a get-acquainted visit you make to their home, that they never want to be poor again. They are going to invest the money, virtually all of it, and do not plan to be so foolish as to give much of it away. They'll surely give some to the church, but hope the other people don't expect large donations. You tell them:

Situation 3: They come to you with a serious family problem. Seems they have informed their teen-aged children that it is their belief that parents who give money to their children as an inheritance inevitably spoil those children. Therefore, they've decided to give each child a modest allowance now, provide some help for college costs, but put the rest in a trust fund to be given exclusively to church and kingdom causes after their death. The kids will receive no inheritance. The kids are furious with their parents, and demand you "talk some sense into them."

What's the problem, and how do you handle it?

Situation 4: Your church is about to embark on a building fund drive for a new sanctuary. You really need substantial donations from wealthier members in the church to enable you to build. The problem is that you alone know of Jorge and Estrella's financial situation; they told you as a friend, in confidence.

How do you handle your knowledge; what would you say to them?

Case Study #18

Wendy is a friend of a recent convert to Christ and new member of your church whose name is Beth. Beth tells you Wendy's life is falling apart; her live-in boyfriend just moved out unannounced; she was fired from her job for using company products for personal use, and has been suicidal lately, saying things like "life isn't worth living any more. I can't handle all these problems. Maybe I should just end it all."

Situation 1: Beth asks you, her district elder, to pay a call on Wendy. Do you go? If so, what do you say?

Situation 2: Beth tells you Wendy is a Christian. "She got saved when she was 8 and went forward in a crusade in her home town." But she also tells you that Wendy has not been active in church for many years, and wonders if your deacons can pay for counseling at a local Christian psychologist's office. The cost could reach several thousand dollars.

You tell Beth:

Situation 3: Wendy shows up at your home one evening, having met you in a visit to church. Wendy is drop-dead gorgeous, has a figure that would stop traffic, and is dressed to kill. When you open the door, you can't help but notice that she is crying and obviously very distraught. Your wife is in the next room, curled up in slippers and robe and reading the paper.

How do you handle the situation?

Situation 4: Wendy meets with a couple of your local elders, and in tears, acknowledges that she has been living in sin and believes that she is suffering the consequences of that sin. She "needs to get right with God," and wants to join your church and be rebaptized as soon as possible to prove she's serious about God.

What do you say to her?

Case Study #19

John and Meg had been "fringe members" of your church for some years, attending just enough to keep the elders from exercising formal discipline. You suspect she never really puts her heart and soul into the service of the Lord, but only comes, when she comes, out of habit. John, you are convinced, is a genuine child of God who is worn out fighting his wife over their religious differences. John's aged mother had recently moved in with them, and today suffered a massive stroke and died. John calls you, in tears, to come over to pray with them and offer your advice about funeral customs and ideas.

Situation 1: During a visit to the grieving couple, Meg asks you to recommend a crematory, since "Mom asked for her ashes to be spread over her favorite flower bed."

Your answer?

Situation 2: John's mother never professed Christ, but Meg keeps referring to her "seeing them from heaven."

How do you handle this question immediately? In light of the question, do you have long term pastoral concerns? How would you address those? (Be specific.)

Case Study #20

Drew, one of the young family men of your church, comes to you as his elder and friend. He is obviously in spiritual agony. He admits that he fell into temptation and had a brief sexual affair with a woman in another city while on a business trip a year ago. He stopped the affair immediately, told the other woman in tears that he had sinned against God and her, that he was deeply sorry, and that he was committed to his Lord, his wife and his family. He tells you that his repentance is genuine and you believe him. Yet he tells you that he can't seem to find relief from his guilty conscience. Upon questioning from you, he makes clear that no one else has any knowledge of the situation, since the sin occurred thousands of miles away and the woman doesn't even know his last name. He asks you: "Must I tell my wife in order to heal my conscience? She doesn't know, and I'm afraid if I tell her she'll throw me out. But I'll tell her if that's what God expects."

- What are the issues, and what would be your counsel to him? What Scriptures would you use?

- Would your advice to Drew differ if you were *not* convinced of the genuineness of his repentance?

- Suppose Drew told *two* elders, of whom you were one, and the other elder took the position that "to stop this pattern of sin, we must make an example of Drew. I believe we must require him to make a public confession of sin before his wife and the whole church." How would you respond to the other elder?

Assignments for Group Discussion

Session #1

What is the Church, according to Scripture? That is a big question today, one for which many individuals and churches have no clear answer. It helps to wrestle with the Biblical word-pictures, or metaphors that God uses to teach us. What is the metaphor used in each of the following passages? How does that metaphor instruct us concerning God's view of the church and how you should view it? (The first one is done for you as an example.)

- Luke 8:21 (The church is a *family*. God's family is defined, not by blood, but by hearing and doing God's Word. Christ thinks of us as His brothers and sisters. I should view church members thus.)

- John 10:11f.

- I Timothy 3:15

- I Corinthians 12:12f.

- Ephesians 2:19; Philippians 3:20

- I Peter 2:9-10

Discuss: Do people in your area or congregation employ worldly concepts or patterns when they think of church leadership? For example, do your people view leaders in the church as trustees of a board? As businessmen in charge of the corporation? As democratic representatives of various interest groups? How can you combat such thinking? (Be specific!)

What do you learn from Matthew 20:20-28 about leadership in the church? Are elders supposed to be "leaders"?

Session #2

Read carefully the following passages:

- I Peter 5:2-4
- I Timothy 3:2-7
- Titus 1:6-11

1. Compile a list of the basic qualifications stipulated in each of these passages as requirements for the office of elder.

<u>I Peter 5:2-4</u>	<u>I Timothy 3:2-7</u>	<u>Titus 1:6-11</u>

2. In what way are the qualifications you've identified *pastoral* in character? (That is, how does each one you've listed enable an elder to do the work of a shepherd? Conversely, how would the absence of each hinder shepherding work?)

3. Does *popularity* in the local church function as an (unwritten) qualification in any of these passages? How about in your church? Are there any steps that you should take to change the way your church selects elders so that the process is based on uniquely Biblical requirements? Be specific, and discuss your ideas.

Session #3

The following **diagnostic tool** can be used to ascertain the health of the Body of Christ, much like a "history and physical" examination is used to determine a person's physical health. Use this tool in your group meeting to discuss the health of your local church. (Option: break up into small groups of 4 or less). Following your assessment, you might consider a separate meeting to devise specific local strategies to correct problems you note.

Assessing the Health of the Body of Christ

Check for the presence of disease. Is there:

Evidence of a lack of true conversion? (Ephesians 4:17-24)

Evidence of a lack of holiness? (Hebrews 12)

Evidence of a lack of repentance? (I Corinthians 7:9-10)

Evidence of a lack of love? (II John)

Evidence of a lack of commitment? (Mark 8:34)

Presence of interpersonal sins? (Matthew 5:23-4)

Unconfessed sin? (Psalm 32:3)

Acceptance of sinful attitudes? (I Timothy 6:3-5, 17)

Toleration of sinful practices? (Ephesians 4:28, 29-31; 5:3-6)

Check the "Dietary" Intake:

Do your people read, study and memorize Scripture? (I Timothy 3:15)

Do your people use the Scriptures visibly and effectively in their lives? (II Timothy 3:14-4:5)

Do your people demonstrate doctrinal/confessional stability? (Ephesians 4:14; Hebrews 5:11f)

Check the Muscle Tone and Function:

What percentage of the members are active in some church ministry? (Ephesians 4:12)

What percentage are active in a Kingdom ministry not sponsored by your local church?

What percentage of the members are active in evangelism among family and friends or the neighborhood? (Matthew 28:19-20)

What percentage of the members are faithful in financial stewardship? (II Corinthians 9)

Identify the characteristics of healthy church life, according to Ephesians 4:13-16.

Note to the Reader

The publisher invites you to respond to us about this book by writing to Reformed Fellowship, Inc., at *president@reformedfellowship.net*

Founded in 1951, Reformed Fellowship, Inc., is a religious and strictly nonprofit organization composed of a group of Christian believers who hold to the biblical Reformed faith. Our purpose is to advocate and propagate this faith, to nurture those who seek to live in obedience to it, to give sharpened expression to it, to stimulate the doctrinal sensitivities of those who profess it, to promote the spiritual welfare and purity of the Reformed churches, and to encourage Christian action.

Members of Reformed Fellowship express their adherence to the Calvinistic creeds as formulated in the *Belgic Confession*, the *Heidelberg Catechism, the Canons of Dort,* and the *Westminster Confession and Catechisms.*

To fulfill our mission, we publish a bimonthly journal, *The Outlook*, and we publish books and Bible study guides. Our website is *www.reformedfellowship.net*